# Contents

*List of Illustrations*  6

*Preface*  8

**1 Attitudes to the Past**  9

Population movement and ethnicity  10
Diffusion  14
Trade  15
Social structure  18
Spatial organisation  20
Chronology  23

**2 The Old Order**  26

The origin of iron working  28
The end of Mycenaean Greece  32
Iron working in Greece  34
Proto-Geometric Greece  34
Late Bronze Age Europe  36

**3 Reawakening in the East**  39

The ninth century  39
Greece and Cyprus in the eighth
  century  46
Italy in the eighth century  58

**4 The Trade Explosion**  62

Greece in the seventh century  62

Etruscan civilisation  65
Situla Art  66
Central and western Europe in the
  seventh century  73
Hallstatt D, 600–475 BC  81

**5 The Tide Turns, 500–250 BC**  103

The classical world of Greece  103
The classical world of Italy  108
Northern Italy and southern France  108
Orientalising in central Europe—La
  Tène A  113
La Tène B–C—the age of migration  126

**6 The Economic Revival**  139

La Tène C, second century BC  145
The oppida  149

**7 The Roman Empire and
Beyond**  158

Britain  158
Germany  173
The impact of conquest  175

*Notes and bibliography*  181

*Index*  189

# List of Illustrations

1 'Celtic' metalwork
a The Gundestrup Cauldron
b Silver cup from Agighiol, Romania
c–f Details of the Gundestrup Cauldron

2 Chronological table

3 Sites mentioned in chapter 2

4 Late Bronze Age swords
a The Erbenheim type
b The Hemigkofen type

5 Alaça Hüyük, Turkey
a Plan of burial k
b–d Objects from burial k

6 Sub-Mycenaean Greece
a Iron knife from Knossos
b–c Objects from Kerameikos tombs, Athens

7 Sites mentioned in chapter 3

8 Zagora, Andros, Greece

9 An early Geometric burial from Athens
a Cross-section of the burial
b–h Iron objects from the burial

10 Lefkandi, Euboea, Greece
a Plan of the settlement and cemeteries
b–n Objects from the settlement and cemeteries

11 Bronze work from Urartu
a Bronze shield from Karmir Blur
b Bronze cauldron and stand from Altintepe
c Protomes on a bronze cauldron from Gordion

12 Salamis, Cyprus
a Plan of Salamis
b Plan of burial 31
c–h Objects from burial 79

13 Early Greek pottery
a Proto-Geometric vase from Kerameikos 12, Athens
b–c Late Geometric pottery from Lefkandi
d–e Late Geometric vessels from the Kerameikos, Dipylon Gate, Athens

14 Veii, Tuscany, Italy
a Plan of Villanovan Veii
b Bronze vessel from burial AA1

c Distribution of Veii type bronze vessels

15 Sites mentioned in chapter 4

16 The orientalising period in Italy
a–c Objects from the Bernardini grave, Palestrina

17 Situla Art
a Distribution of Situla Art
b–c The Benvenuti situla
d The Providence, Rhode Island situla
e Belt plate from Brezje, Yugoslavia

18 Hallstatt, Austria
a Plan of Hallstatt
b–f Objects from burials at Hallstatt
g Distribution of Mindelheim and Gündlingen bronze swords

19 Hallstatt pottery

20 Hallstatt sites in Slovenia and Hungary
a Plan of Stična
b Stamped pot from Sopron

21 The Magdalenenberg, Baden-Württemberg
a Plan of the barrow
b–d Burial 93
e–g Burial 101

22 The Heuneburg, Baden-Württemberg
a–b The Heuneburg and surrounding tumuli
c–f Construction of the Heuneburg
g–h Plans of burials in the Hohmichele

23 Eberdingen–Hochdorf, Baden-Württemberg
a Iron dagger
b Bronze castor

24 Mont Lassois and Vix, Burgundy
a Plan of the Vix burial chamber
b–e Objects from the Vix burial chamber

25 Hirschlanden, Baden-Württemberg
a–b Plan and reconstruction of the tumulus
c Stone figure

26 Sites mentioned in chapter 5

27 The development of Athens
a Proto Geometric Athens
b Geometric Athens
c Classical Athens

28 Early Greek coinage

29 The Etruscan town: Marzabotto

30 Southern France
a Plan of Entremont
b *Têtes coupées* from Entremont

31 The Hunsrück-Eifel, West Germany
a–b Etruscan vessels from Schwarzenbach
c Distribution of Etruscan beaked flagons
d–e Relationship of burials to iron ores

32 The Erstfeld hoard

33 Early La Tène pottery
a–b Wheel-turned and hand-made pottery from the Hunsrück-Eifel
c Jar and cup from Les Jogasses, Marne
d–e Linsenflasche and Braubach bowl from the Dürrnberg bei Hallein
f Decorated Linsenflasche from Matzhausen, Bavaria

34 Early Style La Tène Art
a Gold bowl from Schwarzenbach
b–i Development of lotus flower motif
j–k Attic red-figure ware bowl from Klein Aspergle

35 Waldalgesheim, West Germany
a Bronze vessel
b–c Gold torc and bracelets

36 La Tène flat inhumation cemeteries
a Distribution of flat inhumation cemeteries
b–f Male and female burials

37 Nebringen, Baden-Württemberg
a Plan of the cemetery
b–k Objects from the burials

38 Münsingen, Switzerland
a Plan of the cemetery
b–m Brooches from the cemetery

39 Later La Tène Art
a Decoration on the bronze bucket from Waldalgesheim
b–c Design from gold torc and bronze wagon fitting, Waldalgesheim
d Bronze torc from Jonchery-sur-Suippe (Marne) and their distribution
e–f Scabbards: Hungary and La Tène, Switzerland

40 Sites mentioned in chapters 6 and 7

41 Italian traded goods, second and first centuries BC
a–b Dressel I amphorae
c Sestius stamp
d–f Campanian bronze vessels and their distribution
g–h Black gloss pottery

42 Gallic coinage and its Greek prototypes

43 Mšecké Žehrovice
a Waste from the manufacture of sapropelite bracelets
b Plan of the Viereckschanzen
c Stone head

44 Manching, Bavaria
a–c Development of the oppidum

45 Ramparts of the late La Tène
a The murus gallicus
b The Kelheim construction

46 Buildings inside oppida
a Plan of Villeneuve-St Germain, France
b–c Hrazany, Bohemia
d–e Manching, Bavaria

47 Late La Tène pottery
a–b Vessels from Manching, Bavaria
c–d Bowl and frieze from Roanne, France

48 British La Tène Art
a–k Objects from Stanwick, North Yorkshire
l Bronze mirror from Holcombe, Devon
m–n Gold torcs: Snettisham and Ipswich

49 Hengistbury Head, Dorset
a Plan of Hengistbury Head
b Hinterland of Hengistbury Head
c–e Imported pottery from northern France

50 Britain and the Roman Empire
a–d Changing relationship: first century BC to first century AD

51 Colchester, Essex
a Plan of the settlement
b–c Imported Dressel amphorae
d Imported southern French samian bowl

52 Gallo-Belgic pottery
a–c Beakers and flasks
d Platters
e Potters' stamps

53 Welwyn Garden City, Hertfordshire
a Plan of the burial
b Silver cup

54 The Roman impact on southern Etruria
a The pre-Roman road system
b The imposed Roman system

55 Iron Age and Roman towns
a Mont Beuvray
b–c Pompeii
d Caerwent

# *Preface*

In the ten years or so that I have been teaching undergraduate and extra-mural courses for the universities of Sheffield, Leicester, Birmingham, and Nottingham, I have longed for someone to write a general introduction to the European Iron Age, but no one has, or rather no one has dared, and so I rashly charge into the gap. I hope that the specialists into whose territory I have transgressed will forgive me for any failings in detail which the wide expansion of the literature in recent years makes inevitable. My own doctoral thesis was considered wide, but it dealt with only a century of the development of part of the area covered by this book.

What may have been lost in detail I hope will have been gained in the unity of approach. I believe that for the first time a single author has attempted to describe the processes which underlay the development of European civilisation in the classical world of Greece, Etruria and Rome, and its relationship with the more shadowy areas north of the Alps. As this book demonstrates the histories of Mediterranean and Temperate Europe were inextricably linked throughout the first millennium.

The models that I have used to link the narrative together, of diffusion, trade, social differentiation, urbanisation, and state development are however not the only approaches which could be adopted, but it is the only viable one at present available to us because of the uneven development of archaeological research, and the limited approaches which are still applied especially in certain parts of classical archaeology. However attitudes are changing rapidly, and perhaps in the next decade or two it will prove possible to write from a more social and economic point of view when we know more of the development of the classical towns, or the reaction of the rural economy faced with the rapid changes in trade and industry. This book is thus a first essay of synthesis. I hope in the next decade both I and others will be able to provide rather different viewpoints to those put forward in this book.

# CHAPTER ONE

# Attitudes to the Past

Among the earliest surviving European literature is the poetry of Hesiod, notably his *Works and Days*, in which he describes the hard lot of the farmer – the labour involved in tilling the land to obtain the food needed for survival in a harsh and hostile world. Hesiod lived in the Age of Iron, but in happier days, in the Ages of Gold and Silver, food was plentifully available without the drudgery of farming: it only required gathering and eating. This idealised picture still plays a part in our schizophrenic view of the past and of 'simple societies', be it the concept of the 'noble savage', or what Sahlins has more scientifically documented as 'the original affluent society'.

The opposite view of society is embodied in words such as 'progress' and 'technological advance', popularised in prehistoric terms by Christian Thomsen's *Three Age System*. Who, Thomsen argued, would make axes of stone if they knew of bronze and iron? What had started as a classification of objects in the National Museum at Copenhagen rapidly became the basis for the chronological division of European man's prehistory. Thomsen's idea, coupled later with the concepts of evolution and of 'the survival of the fittest', reflected, if not originated, the self-satisfaction of late nineteenth-century West European society—the belief that it was technologically superior and therefore superior in all other respects to 'less advanced' societies both past and present. This reached its extreme form in the Germanic school of Kossinna whose views on the superiority of the German race formed one of the cornerstones of Nazi ideology.

If the extremist view of the Kossinna school was rejected by the majority of archaeologists, the modes of explanation were shared, except that 'civilisation' was a phenomenon which spread from the south-east rather than the north-west—*ex oriente lux*. Ideas spread by 'diffusion', an ill-defined process which assumed the inevitability of the march of civilisation from one region to the next, and explained the movement of ideas in terms of pseudo-history—invasions and waves of migration of peoples across Europe. The revolution in dating by C14 destroyed the foundation of this approach for some aspects of the neolithic and Bronze Age periods, and in the literature appeared terms such as 'independent development' and 'autonomy' to explain the megalithic tombs of western Europe or the development of European copper and bronze metallurgy. But for the Iron Age at least neither 'diffusion' nor 'autonomy' were adequate explanations; it was clearly a combination of the two—ideas spreading from one area to another, with individual, unique reactions which produced a varied pattern of distinctive regional cultures.

The fashion today is to talk in terms of 'culture change', and to study the mechanics of how this happened in each society. Though each reaction may be unique, the process and mechanics which caused those changes still follow basic rules of explanation. Trade, for instance, can initiate change, but the objects exchanged, the way the trade was organised, the people who participated, and the reactions produced, though often similar, will appear in unique combinations in every case. The economy, the environment, technology, ideology and the social structure will combine in a unique system. In each case we cannot understand one aspect of the system without knowing something of the whole. To gain this knowledge, a study of the entirety of a society is the ideal, but there are practical limitations. The archaeological record represents only a wreckage of former societies in which the archaeologist tries to recognise patterns. Even the aspects of society which we might expect to survive do not always do so. Burials may for some reason not appear or settlements are difficult to locate. Added to this is the bias of the archaeologist. Too often our knowledge is derived from 'treasure hunting' by clandestine tomb robber and archaeologist alike, and the obsession of certain museums for objects of 'art', divorced from their context, has produced a hopelessly one-sided view of, for instance, the Etruscans. They are condemned for their second-rate art, but ignored for the unique development of their urban settlements. Scholarship too readily confines itself to one aspect of a society—its art, its sculpture, its architecture, its trade—but ignores the total context. Thus we have to study the process of urbanisation, or the economic impact of trade on Etruscan society, in terms of art history derived from gravegoods from tombs.

This book has the ambitious aim of studying such reaction and change in southern and central Europe in the first millennium BC. It was the period when European civilisation took its shape, with the appearance of the civilisations of the Greeks, Phoenicians, Etruscans and Romans, and, in more shadowy form, of the Illyrians, Celts and Germans north of the Alps. It starts in a period when Bronze Age Europe, though linked by trade within itself, was isolated from the Near East with the collapse of Mycenaean Greece at the end of the second millennium. We shall see how slowly, through the intermediaries of Phoenicia and Greece, a new network appeared along which trade objects, technology and concepts travelled, gradually embracing the Mediterranean, central Europe and, finally, Britain and Scandinavia. At the end of the period much of the area was united within a common entity, the Roman Empire.

My attitudes are those of a prehistorian viewing the world from central Europe, with a grounding in geography and anthropology rather than the traditions of Mediterranean archaeology. I am more concerned with those developments which

are visible in the archaeological record than written sources, so that we can make direct comparisons between, for instance, the archaic states of Greece and central France. But such aims are not easy to achieve, as the existence of historical evidence has inevitably caused classical archaeologists to lean on these rather than on the archaeology. What did an early Greek state look like in spatial terms, what were the early towns really like—our views are too overlain by classical Greek concepts of what a city and city state was like. It causes problems of nomenclature. Classical archaeologists will call 'kings' and 'tribes' what anthropologists might call 'chiefs' and 'chiefdoms', bringing out our own innate prejudice of what these words mean. The whole of the archaeology is riven with such basic conceptual bias, and I will make no claims to have escaped it myself, but so that the reader can understand better the way in which the data we are considering has been collected in the past, and how different generations and types of archaeologists have attempted to arrange it in meaningful patterns, we must first discuss the basic attitudes from which the period can be viewed.

## Population movement and ethnicity

Invasion and migration have been popular forms of explanation of culture change since the last century, and this has been especially true of the Iron Age, when we have documentary evidence that such migrations happened. However, it has often been too readily invoked, and there are problems with identifying it in the archaeological record even in documented cases. Groups often symbolise themselves in terms of material culture. We can identify pottery styles that are peculiarly Greek during the Geometric and Archaic periods. Though imitations do occur, and the pottery was traded, we can use it to identify Greek colonies, or the presence of Greek potters in Etruscan cities. The problem for the archaeologist is to decide what are the significant signals in the archaeological data. Is the provision of a horse with three tails on certain Iron Age coins in Britain something of overt significance to the users of the coins, was it merely a convention, or was there an

1a

underlying relationship between users of these coins of which even they were not immediately aware?

The problems are most acute when we consider the Celts of central and western Europe. It is regularly assumed that we can equate 'Celts' with La Tène culture and La Tène Art. But what do we mean by 'Celts'? People who spoke a Celtic language, or who were members of a political group who called themselves Celts, or a physical type (blue-eyed, fair haired, etc.), or should we not expect all these definitions to correspond exactly—did all people with La Tène Art speak a Celtic language; did all Celtic speakers have La Tène Art? Without care we can be led into nonsense. In most books on 'Celtic Art' the Gundestrup cauldron is illustrated, on the

**1 'Celtic' metalwork**

The Gundestrup cauldron (a) was found in a bog in northern Jutland in 1891. It had been dismantled and deliberately deposited, and, like many similar finds from Neolithic to Viking times in Denmark, it is probably a ceremonial or ritual offering. It consists of a number of silver plates decorated with repoussé ornament.

The style of the weapons, and especially the fact that the horsemen are wearing spurs, suggests a second or first century BC date. The art style is not local, and it was formerly thought the cauldron was an import from Gaul or more doubtfully from central Europe. The closest parallels, however, come from Romania, for instance the somewhat earlier silver cups from the burial at Agighiol (b), and it seems most likely that the Gundestrup cauldron was made in eastern Europe.

The iconography of the individual plates has attracted

**1b**

**1c**

a wide literature, much of it fanciful. Some of the attributes of the individuals depicted are known from religious sculptures of Roman date from Gaul. Thus the antlered figure (e) is identified with the Celtic god Cernunnos. Some of the weapons (c)—the shields, the trumpet or carnyx—are known in La Tène contexts, but to go further and call this object 'Celtic' is to take archaeology beyond its limits. We cannot know the language spoken by the silversmith—it could have been Celtic, or German, or Thracian or Dacian.

He has taken a wide range of symbolism of different origins. The small figure slaying the bull on the central panel (d) reminds us of the later Persian cult of Mithras, the boy riding on the dolphin (e) appears in Greek mythology, the elephants (f) hint at ideas from further east, while the wearing of torcs found on several of the plates is something by no means confined to the Celtic world.

*Scale: 1:3*

1d

1e

1f

grounds that it depicts items of La Tène material culture (helmets, shields, trumpets), and Celtic deities such as Cernunnos the antlered god. But this object was manufactured in 'Thracian' or 'Dacian' Romania, and buried in 'Germanic' Denmark. The scenes mentioned do not make it 'Celtic' any more than the bull-slaying scene makes it 'Persian', or the elephant makes it 'Indian'. Though we should be aware that items such as La Tène brooches *may* have an ethnic significance, we must be firmly aware of alternative explanations.

## Diffusion

Diffusion implies the gradual adoption of new ideas and their general spread. It is a phenomenon which we can detect in, for instance, the spread of techniques of iron working, in the adoption of coinage, of urbanisation, of the potter's wheel, and it lies behind the layout of this book. But it is a dangerous and misleading concept. On the one hand, it can lead to false assumptions in the source and direction of diffused ideas, such as the 'hyper-diffusionism' of Elliot and Perry which sought to derive all concepts of civilisation, even of Meso-American civilisation, from Egypt, views based on a number of fallacies, still, unhappily, perpetuated by Thor Heyerdahl

in his Ra expedition. Secondly, it is in itself no explanation of why an idea spread, why it might be adopted by one society and not another, or indeed whether it necessarily played the same role in all societies. To take a concrete example: a type of knife or dagger may be in daily use by all members of society in the area where it is manufactured; it may be traded to a neighbouring society where its rarity makes it an item of prestige; it may be traded even further, into societies where it is considered so exotic that it is only used in ritual and ceremonial circumstances. Such changes of meaning can be documented in the modern anthropological record, we must assume that similar phenomena occurred in prehistory, as for instance the bronze vessels traded from Italy to southern Germany in the sixth century BC. In other words we must study the context of any object or innovation as it occurs in a society, and try to understand the role that it played and the message that it carried. We must also understand the social and economic context. The potter's wheel will not be adopted if there is no tradition for making fine pottery or no way in which a specialist can be supported. Towns are not something which can suddenly spring up without the necessary social, political and economic institutions to support it. Diffusion is only a description, it does not tell us why.

The spread of the knowledge of iron working, especially the technology which allowed the production of functional tools and weapons, shows a classic pattern of diffusion, and other examples can be clearly identified in the archaeological record during the Iron Age. The ideas mostly emanated from the technologically and socially more advanced areas of the Near East and the east Mediterranean. We must, however, beware of assuming that all advances necessarily moved in a westward and northward direction. For instance, fortification techniques in the first century BC spread from Britain into neighbouring areas of the continent; bronze swords of early Hallstatt type may have spread in the seventh century BC from Britain towards central Europe. Indeed, in certain aspects central Europe was technologically more advanced at various periods in prehistory than the Near East, as in the production of long bronze swords at the beginning of the late Bronze Age, or the high-quality iron work which was being produced in the Alpine region in the second and first centuries BC.

However, the majority of technological innovations do have their origin in the Near East. The use, for instance, of the potter's wheel is something we see appearing in Greece around 1050 to 1000 BC, and then appearing alongside other evidence of Greek contact in central Italy in the period about 750 to 700 BC. Thence it spread into northern Italy by around 700 BC, and we find its first introduction into central Europe at the major trading centres of the Heuneburg and Mont Lassois around 550 to 500 BC. Not until the end of the second or beginning of the first century BC did this new technology reach southern England, and other areas such as northern Britain and Scandinavia were not to adopt the potter's wheel until the Roman Iron Age, if not even later. In this particular case the adoption of a more advanced technology was hindered by the low level of economic development in various societies, which did not have the institutions which could support specialised industries. It is also connected with the organisation of society, especially the presence of an elite clientele who could form a market for high-quality goods.

The most far reaching and complex of these diffusion patterns is that associated with the so-called 'orientalising' process visible in the artistic styles of the Mediterranean and central Europe. This was connected with the trade patterns which emanated from the developing civilisations of the Near East, Greece, North Africa and Italy. It is characterised by the adoption in local art forms of floral motifs, such as the lotus bud and palmette, and animal motifs whose origin can be seen in the Near East. Most obvious are the various mythical beasts, often mixtures of various animals, or animals and humans, such as the sphinx, the winged horse, centaurs, fawns, chimaeras and gryphons. With these ideas also moved technological information, especially in the production of beaten bronze metalwork on which many of these artistic motifs are depicted. But artistic change may reflect more fundamental changes within society, and we find that the same creatures appear in myths explaining the nature and structure of Greek society—such as the role of the sphinx in Thebes, or the minotaur in Athens—to confirm the dominant position of certain of the leading families.

## Trade

Trade falls into three main categories: long-distance, inter-regional, and local. It is the long-distance trade that is easiest to detect in the archaeological record because foreign and exotic goods are readily identified from more local objects. By inter-regional is meant the exchange of goods often over long distances, but within a similar cultural milieu, and which may involve objects which are similar, at least in outward form, to local products. In the case of pottery, for instance, it may only be the composition of the clay which betrays a foreign object.

The motivations for trade varied, and, though there is obviously a general economic context within which trade is going on, to understand the nature of prehistoric trade we must try to identify which sectors of society were engaged in the trade, and what their motivations might have been. Within the general economic context, it is the lack of basic raw materials which will motivate trade in the first place. Certainly by the end of our period we can identify societies which cannot exist without trade in some form or another, not merely for raw materials, but even for their basic food supplies, and into this category come some of the Greek cities like Athens, and later, Rome. The major cities of the Near East, especially those of the Mesopotamian Plain, were equally reliant upon trade for their very existence; although food was no major problem, all other raw materials especially metals and wood had to come from outside the Mesopotamian Plain. But the pattern is not quite as simple as one might imagine, as often the trade was not controlled by the large city states and empires where the need and the wealth resided, nor necessarily in the source areas of the raw materials. It is not uncommon for peoples peripheral to the main trade route to gain control of it and to act as middlemen—a characteristic we find in the trade networks of both the Greeks and the Phoenicians.

This brings us to the question of who within society was engaging in trade. Trading is an activity which is carried on by individuals for two reasons—either to acquire wealth, or to acquire status. In societies where hereditary power is based upon land ownership, as in the classical societies of Greece and Rome, an independent class of merchants who are acquiring wealth by trade and industry can represent a threat to the ruling class, and various alternative strategies have been adopted in the past to counteract this problem. In some societies, for instance, external trade is left in the hands of foreign merchants, who must pay tolls to the state, and who may be restricted in their movements to specific ports or trading centres, but who, by being foreigners, represent no threat to the power structure within the society. Foreign influences themselves can be capable of undermining society, and in certain cases, as with the Phoenician sites of Tyre and Sidon, neighbouring powers such as Assyria were willing to leave them independent, so that all foreign trade could be channelled through them—the so-called 'ports of trade'. China provides a modern parallel, with the independent ports of Shanghai and Hong Kong, but a 'port of trade' need not necessarily be a coastal site; it can be a neutral inland site on the boundary between two conflicting states. An alternative is to attempt to emasculate the merchants' political power by restricting office to the landowning class. Although the wealth may be gradually absorbed by intermarriage into the upper classes, in Rome for instance, the senatorial class—the traditional landowners—were forbidden to engage in trade, whereas the merchant class—the Equestrian order—were not eligible under the constitution of the Republic for election to the senate.

An alternative was for the ruling class themselves to keep very tight control over trade, but this could only be done when the trade was not so extensive that control was impossible. It also depended on limiting the channels whereby trade entered the country. This was clearly easiest where connection was by sea, so that trade could be forced through a small number of ports. But the trade routes over the Alpine passes, or along the major river routes such as the Rhône, offered equal opportunities. Such centralised control is, however, a relatively rare phenomenon in the areas which we are considering. There is evidence that it may have existed in the late Bronze Age in Greece and Crete, with the Minoan and Mycenaean palaces controlling the trade and redistribution of goods by means of a developed, literate bureaucracy. In less developed forms we may detect centralised control on the sites of the late Hallstatt period of the sixth century BC, sites such as the Heuneburg and Mont Lassois in western Europe. Yet other examples may be the late Iron Age trade centre on the Magdalensberg in Austria, or the port site of Colchester in England. In these cases the trader may again be a foreigner, and this is the most likely in the cases I have cited; alternatively he could be a low-class individual, who merely acted as transporter for goods on behalf of members of the aristocracy.

So far we have been assuming the existence of a group within society whom we can class as 'merchants', but this assumption is only applicable to the more complex societies that existed by the late Iron Age. Other mechanisms can be used to explain long-distance trade, for instance 'down-the-line' trade whereby goods pass from community to community on a reciprocal basis along kinship channels, or through trading partnerships. Alternatively, trading may only be an irregular activity, on a seasonal basis, but possibly more erratic, through the instigation of an individual, as for instance happened in Viking society. Under these circumstances, individuals could travel considerable distances. One possible example is the trade link which developed between the central Rhine and the southern Alpine valleys in the early La Tène period in the fifth century BC.

Inter-regional trade was probably organised along very similar lines to that of the long-distance trade we have been describing, except that in the Iron Age the mechanisms of down-the-line trade and seasonal trade were more likely than trade through a specialised merchant class. Social links of a political and family nature were much more likely between societies sharing similar cultures, and presumably languages, and would be capable of producing all the basic commodities that might have been necessary to sustain a given society. For Temperate Europe, at least, long-distance trade was generally not necessary, except to acquire luxury goods like wine and silk. Otherwise these areas were largely self-sufficient through inter-regional trade.

It is, therefore, perhaps not surprising that the main stimulus for long-distance trade came from the Mediterranean and from the Near East. True, within Temperate Europe there had already existed in the late Bronze Age a system of contacts which extended from central Italy in the south up to Denmark in the north, which resulted in close similarity over a very wide area between prestige items such as beaten bronze cups and buckets. But it is not clear to what extent individual objects were moving, or were merely local imitations. It seems most likely that this was down-the-line trade, with reciprocal arrangements between members of the upper classes of late Bronze Age society. It is very different from the Iron Age trade between the classical worlds of Greece and Etruria with central and western Europe, where the goods—be they fine pottery, textiles, or more especially wine—could not at this stage be imitated locally, and where, in certain cases at least, the Greek and Etruscan trade seems to have been in the hands of full-time merchants.

In the late Bronze Age there had existed in the East Mediterranean a trade system in the Mycenaean world which linked together the Near Eastern civilisations of Mesopotamia and the Anatolian highlands with Greece and the central Mediterranean, with ramifications which were even influencing central and western Europe. But this had collapsed by about 1000 BC. In the succeeding centuries we see the appearance, first in Cyprus and Greece and then again extending on into Italy and eventually central Europe, of a trade system largely under Greek and Phoenician control which first supplied the Near Eastern markets, and then became essential for the developing classical cities of the Greeks, the Carthaginians and the Etruscans. This trading system was to reach Greece by about 900–850 BC, Etruria by 800–750 BC, southern Germany by 700–650 BC, and Britain and Scandinavia in the first century BC. Though the emphasis changed from one period to another (for instance, a switch in the seventh/sixth centuries BC from the development of a western market to a development in the fifth century of the Black Sea ports by the Greek cities), nonetheless—this interchange between the Mediterranean world and Temperate Europe was to remain a major theme throughout the Iron Age, culminating in the Imperial conquest of much of the area by Rome at the end of millennium.

Local trade systems have been very much less studied because there has always been a tacit assumption that we understood the mechanics of local exchange. It is only with the work of Polanyi and Sahlins that we have realised that the mechanisms of barter and especially the market are relatively new innovations, and that other mechanisms which can still be found in our own society were very much more important if not exclusive in early societies. The first of these was 'reciprocity'—the exchange of goods between individuals of a balanced nature whereby gifts are given to fulfil obligations of a social or familial nature. Such exchange can be found within all societies, be it the partitioning of a dead animal by a hunter, or the social exchange of tobacco and alcohol or giving of Christmas presents within our own society. Secondly there is 'redistribution' whereby an individual or institution acts as the focus of the exchange. Some societies have an individual who is free to obtain status by means of exchange, the so-called 'Big Man' or, if it is a status inherited by birth, the 'Chieftain', though this varies from an individual who is merely tolerated by his society to situations where power is also concentrated in his hands. Gift-giving is then a right expected by the chieftain in the form of tribute, with little reciprocal return. These forms of movements of goods are personalised, taking place between individuals who share other connections of social, political or familial nature. 'Barter' is a form of exchange which implies that there are no other relationships, and can only take place when there are individuals who wish to engage in direct exchange of goods, a form of exchange which was probably much rarer than has often been assumed.

The advent of market exchange for the first time allowed impersonal exchange to take place, usually using some medium of exchange, of which coinage is the most common form, though other items such as shells or food stuffs have been known to perform similar functions. Polanyi has suggested that the beginning of a market-style economy was a late feature, which appeared in Greece in the fifth and fourth centuries BC, beginning in the classical towns such as Athens, where coins were being produced for state purposes such as paying for military or jury service, but which was rapidly developed for use for impersonalised exchange. But we can assume that coinage was probably never produced in ancient societies to facilitate exchange. The earliest coins we possess from Asia Minor are all of high values, of gold and later of silver, which could only have been used in a limited set of circumstances, for the payment, for instance, of tribute or bride wealth and for other political or social needs. The use of coinage spread rapidly throughout the Greek world, and by the third century BC had spread to much of Temperate Europe as well; but wherever it was adopted, the early stage is represented by these high-value coins, and only at the end of the Iron Age in Temperate Europe were lower-value coins being minted. Again we can assume that they were not made to facilitate exchange, as no issuer would

have seen much immediate return for encouraging trade in this way, and the use of low-value coins for direct exchange is probably in all of these areas a matter of secondary usage.

It is difficult to distinguish between the different kinds of exchange at a local level. It is essential to know something of the social and economic organisation of the society; are there, for instance, individuals who seem to be much wealthier, and who may have been acting as the centres of exchange systems? Some clear examples of this exist in the archaeological record, such as the rich burials associated with Mont Lassois and the Heuneburg. But it may be easy to confuse such rich burials with those of a land-owning elite, who may have played no part in the exchange, other than that of being the eventual recipients of the traded goods. Another problem is the identification of 'central places' where exchange could and did take place. Though the role of the Greek and Roman towns in this respect is well documented from later sources, we are less clear about the role of sites such as the hillforts of central and western Europe. These sites could have been the centre of exchange, but likewise they could have been peripheral, with exchange passing through members of the upper classes of society, who may have been resident elsewhere than on the hillfort. Our only hope in identifying 'central places' lies in the recognition of special items such as weights or unusual concentrations of items traded from a larger distance. The nature of local trade systems is going to be a major area of research in the next decade.

## Social structure

As suggested above, it is impossible to understand how trade and production were organised without understanding something of social organisation, though this is never easy from archaeological data, and often is more of a likely guess than anything that can be proven, even at the level of generalisation which is all the prehistorian can hope for. The terminology in this book is that of the evolutionary school of anthropologists in America such as Service and Fried, as they do offer us some possibility of applying a more uniform terminology across the various societies discussed in this book.

The simplest level of *band* applies primarily to hunting-gathering groups and does not concern us in Iron Age society. Neither should Service's second level of social integration, the *tribe*, except that this is a term used traditionally to describe many European societies in the Iron Age which had not reached an advanced level of state organisation. Anthropologically, the tribe is an egalitarian organisation based upon lineages, bound together by other social institutions ('sodalities') such as age-sets and secret societies which cross-cut lineage affiliations. The third level is the *chiefdom* which is organised in a social hierarchy or pyramid structure based on lineages. Social status is inherited, and power based upon authority. But it may be worthwhile distinguishing simple from complex chiefdoms, the latter with more tiers in the hierarchy, larger geographical territory, and, as we shall see in the next section, a rather different form of spatial configuration. Complex chiefdoms lead on to *archaic states*, a division not easy to make on purely archaeological grounds, in which institutionalised offices appear, with power invested in them to impose the will of the state by force. Positions may be inherited, as in kingship, but magistrates are often elected. Groups of states may be linked together to form leagues, as in Greek and Etruscan society, but where one state achieves dominance and exacts tribute from the others, as Athens did from the Delian League in the fifth century, the word *Empire* might be more applicable. Properly, however, this term should be used for a state organisation which unites a number of different territorally based ethnic and cultural groups, as did the empires of Macedonia and Rome.

These various levels of social integration are associated with developments in the roles of individuals, though the terminology developed by Fried does not correspond exactly with Service's classification. At the simplest level, status is *egalitarian*, within the limitations of age, sex, and personal ability; *ranked society* is based essentially upon *achieved status* by an individual through his position within a lineage or a sodality; *stratified society* is based upon *inherited status*, as is typical of many chiefdoms and archaic states. Within the classes of social complexity there is often a centralisation based upon individuals. At the tribal level it might be epitomised by the 'big men' of New Guinea society—an individual who acts as a nodal point for exchange within a region, and who, though of great prestige, does not necessarily have any other status within society. The role may be passed from father to son, but each individual has to establish his own prestige. At the chiefdom level the central individual is the chief, of complex chiefdom the paramount chief, while the terms king, tyrant or dictator might be reserved for the state level, and emperor for the multinational state. This avoids confused terminology, for instance, for the translation of the Greek word βασιλευs (basileus) as 'king' as it is used by Greek historians for everything from chief to emperor, and immediately prejudices our concept of the level of early Greek society. All these terms, however, are only used in a generalised way—there are many different forms of chiefdom or early state, and the terminology and classification will not tell us how any individual society actually functioned, though it does suggest what may be the key features we should be investigating.

It is at the level of the individual that the archaeologist may best be able to operate, as his status within society may well be fossilised at his death in terms of the burial rite. Different levels of organisation may be identifiable in spatial terms, as will be discussed in the next section, but settlement evidence can be ambiguous, and key sites may be missed, whereas the more ubiquitous burial evidence may allow us to predict the existence of undiscovered sites. Burials, however, have their own drawbacks. Archaeologists assume that status is indicated by gravegoods, grave-structure and siting of the tomb; the problem is that each individual may have many statuses, and which is being symbolised? Is a grave with many pots a person who was himself wealthy, or one who had many relatives each of whom gave a pot? Sometimes several statuses may be symbolised—in sixth-century southern Germany gravegoods may indicate both wealth, age, and marital status; in the male Germanic cemetery of Gross Romstedt trade/social status, and rank within the military hierarchy, may both be indicated by different sets of gravegoods. Such details are not available for the majority of areas, even the basic divisions of age and sex, and so we are forced back to assuming that rich gravegoods mean rich individuals, and directly comparing one society with another, though as we should realise from our own society, a lack of gravegoods does not mean poor people—ideology plays a role as well.

Though anthropologists commonly issue warnings about exceptional cases, the archaeologist's experience with large numbers of burials shows that there is usually considerable standardisation of burial practice within individual societies, and patterns are visible. Large numbers of wealthy gravegoods represent a deliberate, ostentatious destruction of wealth, presumably by those wishing to inherit the dead man's status, a combination of 'potlatch' and 'rite of passage' (ceremonial activity to mark an individual's change of status—birth, initiation, marriage, death, etc), in cases where inheritance may not be entirely ensured or where power needs to be reaffirmed. Adult gravegoods with young children may likewise imply inherited rather than achieved status, but every case needs arguing within its own cultural context, and such studies are generally rarely available.

The general trend throughout the first millennium is for social differentiation to increase, though this was by no means a simple unilinear trend—north of the Alps the richest prehistoric burials belong to the sixth century BC, and there is no evidence of anyone with wealth comparable to these individuals for several centuries. Where social differentiation was taking place, we must ask what is causing it, and what the basis of elite power may be. In Greek and Roman society the basis of power was land, and though money might be invested by these elite in production and trade, in Roman society at least the senatorial class was debarred from engaging in such sordid activities. The Hallstatt chieftains, on the other hand, may well have gained ascendancy by monopoly control of trade, for those of La Tène A production of raw materials may be the key, and military conquest is a fourth possibility, but normally combinations of all four may be found, as in medieval feudal society when local power rested in control of land, and regional and national power in military force. Checks on absolute power might exist, as appears to be the case in Archaic Greek society, when military control by an individual or class was impossible, as warfare depended on putting large armies of citizen soldiers in the field.

## Spatial organisation

The organisation of trade and production, the social structure and the complexity of a society all combine to show themselves in one way which archaeologists can identify, in terms of spatial organisation. These are based on geographical models, in what anthropologists term 'regional analysis', which attempts to understand the economic and social functioning of an area as a whole.

The first question to ask of any society is what evidence is there for centralisation of any sort—concentrations of wealth, population, industry, trade, ritual, ceremonial and cultural activity, everything that can be termed *central-place activities*. At the lowest level of social organisation this may not be easy to identify. In the fourth and third centuries BC in central Europe, for instance, there is little difference detectable in terms of wealth or size between one settlement or cemetery and another, though there was certainly craft specialism, implying that individual sites may have had their own speciality, like the production of bronze fittings for chariots and harness at Gussage All Saints in Dorset, or that specialists would be called in when needed to superintend some specialist activity. We cannot envisage each village as a separate independent entity, but social, religious or political activities which helped to bind together a tribal group may not always be identifiable in the archaeological record, and without documentary evidence we may not realise their precise significance, like, for instance, the major shrines of Greece at Delphi, Delos, Olympia, Dodona and elsewhere, which gave the Greeks a sense of ethnic unity, but little more.

Even when we can identify evidence of communal activities, we must be careful not to assume that other aspects of society may also be centralised. A hillfort, for instance, represents a group response to the need for defence, it may even have had a permanent population within it, but it does not necessarily mean that industry or trade were centred in it, or that the elite members of society were resident within it. The geographer's concept of 'central place', though useful for interpreting ancient societies, holds dangers, and should only be used in situations where urban communities are fully developed, as it can lead to false assumptions about the level of social organisation that has been achieved.

At the 'chiefdom' level of society we should be able to identify some sort of social hierarchy, at least in terms of relative wealth of sites, and possibly in terms of population concentrations, and increased specialisation of industry, and generally denser population than at the tribal level. Agriculture may become more specialised, new farms established where they need only exploit one specialised environmental niche, acquiring other necessary foodstuffs by trade rather than producing it themselves. It can also lead to permanent occupation of marginal land which could only be exploited seasonally before, such as summer grazing areas. Chiefdoms will most naturally arise where the environment and topography is diverse.

The complex chiefdom has rather different spatial characteristics. If an individual's power is based on his position in a lineage rather than control of land or industrial production, he will rely on payment of tribute from those under him, in return for protection and other often minimal assistance. A chief in turn will owe allegiance and pay tribute to the paramount chief. In this situation transport costs are kept to a minimum if the chiefs' residences are close to that of the paramount chief, though not necessarily on the same settlement. This clustering around the main site forms a marked contrast to the situation we shall encounter where there is competitive marketing. The settlements of Hallstatt D such as the Heuneburg represent the classic European example of this phenomenon, but it could possibly explain the clusterings of settlement which charac-

terise the earliest phase in the development of Greek and Etruscan towns.

With the appearance of urban settlements, there are three sorts of central-place system which we may expect to encounter. The *dendritic* system is a term properly developed for exploitation of a peripheral area by means of a linked system of nodal points. The primary town is usually a port, linked to one or more secondary centres, themselves connected to tertiary points. In its developed state it is a product of colonial exploitation for the export of raw materials and agricultural produce to a 'core area' (in recent times western Europe or north America), and can lead to a collapse of native institutions and poverty in the hinterland, as in the best-documented case in northern Guatemala. The system is controlled from outside, though individuals, especially in the primary town, may acquire a considerable wealth because of their external contacts, and the town dwellers are often ethnically separate from the surrounding rural population.

Such systems in simpler form are readily distinguishable in the Mediterranean in the first millennium BC, though they varied in their level of exploitation. The relationship between the Greek colonies of southern Italy and Sicily clearly fit this pattern, with the subjugated natives in some cases virtually slaves. However, a less exploitative version was more common, for instance the links of Marseilles with its hinterland, or possibly Colchester in the early first century AD. At the other extreme is the port-of-trade, which may even have been beneficial to its hinterland in introducing luxury goods to undeveloped areas (as Hengistbury Head in southern England), or necessary trade contacts to major empires, as the Greek entrepôt of Naucratis in Egypt.

The second group are the *solar central places*, usually major administrative centres, which possess a monopoly for their surrounding area, in terms of marketing and trade facilities, and often industrial production as well. Characteristically they are very large, especially in comparison to towns in more developed competitive systems. Early Etruscan towns may have fallen into this category, but the classic examples in Iron Age Europe are the oppida of central and western

Temperate Europe, which are often much larger than their Roman and medieval successors— Manching for instance had a densely occupied area twice that of Roman London, itself one of the largest Roman towns north of the Alps.

In both the dendritic and solar central-place systems, access to market is restricted by the lack of subsidiary centres. At a more developed stage competitive central-place systems appear, with the appearance of subsidiary centres offering more localised market facilities for the agricultural population. Often attempts are made to suppress this development, as for instance in late Saxon England where laws were introduced to restrict market transactions to authorised sites and thus maintain monopolies, but usually the economic forces prove too strong. There are various competitive central-place systems, which differ in the siting of the subsidiary centres, and in their relationship to the primary centres. In the market principle the secondary centres will develop at the points furthest from the major centres, as it were filling in the gaps, and this is likely to evolve from the solar central-place system. The second is the transport principle, where the secondary sites appear on the routes mid-way between the primary centres, presumably a development of the dendritic system.

To what extent competitive systems had come into existence before the Roman period is unclear, but a competitive system may well have been developing in Etruria, and presumably based on the marketing principle. Over most of Temperate Europe, however, it was an introduction of the Roman period. The only detailed analysis is of southeast England, and relates to the second-third century AD, when the hierarchy and spacing of the settlements forms a classic case of the 'transport' principle, caused by the imposition of the Roman road system.

The appearance of urban 'central places' was one of the major innovations in Europe of the first millennium BC. Even if we reject centres such as the Heuneburg as truly urban, despite the concentration of wealth, trade and industry on them (the social structure would have prevented the full development of exchange as we know it on later sites), we still have a number of different urban types; administrative centres, market centres, colonies, and entrepôts for long-distance trade including ports-of-trade. Each of these classes would have its own characteristics in terms of who was resident, what public amenities were present, and in the spatial layout of the town.

The administrative centres might be expected to conform to the concept of the *pre-industrial city*. At its centre the administrative buildings— forum, basilica, major temples—and around it the courtyard dwellings of the social elite who provided the priests, magistrates and administrators who ran the city. Around this, arranged in residental quarters according to ethnic origin, occupation and wealth, would be the lower echelons of society—traders, merchants, artisans, and, on the outskirts, the urban poor who provided labour for the menial unskilled tasks. This extreme pattern—the reverse from that found in industrial and post-industrial cities, where the rich live in the periphery and the poor around the central business area—may have only been fully developed in major urban agglomerations such as Rome. In smaller towns, such as Roman civitas capitals where no-one lived far from the centre of the city, a different pattern might emerge, with the artisans clustered along the main access routes, and the wealthy in the secluded areas off the main roads.

The market centres and entrepôts might be expected to form a different pattern. The elite land-owning class would presumably not be resident, and political control of the town would lie in the hands of the wealthy merchant class. We would not expect the same range of public buildings—only those required for economic functions such as the market place—and for the administration of the town itself, and religious buildings too, but not the senate house or major buildings. These institutions, however, are those that we associate with a fully developed town, and one problem we shall have to consider is how and when these various institutions came into existence, though they are not questions we can always answer due to a lack of work on urban origins, especially in Greece and Etruria.

The basic characteristic we must expect of true urban sites should be variability: a wide range of different social groups present, from rich patrician to poor plebeian, a wide range of activities—trade, industry, religion, and 'culture' (theatres, baths etc)—and possibly also ethnic variability, such as the Italian trading quarters on the Magdalensberg, or Jewish ghettos in medieval towns. We might expect to find evidence of guilds, which express themselves spatially by the concentration of individual crafts in specific areas of the town, as for instance in classical Athens, or at Manching. The nature and variability of early towns is a subject which has been little explored.

## Chronology

As this book deals with trends and processes, a precise chronology is hardly necessary, though even for periods relatively late in the first millennium we cannot date within a century or so. All the dates used in this book are derived from historical documentation—dates provided by written records initially of Assyria and Egypt, but increasingly of Greece and Rome. These still provide more precise dates than scientific methods such as C14, though in the next decade tree-ring dating (dendrochronology) is going to revolutionise dating of the central European sequence.

The relative sequence in each area is derived from such methods as typology—the gradual change through time of pottery styles, ornaments such as brooches—supported by association in grave-groups, hoards or other deposits, or by stratigraphical sequences from long-lived sites. These are then given absolute dates by cross-dating either by the occurrence of imports from dated sequences elsewhere, or by exports occurring on historically dated sites, or preferably both.

The late Mycenaean period is fairly well dated by correlation with the Egyptian sequence, and by associations of Mycenaean pottery with the settlement of the Philistines in southern Palestine. After this the relative sequence of Proto-Geometric and Geometric Greece is well established, especially in Athens, based on the developing geometric styles of painted pottery which give the period its name. Between about 1100 and 750, however, contacts between Greece and the out-side world were meagre, and absolute dating for this sequence is a matter of informed guesswork, until the earliest occurrence of exported pottery on historically dated Near Eastern sites such as Hama in Syria. From the end of the eighth century the major sequences of Corinth and Athens can be given greater precision, based on the earliest pottery from Greek colonies with known foundation dates. The idiosyncracies of style of individual potters provides even greater precision in the black- and red-figure wares of late Archaic and Classical Greece of the sixth and fifth centuries, allowing us to date individual vessels within a few decades.

The central European sequence both for the late Bronze Age and for the Iron Age is based primarily on the development of metal objects, and for the Bronze Age this includes Italy as well. Broad sequences applicable over wide areas from Scandinavia to Sicily have been established, but absolute dating relies on the Greek sequence. The occurrence of swords of central European type in Mycenaean contexts allows the beginning of the sequence in the thirteenth–twelfth centuries to be dated, but then there is a gap until the Greek colonisation of Italy—the colony of Cumae founded c. 750–730 BC overlies a cemetery with bronze types related to those of central Europe.

The nomenclature for central Europe used in this book is based on that developed by Reinecke for southern Germany earlier this century. He used the nomenclature of the Scandinavian scholar Hildebrand, who identified the stylistic differences in the weapons and ornaments from the Alpine sites of Hallstatt and La Tène. Reinecke recognised the continuity of the earlier Iron Age with the preceeding 'Urnfield' Bronze Age, and applied the term 'Hallstatt' to both: phases C and D specifically refer to the Iron Age. The sequence for the Bronze Age is essentially established from hoard finds, for the Iron Age from burials, mainly from Hallstatt itself and from Bavaria and from the La Tène cemetery of Münsingen in Switzerland. Scholars have successively redefined and subdivided these periods, and for some phases such as Hallstatt D, it is almost possible to talk of individual generations. The sixth and fifth centuries are especially well dated

| | NEAR EAST | GREECE | CENTRAL ITALY | SOUTHERN GERMANY | CENTRAL FRANCE | SOUTHERN ENGLAND |
|---|---|---|---|---|---|---|
| 1200 | ASSYRIA / URARTU | MYCENEAN | PROTO-VILLANOVAN | HALLSTATT A 1 2 | URNFIELDS / BRONZE | LATE |
| 1100 | | SUB-MYCENEAN | | | | |
| 1000 | | PROTO-GEOMETRIC | | HALLSTATT B 1 2 3 | FINAL | BRONZE |
| 900 | | | VILLANOVAN | | | |
| 800 | | GEOMETRIC e m l | | | | AGE |
| 700 | | | | HALLSTATT C 1 2 | HALLSTATT I | |
| 600 | PERSIANS | ARCHAIC | ETRUSCAN | HALLSTATT D 1 2 3 | HALLSTATT II | EARLY IRON |
| 500 | | | | | | AGE ? |
| 400 | | CLASSICAL | | LA TENE A | a | |
| 300 | HELLENISTIC | Alexander / HELLENISTIC | | LA TENE B 1 2 | LA TENE I b c | MIDDLE IRON |
| 200 | | | | LA TENE C 1 2 | LA TENE II a b | AGE |
| 100 | PARTHIANS | ROMAN | ROMAN / Augustus | LA TENE D 1 2 | LA TENE III | LATE IRON AGE |
| BC | | | | | | |
| 0 | | | | ROMAN | ROMAN | GALLO-BELGIC |
| AD | | | | | | |
| 100 | | | | | | ROMAN |

•••••• iron working   〰〰〰 orientalizing   ▥ urbanising   ▨ imperial

**2** Chronological table

by means of Greek and Etruscan imports.

After about 400 in both the Mediterranean and central Europe the chronology is much less precise. The elaborate Greek painted wares disappear, and the simpler mass-produced plain wares of the Hellenistic period are not so readily diagnostic nor do we have new Greek colonies to give us absolute dates. In central Europe initially, imports are unknown anyway, and when they reapppear, are not readily dated. The horizontal stratigraphy of the Münsingen cemetery allows a fair amount of precision in the relative sequence, which can be applied with lesser or greater confidence from Romania to Britain, based on similarity of brooch types over the whole area. But absolute dating is not precise within a century until we reach the second half of the first century BC. Not until after 30 BC do datable coins become common in the archaeological record, and from 20 BC samian ware appears first from Arrezzo in Etruria and later from southern Gaul, which not only bears elaborate decoration but the stamps of individual potters and firms. These in turn occur on Roman forts in Germany which can be assigned to specific campaigns, with the result that dating within a decade, even five years, becomes a possibility on all classes of site where samian is found.

# CHAPTER TWO

# The Old Order

Contact between the Mediterranean and Temperate Europe was no new phenomenon. As early as the neolithic in the fifth–fourth millennium spondylus shells, probably from the Aegean, were circulating among the early farming communities of the Danube valley. The diffusion of the techniques of agriculture can be taken as an analogy for later diffusion patterns. Agriculture could not be simply transplanted from the Near East to central Europe—it required modification, new and hardier breeds of animals and plants, new domesticated species, and new methods of farming. In the same way, urbanism had to adapt to central Europe a few millennia later.

It was, however, the advent of bronze metallurgy that started the symbiotic relationship between the two areas. Copper, and more especially tin, are of localised occurrence, and areas such as the Aegean or Scandinavia were forced to rely on long-distance trade to obtain their metal supplies. Unfortunately, even using modern methods of analysis for the identification of trace elements, so complex is the pattern caused by the variability of the original ores even from a single mine, and of the processing of the metal, alloying, and reuse, that only rarely is it possible to identify the source of the metal outside its areas of origin. So, although we can be fairly sure metals from the north were reaching the east Mediterranean, the precise routes and the mechanisms of the trade still elude us.

Doubtless this trade, both local and inter-regional, was one of the causes behind the ever-increasing input of labour and destruction of wealth associated with the burial of specific individuals. At the end of the third millennium in central Europe bodies might be accompanied by an elaborate pot or one or two metal ornaments, and be buried under a small round barrow. Early in the following millennium, for instance at Leubingen in East Germany, an elaborate timber structure under an ostentatious barrow might include axes and halberds, gold pins, even possibly human sacrifice. By the thirteenth–twelfth century wagons accompanied the wealthiest, like the pyre burial of Hart-an-der Alz in Bavaria with its rich collection of bronze vessels, some possibly of North Italian origin; or the warrior at Čaka in Slovakia, interred with a corselet of bronze—a display of funerary wealth that would not reappear again in central and western Europe until the beginning of the Iron Age in the seventh century BC.

Other goods and materials were being traded. Amber from the Baltic is one of the easiest to identify archaeologically, passing down the river routes of the Elbe and Oder, and reaching the Aegean, while in return from central Europe bronze reached Scandinavia in increasing quantities. Salt was also being produced at Halle on the Saale in East Germany—probably the basis of the wealth of the Leubingen burial. With this centralisation of surplus came greater specialisation in craft products—gold ornaments and cups, beads of faience, jet and shale, which too are found in the wealthier burials.

In Temperate Europe this centralisation of wealth mainly found expression in archaeological terms in burials, hoards (some of which were deliberately deposited rather than accidentally not recovered), or more rarely in ceremonial monuments such as Stonehenge. But in one area

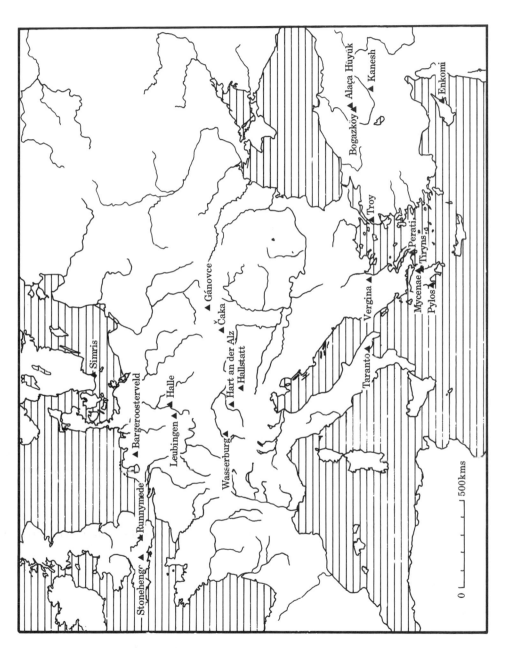

3  Sites mentioned in chapter 2

of Europe, the Aegean, this centralisation of wealth and power took on a more extreme version, in the palaces of Minoan Crete and Mycenaean Greece. What caused this lies outside the realms of this book, but clearly trade and the proximity of the great irrigation civilisations of Mesopotamia, Turkey and Egypt were contributory factors.

The palaces acted as centralised stores for grain, olive oil and other agricultural surplus, and this in turn was used to support specialists of many kinds, indeed the palaces may also have been able to control production of both prestige and many utilitarian goods. Potters were producing fine ceramics of a kind which had no equal in the rest of Europe or even the east Mediterranean. Mycenaean pottery appears in Egypt and the Levant in historically dated contexts, which allows us to fix fairly precise dates for the Mycenaean world up to about 1100 BC. Metalsmiths were working bronze, silver and gold, inlaying bronze dagger blades with hunting scenes. Architecture developed with ashlar construction for both the palace buildings and the collective tholos tombs, while around the Minoan palaces and Mycenaean citadels there clustered stone-built houses, agglomerations of population which we might well describe as urban. And to run the whole system there appeared a class of bureaucrats who inscribed their accounts on tablets of clay, in Greek.

All this is evidence for a concentration of power and a level of specialisation unparalleled outside the Near East. Some of the specialisms (ashlar building, writing) were unique in Europe to the Mycenaean world, and the surrounding societies to the north and west were incapable of emulating the production of the luxury goods. But Mycenaean Greece did not hold a monopoly of innovation, and in one sphere at least it was surpassed, in the production of weapons. The major innovation in fighting in the thirteenth–twelfth centuries BC was the flange-hilted sword. Various early varieties are known, with different shapes of hilts, the best known being the Hemigkofen and the Erbenheim varieties. Partly these swords owe their appearance to technological developments, the ability of bronze-smiths to make larger and more elaborate cast-

ings, including the addition of lead to the bronze alloys. Between the fifteenth and thirteenth centuries the short dagger became longer, firstly a rapier and finally a true sword. The second innovation was the leaf-shape of the blade which placed all the weight at the point, allowing the warrior to fight by slashing rather than fencing. The flange-hilt to hold the wooden handle was the third innovation, improving the warrior's grip on the sword,. These swords have a pan-European distribution—from Britain and Scandinavia in the west to Cyprus in the east—and they are the predecessors of the swords of the late Bronze Age and early Iron Age from Syria to Ireland.

The typological ancestors of these swords are only found in and around the Hungarian Plain, and this area may have been the origin of other metalworking innovations, such as the safety-pin brooch, defensive armour (greaves, corselets, and helmets) and possibly bronze vessels. But these items were also rapidly adopted in Greece, and their development is not so clear as that of the swords.

The flange-hilted swords are found in the final phases of the Mycenaean civilisation (Late Helladic IIIb–IIIc), which has led some scholars to suggest that it was destroyed by invaders from the north, but they are in fact found in normal Mycenaean graves, and had clearly been adopted before the civilisation collapsed. It is with the fall of Mycenae that our enquiry will begin, but first we should discuss the development of iron working which makes its appearance in Greece in the same contexts as the flange-hilted swords.

## The origin of iron working

Iron has such obvious advantages over bronze that one must explain why iron working was not adopted earlier. In comparison to copper, especially the tin ores required to make bronze, the basic iron ores are widely spread and available in most areas. The simplest oxides such as haematite ($Fe_2O_3$) are available in various forms either as rock ores or as bog iron, and these were the most sought after. The sulphide ores such as pyrites ($FeS_2$) were less popular as small amounts of sulphur would make the iron brittle. But the

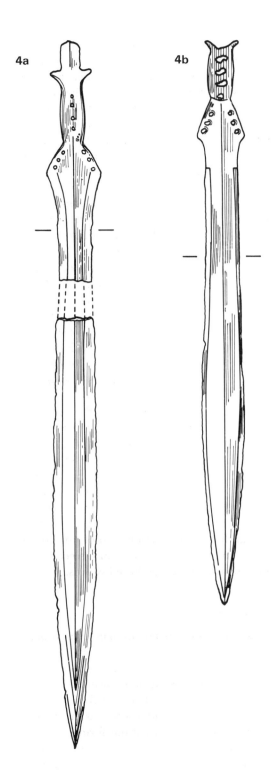

**4a**

**4b**

**4** Late Bronze Age swords

The Erbenheim (a) and Hemigkofen (b) sword types represented a great innovation in fighting techniques. With previous technologies it had only been possible to make short blades (daggers and 'rapiers') which had to be rivetted to the hilts. Improved casting techniques, including the addition of lead to the bronze, allowed large and elaborate castings to be made. The hilt was cast in one with the blade, and the handle secured by side flanges and rivets, making it possible to grip the sword better, and to swing it. The thickening of the end of the blade ('leaf-shaped') placed all the weight at the pointed end, producing a change in fighting techniques with slashing as well as thrusting.

From their area of origin in the Hungarian Plain, these sword types spread across Europe to Britain in the West and Scandinavia in the north and they turn up sporadically in Mycenaean Greece, for instance in burials of Mycenaean IIIb–c at Enkomi on Cyprus, datable to about 1250–1200 BC. They represent one of the last contacts between Greece and the rest of Europe for three or four centuries.

These flange-hilted swords were the predecessors of a long series of local types which continued until the seventh century BC. In Greece their successors were of iron (e.g. fig 9), and these are found widely in the eastern Mediterranean. In Europe bronze continued in use until the final years of the leaf-shaped sword, with the Gündlingen and Mindelheim types of Hallstatt C (fig 18), though the latter are also known in iron.

*Actual sizes: a—length 74cm; b—length 59.5cm*

ubiquity of the ores meant that implements could be made more locally and so more cheaply. The second advantage of iron is that it can produce a harder, tougher and sharper cutting edge. If we compare the relative hardness of iron and bronze on the Brinell scale of hardness, we obtain the following figures:

Cast bronze: 88; Hammered bronze: 228; Wrought iron: 100; Forged iron: 246+

The problem with iron lay in the technology needed to produce an implement. The techniques of manufacture were different from those required for the other metals familiar to prehistoric man— gold, copper, tin, silver and lead. All these had a relatively low melting temperature which meant that impurities could be removed at the smelting stage, and the molten metal cast in moulds. The basic techniques required for these metals were smelting, alloying with one another, casting, and hammering. Iron ore is not difficult to smelt. After pounding and roasting, it needs to be mixed with charcoal and heated to a temperature of about 1100C in a reducing atmosphere. The charcoal combines with oxygen in the air to form carbon monoxide ($2CO_2$ to $2CO$), and this in turn reduces the iron oxide ($Fe_2O_3 + 3CO = 2Fe + 2CO_2$), giving off carbon dioxide, and leaving behind the smelted iron.

The resulting iron 'bloom' left in the bottom of the furnace is a spongy mass of iron full of impurities. It first required extensive forging to remove the slag. As temperatures sufficiently high to melt the iron were unattainable, casting was impossible; the iron could only be formed into a useful implement by forging, and the hammering would both shape the object and force out some of the impurities. Even so this did not produce a hard enough cutting edge. The iron needs alloying with a small amount of carbon to produce steel, and this could only be done by heating the blade in a charcoal furnace, hammering when hot, and then quenching in water. This process needs to be repeated several times before sufficient carbon is absorbed.

With primitive technology, however, only the outer skin of iron would absorb any carbon; the core would remain pure iron with slag inclusions, and so relatively soft. The earliest answer to this problem was 'piling' the forging of slabs of iron together, each with a 'skin' of steel, so forming a composite blade of alternating iron and mild steel. Towards the end of the Iron Age, in the Alpine region, more sophisticated techniques were evolved. To form sword blades, long fine rods were welded together to give a laminated blade, while in Austria a technique of producing a mild steel containing 1.5 per cent carbon was achieved.

The adoption of iron working thus involved the smith acquiring a new range of technical skills, and the blacksmith quickly became a specialist divorced from other metalworkers. Initially it was difficult to produce iron blades which were technically superior to contemporary bronzes, so at first it was mostly adopted more for reasons of prestige rather than usability.

As with many of the major advances in prehistory, we have no idea exactly how the techniques of iron working were discovered. There is nothing in each step which involved the development of a higher technology than was already known in the third millennium BC. What was needed was to put each step into a new combination which would produce a usable implement. The advances that were being made at the same time in other aspects of metallurgy and pottery manufacture suggest that experimentation was going on to discover new ores, metals and techniques, but the earliest phase of experiment cannot be documented in the archaeological record.

We can, however, say approximately when and where the discovery was made, from the occurrence of early iron objects. The best authenticated find comes from a burial at the early Bronze Age town of Alaça Hüyük near Ankara in central Turkey, dating to around 2500–2300 BC. It is a dagger with a short iron blade; the hilt was organic, probably wood, which had been overlaid with gold sheet. The burial was found flexed in a small partition in an area defined by stone blocks which had apparently been covered over by wooden planks. Also in the burial was a bronze stag inlaid with silver, and a number of pottery and metal vessels. The burial was one of thirteen discovered in this phase of the settlement, and gravegoods from these other graves included elaborate bronze 'standards' formed of a grid of

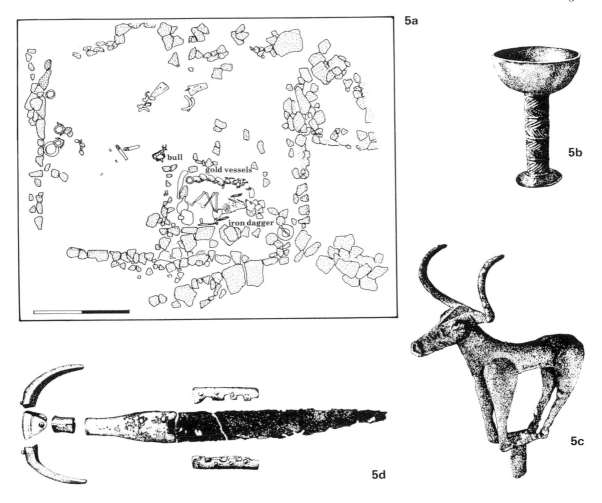

**5 Alaça Hüyük, Turkey**

Alaça Hüyük is a small tell in central Turkey not far north of the Hittite capital Hatussas (*Bogazköy*). Excavations in the 1930s revealed a Hittite town, and, underlying it, an early Bronze Age settlement, with a series of thirteen rich burials. The graves were stone-lined, with a separate compartment for the body, and apparently covered with timber planking. Some had a second level of gravegoods consisting mainly of the heads of cattle. All the burials were of high social status, and included ceremonial objects, such as cast copper figures of bulls or stags, some inlaid with precious metals, or elaborate 'standards' made of a grid of copper bars with hanging ring pendants.

Burial K was amongst the richest (a). The body was furnished with a diadem made of gold sheet, six gold vessels (b), two silver vessels, several gold and silver pins and beads, a silver dagger, a copper rapier, and a copper bull with eyes, tail and forehead inlaid with silver (c). The iron dagger (d) lay by the hip of the crouched skeleton. The hilt was of wood overlaid with gold and the scabbard fittings were also of gold. The burial dates to about 2500–2300 BC.

*Actual sizes: b—height 12.5cm; c—height 23cm, length 29.5cm; d—total length of blade and handle 30cm*

bronze bars with wheel pendants attached, and a
gold diadem. Two points emerge. Firstly, the find
is in a context of high social status—the burials are
comparable with those from contemporary Mesopotamian towns such as Ur; secondly, the technology of the bronze work is as high as anywhere
else in the world at this time: elaborate bivalve
casting and inlay with different metals—a technology sufficiently high to permit iron working.

Comparable early finds are not well documented, partly due to lack of interest in finds of iron by
early excavators, partly due to poor preservation.
Fragments of iron have been found in hoards of
third millennium date at Troy, again associated
with high-prestige objects such as bronze and
polished stone axes of serpentine and lapis lazuli.
These discoveries from Troy and Alaça Hüyük
demonstrate that iron was known and worked in
small quantities over much of modern Asia Minor
at the end of the third millennium BC, and that
knowledge was sufficiently advanced to produce
usable tools and weapons.

For the following millennium we rely mainly on
documentary evidence. The sources are the clay
tablets incised with cuneiform writing from the
Hittite capital of Bogazköy, the ancient Hattusas,
and from the Hittite town of Kanesh (Kultepe)
where a residential suburb was occupied in the
seventeenth century BC by an enclave of Assyrian
merchants. In the latter case we are told of the
materials traded, and it is possible to work out the
approximate relative value by weight of the
different metals being traded. The most valuable,
worth five times more than gold, was iron. The
merchants were dealing mainly with prestigious
substances—copper, tin, gold and lapis lazuli—
often as agents of the Hittite and Assyrian kings
and aristocracy.

From Hattasus we possess a letter written by
King Hattusilis III (1275–1255) to another,
unnamed, king:

> As for the good iron which you wrote about to me,
> good iron is not available in my seal-house at Kizzu-
> watna. That it is a bad time for producing iron I have
> written. They will produce good iron, but as yet they
> will not have finished. When they have finished I shall
> send it to you. Today now I am dispatching an iron
> dagger-blade to you.

A number of points emerge from this letter.
Firstly, iron was a subject worthy of discussion
between the most powerful rulers in the Near East
and even such small items as dagger blades made
worthy royal gifts. Secondly, the reference to the
'seal-house' in Kizzuwatna (apparently an area
in south east Turkey) implies that there was direct
royal control of iron production. Further evidence
of the royal status of iron comes from the tomb of
Tutankhamun, where one of the two gold-hilted
daggers possessed a gold blade, the other being of
iron. The Hittite and Egyptian royal houses were
linked by marriage, and the iron blade is presumably of Hittite origin.

Around 1200 BC the Hittite empire collapsed,
at about the time when iron working appeared in
Cyprus and Greece. This could be interpreted as
iron working spreading only with the collapse of
the Hittite monopoly over its production. However, the pattern of archaeological discoveries
casts doubt on this simple interpretation. Iron
objects are virtually unknown in Hittite contexts,
whereas they are known in second millennium
contexts too far distant for them to have been
traded from Turkey–Simris in Sweden (a fragment), Bargeroosterveld in Holland (an awl),
Gánovce in Czechoslovakia (an iron-hilted bronze
dagger) dating between the eleventh and fifteenth
centuries BC. The problem with these finds is that
it is not clear what expertise in iron working they
represent—only smelting or hammering, or had
carburisation been discovered, as is implied by the
Hittite documents? Only with the rise of the
Greek iron industry can we be sure that service-
able tools and weapons of iron could be produced
in quantity.

## The end of Mycenaean Greece

It is at the end of the second and first millennia BC
that we can detect fundamental changes which
were to lead gradually to the climax of Mediterranean civilisation. These developments have
their roots in, and indeed must be compared with,
what had preceded them. When, for instance, we
look at trade networks, we must suspect that the
Greek trade was developing along the routes
followed by its Mycenaean predecessor, which

may not have been entirely forgotten, even though it may only have been retained in the form of myth and half-garbled stories. The east Mediterranean had been dominated in the second millennium by three fairly stable civilisations—Egypt, the Hittites based in central Turkey, and Mycenaean Greece. Whatever the cause and nature of the period of unrest which finally brought the Hittite and Mycenaean empires to an end, the universal picture of the east Mediterranean, from 1200 BC onwards, is one of decline and depopulation. In mainland Greece the centres of power, based on the defended citadel palaces of Pylos, Mycenae, Tiryns and other such centres, were deserted somewhere in the period around 1200–1100 BC. A number of causes have been postulated for this collapse: an invasion from the north, which has been tied in with the mythical Danaïds (though archaeologically this has generally been discredited); the involvement of the Greeks themselves in the so-called 'Peoples of the Sea', which included the Pelesta, the historical Philistines, who used pottery of Mycenaean origin; models of climatic deterioration, with a series of major droughts similar to some which are historically documented for Greece; or an attempted over-exploitation of the agricultural resources which led to a final and sudden catastrophic collapse of the centralised kingdoms. Certainly we see the disappearance of many aspects of civilisation: the production of fine pottery and metalwork; the importation of luxury goods such as ivory, gold and faience; developed stone ashlar building techniques; and the Linear B tablets which had been used to keep the palaces' accounts. There is evidence of a major drop in population, though this comes mainly from evidence of field surveys, which are themselves largely based on the availability of pottery sherds. It has been suggested, for instance, in the field survey of Messenia in south western Peloponnese that the population may have dropped by as much as to one tenth of its former size. Although this general pattern is undoubtedly true, it is difficult to translate potsherds into population sizes, and we may be seeing the collapse of the pottery industry, and indeed a period when pottery was not in great use, as much as a decline

in the actual population using it. If we are to take these figures in absolute terms, then it is difficult to explain the origin of, for instance, the kingdom of Sparta, for which we have virtually no archaeological evidence until the eighth century—by which time it was already a dynamic and expanding society.

It is only in certain areas of Greece that we have a full sequence of pottery styles, and to a lesser extent of burial evidence. The main area is Attica, and especially Athens, which gives some hints of the complexity surrounding the demise of the Mycenaean civilisation. A major setback seems to have been suffered in the Mycenaean world between Mycenaean IIIb and Mycenaean IIIc, datable to somewhere around 1200 BC. In Attica Mycenaean IIIc pottery is found in certain areas, notably at Perati in eastern Attica, whereas it does not occur at Athens. Instead we find coarse handmade pottery of a much lower quality, in both production and decoration, which is generally termed sub-Mycenaean. This term implies that this coarse pottery was both a successor and a degenerate form of a preceding Mycenaean pottery, but the differing distribution within Attica of Mycenaean IIIc and sub-Mycenaean pottery had led some specialists to suggest that the two pottery forms were contemporary. In other words not all aspects of Mycenaean civilisation disappeared at the same time in all areas, and in certain areas the production of fine pottery, for instance, and indeed the building of palatial buildings may have continued on into Mycenaean IIIc. This is especially true of Cyprus, where the town of Enkomi, established during Mycenaean IIIb, continued as a flourishing settlement until as late as about 1050 BC, when it seems to have been finally destroyed by an earthquake. In this late period it still had stone buildings and stone-paved streets, and was still importing exotic goods from the Egyptian and Near Eastern world. It also seems to have maintained contacts with central Europe, as Enkomi is one of the sites to produce the flange-hilted swords of Hungarian form discussed above.

To some extent similar problems surround the situation in southern Italy and Sicily, though from here the archaeology is dependent on typology for dating, as much of the meagre evidence comes from collective tombs and cannot be placed within tight chronological sequences. But the inheritance of Mycenaean influence is fairly clear in both metal types, and in certain areas in the pottery as well. Southern Italy and Sicily had been exploited by the Mycenaean world, with the establishment of defended sites, which were perhaps trading outlets or colonies at such key points as river mouths (for instance, the site of Scoglio del Tonno, at Taranto)—sites which in some ways resembled the later Greek colonies. In south eastern Italy the pottery styles of the post-Mycenaean period represent a continuation of Mycenaean traditions, with fine painted wares which run parallel with the Geometric sequence of Greek proper. The Mycenaean influence penetrated at least as far as central Italy, as fragments of imported pots are not unkown in, for instance, Tuscany, but the links of northern Italy and especially the Po valley had traditionally been with central Europe and with the demise of the Mycenaean civilisation, it is the central European connection that becomes dominant.

## Iron working in Greece

It is in this sub-Mycenaean context that iron working first became common in the eastern Mediterranean. The earliest objects turn up in a Late Helladic IIIc context, in the decades either side of 1200 BC, in cemeteries such as Perati. However, as these objects are usually found in collective tombs, in which it is difficult to assign gravegoods to individual interments, precise dating is generally impossible. The earliest objects are mostly simple, and include iron rings, and short iron knives, some of which have handles fixed with bronze rivets while others have iron rivets—which suggests a greater mastery of iron working techniques. It has been suggested that the origin of these knives is Cyprus where they also occur at sites such as Enkomi. If we follow a diffusion model for the spread of iron working from Asia Minor, Cyprus might be the logical meeting point between the Hittite and Mycenaean spheres of influence. But the majority of tools and weapons at this period are still made of

bronze, such as the flange-hilted leaf-shaped swords from Enkomi.

Though Late Helladic IIIc may in some areas run on contemporary with sub-Mycenaean, and therefore these iron objects may be contemporary with sub-Mycenaean elsewhere, iron objects are notably more common in sub-Mycenaean contexts. In Athens, for instance, a number of iron brooches and iron rings are known from inhumation graves belonging to this period. In Athens and adjacent areas in the north western Peloponnese, there is a marked shift in burial practice; single inhumation, which, though known previously had not been common, replaced the more normal collective tholos tomb burial typical of the later Mycenaean period. In other areas such as Crete and Thessaly, however, the tholos burial rite continued well into the early Iron Age. In the sub-Mycenaean period, rich gravegoods are notable by their absence; gold and silver, if they occur, are limited to one or two finger-rings. The pottery at Athens is noticeably crude, decorated in simple motifs of geometric character, and the ornate freehand decoration of the Mycenaean period has almost totally disappeared.

## Proto-Geometric Greece

This period is succeeded by the Proto-Geometric, datable to around 1150–1050 BC—though the chronology for this period and the succeeding Early Geometric is vague due to a lack of contact with areas with a firm historical chronology. The graves of this period at Athens show yet greater poverty, while precious metals, even bronze, are notable by their general absence. Settlement evidence is virtually unknown. Some trade contacts had been maintained, notably with Cyprus during the sub-Mycenaean, and the end of this period brought in major innovations, at least in the manufacture of pottery. Firstly, the potter's wheel was introduced, and with it improvement in the quality and the treatment of the clay. Secondly, there is an innovation in the decorative techniques; though the motifs are still geometric and derived from those of the previous sub-Mycenaean period, there is much greater care taken. In the circles we see the introduction of the

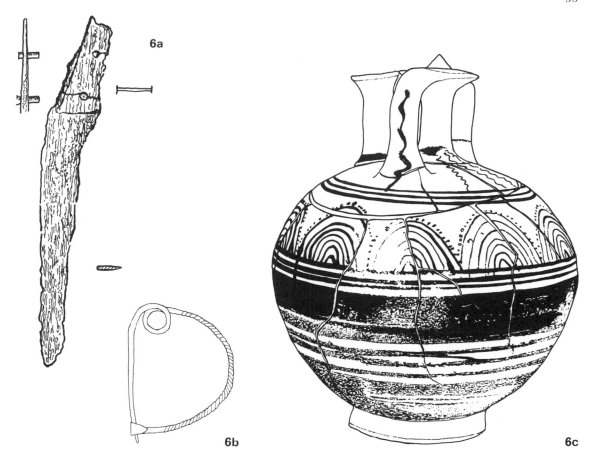

**6a**

**6b**

**6c**

## 6 Sub-Mycenaean Greece

The earliest iron objects in Greece include small iron knives (a), with bronze or iron rivets, but these are mainly found in Crete and Cyprus, and are probably of Cypriot origin. They, and small iron rings, are unfortunately poorly dated as they tend to be found in collective tombs, but they appear to belong to late Helladic IIIc (late 12th–early 11th centuries BC). Simple iron objects also appear in the partly contemporary, partly subsequent Sub-Mycenaean period, for instance in Athens, in single graves with a limited range of personal jewellery such as the arc brooch (b). Increasingly in the Sub-Mycenaean, and especially during the Proto-Geometric, brooches and pins are made of iron, even for objects which in later times would normally be made of bronze. This suggests that bronze may have become more difficult to obtain, and objects of any metal other than iron are

rare in the Proto-Geometric.

Mycenaean IIIc pottery had been of high quality, but Sub-Mycenaean pottery (c) is, in comparison, poorly made, with ill-prepared and ill-fired clay. The repertoire of decorative motifs becomes very restricted, with only the simplest geometric motifs, generally poorly executed. These do however form the basis for the Proto-Geometric style, which saw a revival in the quality of preparation and firing, and more carefully designed painted decoration using the compass and the multiple brush. The potter's wheel also reappears, an investment in time and equipment that implies a clientele capable of supporting specialist crafts, and gives a picture which contrasts somewhat with the poverty of the burials of this period.

*Actual sizes: a—length 15.4cm; c—height 20.6cm*
*Scale: b—1 : 2*

compass, and also of the multiple brush, which was a device by which several brushes were attached together, so that exactly parallel lines and truly concentric circles could be drawn in one operation. High-quality prestige pottery was thus established—a tradition which was to survive through into the Classical period.

The evidence for trade contacts in the Proto-Geometric period is, however, considerably less than in any previous or succeeding period of the Bronze Age or Iron Age. Indeed, it seems as though Greece was almost completely isolated both from its more powerful eastern neighbours, and also from central Europe and Italy. Bronze is extremely rare; the sources of both copper and tin were apparently cut off by this loss of trading contact. On the other hand, iron became the standard material for producing both weapons and tools. It has been suggested that the lack of bronze is due to the adoption wholescale of an iron technology, but, as we shall see elsewhere, the introduction does not usually mean the demise of the bronze industry—rather the opposite. It is more likely that the concentration on iron was due to the difficulty in obtaining bronze. There may also have been technological innovations in iron working which led to its adoption. No longer are the objects confined to minor trinkets and knives, but for the first time full-scale weapons, like the flange-hilted iron sword from a warrior burial at Tiryns, appear, datable to about 1050 BC. The technique of 'piling' had perhaps already been mastered, whereby slabs of steel were welded together to produce a blade which had steel in its core rather than plain soft iron. The distribution of iron objects is, however, still largely confined to the islands such as Crete and, on the Greek mainland, to the north western part of the Peloponnese and to Attica. Though iron objects do occur sporadically elsewhere, usually in not closely datable contexts, one other area at least had adopted a fairly extensive iron-using economy—the area of the north western Aegean, in Macedonia, where the cemetery at Vergina has produced a number of iron swords, in a context which is perhaps as early as those in Greece. In this case, however, there was no lack of bronze, as this area seems to have maintained links with

central Europe, and much of the other bronze material from the burials is closely similar to Urnfield types further north.

The burial rite of this period continues to be mainly single inhumation, though in Athens there is a notable move towards cremation burial rite, which was to remain the standard burial rite in Attica into classical times. Despite the poverty of the gravegoods, despite the lack of information that we have for this period generally, and despite the general lack of contact with the outside world, this is the period when we can see the beginnings of a civilisation which is noticeably Greek and which leads on to the classical world. In all areas the Mycenaean social structure had broken down completely, the palaces and citadels had all but been deserted, the bureaucracies, with their writing and their centralised control, had disappeared. Although society was not classless, evidence of social differentiation is meagre. Although there is as yet no evidence for the rise of any centres, the growing number of burials at Athens in this period demonstrates an increased density of occupation. It was not, however, centralised around the acropolis. This was an essentially agricultural society based on small villages or single farms.

## Late Bronze Age Europe

The demise of the Mycenaean world must have had some effect on southern Italy and Sicily with the breakdown of trade, but we know too little of the native Bronze Age settlements to identify change. The Mycenaean styles of bronze work and pottery continued for some centuries. Otherwise there is no obvious sign that the disappearance of the east Mediterranean market for metals and amber had any influence on central and northern Europe, though ultimately it may have delayed the processes which came into play in the sixth and fifth centuries. No prestige goods from the Aegean were passing north and there was no dependence on external trade. The expanding economy and population were well able to absorb and sustain the production of raw materials.

The only obvious change is in the disappearance of exceptionally rich burials. But the rich items which accompanied the dead do not disappear. Bronze body armour, shields, swords, bronze vessels, harness and wagon fittings are still relatively common, though now they occur in hoards or as stray finds in rivers. A hierarchical society still existed, but it was no longer clearly symbolised in the burial rite.

The period 1200–700 BC is one of gradual evolution of the bronze industry with no marked technological innovations, but with an ever increasing range of types, not merely weapons, tools and metal containers, but also ritual implements and musical instruments. The Irish bronze industry was particularly innovative, and its products included trumpets, rattles, and elaborate flesh forks decorated with little bronze animals, while the gold work included an exciting range of dress fastenings, gorgets, and fittings such as those on the model boat from Caergwyle, all decorated with geometric patterns of concentric circles. It is only rivalled by the Danish industry which was producing masterpieces such as the paired horns (lyrer), or the Trundholm 'sun-chariot'. All these objects betray a rich cultural and ceremonial life behind the dull typologies of bronze objects that archaeologists produce for this period.

The bronze industries form a number of overlapping zones—in the north encompassing the north German plain and Scandinavia; in the west from Britain to southern Spain; in the south Italy; and in the centre the Urnfield groups. Each is defined in terms of decorative motifs, and types of socketed axes, palstaves, chisels and spears of localised distribution, the product of small-scale industries mass-producing every-day items. Only rarely did such items travel far from their place of manufacture. In contrast, there is a range of prestige items that often crossed from one zone to another. The various types of cups—Müllendorf, Sartrup and Jenišovice—have a distribution that extends from central Italy through Czechoslovakia and Germany into southern Scandinavia. Though there must have been a number of workshops over a wide area producing a range of almost identical products, their distribution does imply extensive contacts including trans-Alpine, in the higher echelons of society. Bronze buckets

made of sheets rivetted together show a more east-west distribution, and though these are likely to be an innovation of the Hungarian Plain, they were closely imitated in western Britain, which went on to produce its own distinctive forms. These buckets were the ancestors of the bronze situlae of the Iron Age, which in northern Italy would give their name to a distinctive orientalising art form. Distributions of sword types had an intermediate apportionment. No single type was to reach anything like the area of the Hemigkofen and Erbenheim types of the twelfth–eleventh centuries until the advent of iron swords in the seventh century. Nonetheless, types such as the Ewart Park in Britain were extensively distributed within their zones.

These extensive contacts within central Europe, and extending down into Italy and Catalonia, were echoed by two other features, firstly the burial rite of cremation, and secondly by the distinctive pottery found in the graves, especially the urn itself. Typically the graves are concentrated in flat cemeteries (Urnfields), or at most under a small low tumulus, and though there may in certain cases be a range of accessory vessels, metal objects are not common, and generally the burials are marked by their lack of ostentation.

The settlement hierarchy seems rarely if ever to extend above the size of a village, and cemeteries too indicate no marked concentrations of population. Hillforts are not uncommon, but like their Iron Age successors, they do not seem to be centres of wealth, trade or industry. Though there is some evidence of differential house sizes, especially on the open settlements, it is not always clear whether this is due to different functions or social differentiation. Certain individuals did possess substantial houses, like the inhabitants of the marsh fort of the Wasserburg in Buchau in the Federsee in southern Germany and, like the burial evidence suggests, some, but not highly marked social differentiation.

The larger open settlements are often situated in the river valleys, and settlements such as Runnymede on the Thames were places where metalworking, and presumably other industrial activities were carried out. The 'industrial villages' were to remain a common feature of the settlement pattern of Temperate Europe as late as the first century BC. Etruria, however, was already slightly different, with clusters of villages on defensive plateaux, a phenomenon which will be discussed further in the next chapter. Only rarely did anything more specialised appear, and this was usually connected with mineral extraction. Specialist communities were already mining copper ores in elaborate underground mines in the Austrian Tyrol, and around 1000 BC, this mining skill was extended to salt extraction with the earliest phase of mining at Hallstatt. This first period of mining was to last at Hallstatt for about 200 years before the entrance was blocked off, apparently deliberately.

It is difficult with such societies to say much of the social and political organisation. Each village or hillfort seems to be an independent unit, equal in status to its neighbours, though presumably they were linked into larger groupings. Only in the Lausitz Urnfield groups of southern Poland are there hints of larger regional organisation with defended lakeside forts such as Biskupin, with a cluster of small settlements and villages around, and also clusters of hillforts, separated by areas of unsettled land. But the major phase of these Lausitz societies is the seventh century, taking us already into the Iron Age. Other than hillforts, there is no construction of communal buildings or ceremonial centres.

Temperate Europe in the late Bronze Age thus presents a picture of steady, but unspectacular growth. Local disasters there may have been, like the flooding and abandonment of the Swiss lake villages, or the eventual desertion of the Lausitz settlements of southern Poland, confirmed by the forest regeneration in the pollen record. But these had little or no impact outside their immediate areas. Warfare was rife, as both weapons and hillforts testify, but again this was localised, and there is no evidence for widescale transplantation of the population which occasionally occurred in the Iron Age.

# CHAPTER THREE

# *Reawakening in the East*

## The ninth century

The Proto-Geometric period in Greece can be looked upon both as the first intimation of Greek society and civilisation, and also as the period of minimal external contact in the eastern Mediterranean. But from about 900 BC, we see in the archaeological record the gradual rebirth of contact between various areas of the eastern Mediterranean which was to infiltrate towards the centre and west. The initial impulse for these changes came from the Levant, especially in the development of the trading cities of the east Mediterranean coast which were supplying goods to the established civilisations of the Mesopotamian world, now dominated by the Assyrian empire. Pride of place is always given to the two cities of Tyre and Sidon which initiated the Phoenician trade network, soon to spread as far as Spain and Portugal, but other cities such as Byblos and Al Mina also developed rapidly, dominating coastal harbours, or routes into the interior. The date for the development and the foundation for the Phoenician network is something of a problem, as the mythical foundation dates for many of the colonies receive no support in the archaeological record. Kition in Cyprus, for instance, is supposed to have been founded around 1200 BC, but the excavations have produced no evidence for activity before about 800 BC, while Carthage, which has a traditional foundation date of around 900 BC, archaeologically only starts at 700 BC. The truth probably lies somewhere between the two sets of evidence. Greece was affected fairly early by this trade system, and we can see in the archaeological record the first glimmerings of foreign influences appearing in burials such as those from Athens in the early Geometric period around 900 BC. From the Kerameikos cemetery in Athens there is an embossed bronze bowl with human figures and animals in a style which certainly originates from the Levant, though no precise origin can be suggested.

By this period the Greek sphere of influence had considerably expanded from that of the sub-Mycenaean and the Proto-Geometric periods. Geometric style pottery is now found on the eastern coast of the Aegean, as well as on many of the islands such as Rhodes and Samos. To what extent there had been continuity of a Greek-speaking population in these areas from the Mycenaean period, or to what extent it was new colonisation is a matter of debate. The intervening period, both here and in other parts of Greece such as the Peloponnese is an archaeological blank, but that colonisation was part of the process is suggested by a number of factors. Firstly, there is the evidence of dialects. The Aeolic dialects are found extending from Attica in the west across to the opposite coast of modern-day Turkey, while in the south the Doric dialect shows a similar east-west spread through the Peloponnese and the southern islands and Crete. This could perhaps reflect the Mycenaean dialects, but the usual interpretation is one of colonisation from west to the east. The second set of evidence is that of defended sites, or sites which have been deliberately founded. One such site is the defended headland at Old Smyrna on the coast of Turkey, whose defences date back to as early as the ninth century BC, the earliest known defences in the post-Mycenaean Greek world.

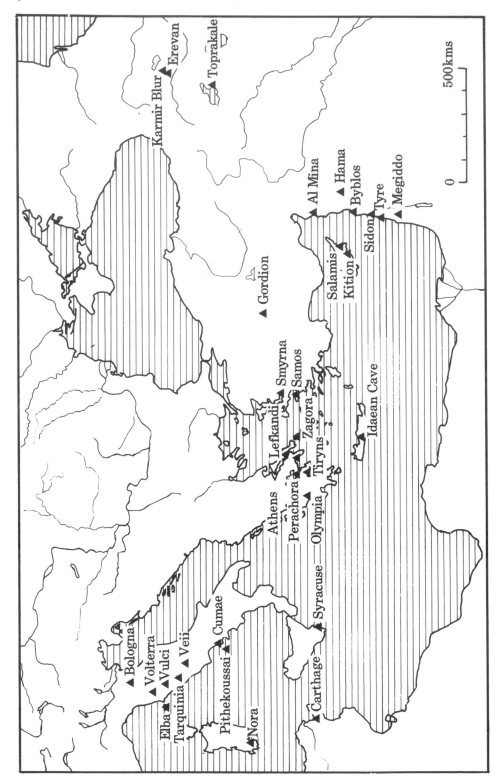

7  Sites mentioned in chapter 3

These defences may represent a Greek colony defending itself from hostile, non-Greek inhabitants of the area. Little is known of the internal layout of the site at this period: it does not seem to have contained substantial houses of an urban nature, and it is not until considerably later that its urban character can be demonstrated. A second site that looks like a deliberate foundation belonging to about the eighth century, and in a situation which is essentially defensive, is Zagora on the island of Andros. Here a relatively short-lived settlement shows signs of being deliberately laid out, as many of the houses were built as a continuous block of buildings.

From the mainland, evidence for this period mainly comes from burials. Again it is Athens which provides the main sequence of events. Among the burials one or two show evidence of the development of marked social differentiation, such as the one from the Agora with sword and horse bit, the latter perhaps symbolising in funerary ritual the existence of a knightly horse-riding class.

A number of the burials contained prestigious pottery vessels which show the increasing mastery of the Athenian potters. The early Geometric period is notable for the sparseness of decoration in comparison with the later periods, but already many of the standard forms of the later Geometric period had made their appearance, as had some of the Geometric designs. Though Athens may have been in the lead in pottery design and production, similar wealth is hinted at in other centres such as Corinth and Tiryns and Mycenae.

However, the wealthiest burials are not found on the mainland, but on the island Euboea, where recent excavations have revealed a settlement at Lefkandi on the south west coast of the island, controlling the straits between the island and Attica. Its siting suggests that trading formed a major part of the economy of this community. Several of the burials have produced gold objects, notably finger-rings, as well as imported phials and a rich selection of local bronzes, including brooches, and local pottery. The contemporary settlement has also been tested. Above the Mycenaean level is evidence of a tenth-century occupation, which included the production of

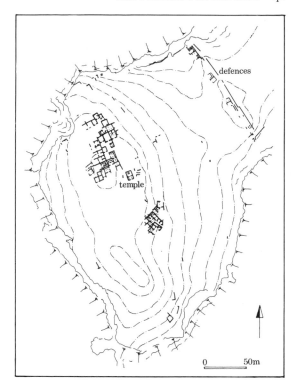

**8** Zagora, Andros, Greece

The only extensive plan we possess of an early Greek defended site comes from the site of Zagora on the island of Andros in the central Aegean. It was established primarily for defensive reasons, as it lies on a 150m high promontory defended on three sides by cliffs, some distance from the nearest water supply. An area of 6.7ha was cut off by a wall 2m wide and 470m long. It was only occupied for a brief time in the 9th–8th centuries BC, and later activity is confined to the construction of a temple in the late to mid-sixth century. The houses are stone built. They form a number of agglomerations without streets, and show considerable planning in the layout of the settlement. Whether this site represents the local inhabitants defending themselves in a period of unrest, or Greek colonisation in a hostile environment is still unclear.

9a

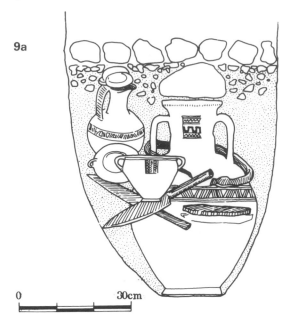

0        30cm

9c

9b

9d

9e

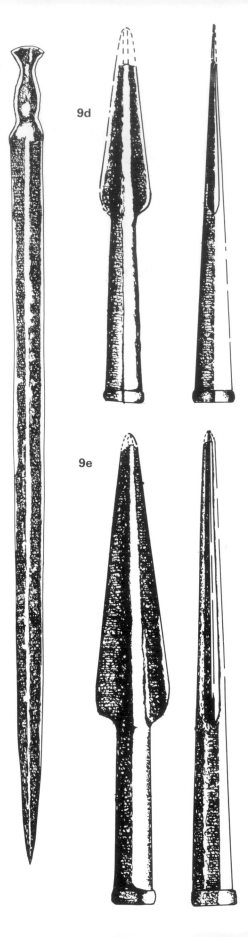

**9** An early Geometric burial from Athens

The early Geometric period burial D16:4 from the
Areopagus cemetery at Athens (a) was of a man in his
mid-thirties. Dating to the early ninth century, this
burial shows the increasing definition of rank
demonstrated through gravegoods. Many of the items
can be found individually in earlier graves, but this
man was given a fairly complete set of weapons and
other equipment: a flanged iron sword (b) which had
been wrapped round the urn; two spears (c, d); a
javelin point (e); a whetstone; a knife (f); an axehead
(g), and perhaps most significantly of all, two iron
horse bits (h) which may signify membership of the
emerging class of 'knights'.

*Actual size: b—length 86cm*
*Scale: rest 2:5*

**9f**

**9g**

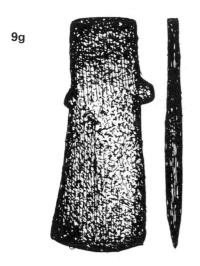

**9h**

bronze cauldrons, as fragments of moulds for tripod feet were found in a pit on the settlement. One of the major elements of the economy may have been iron production and the surrounding area is certainly one of the more productive areas in Greece for surface deposits of iron ore. But iron ore itself is not enough, and there may have been major technological developments, with the adoption of the technique of piling allowing the production of larger and stronger iron objects. This area of Euboea was perhaps the pioneer and main production area of these high-quality iron tools and weapons. Certainly when we come into the period of expansion of the Greek trade network, Euboea was in the forefront of development, when the two major sites were Eretrea and Chalkis. The latter was possibly the successor of Lefkandi, which was abandoned for some reason in the eighth century BC. There are whispers in the historical record of a major war, the Lelantine war, involving these two towns, which may have caused the retreat of the inhabitants of Lefkandi to a more defensive site.

However, the archaeological record remains extremely faulty. There are still large areas which are a total blank, including much of the southern part of the Peloponnese. Nor do we know much about the eastern islands, which seem to have been important in the early trade development. Among the few finds is a number of imported objects such as faience beads, which are some of the earliest traded goods which we have in the Phoenician trade network. The eastern Aegean was also one of the earliest areas to start imitating Phoenician vessels, notably small phials which were used to carry precious ointments and unguents. Crete too was probably included in this early trade network. Among the finds from the Idaean cave, the sanctuary associated with the birth of Zeus, there is a number of beaten bronze shields of types which are closely similar to those in Asia Minor, especially from the kingdom of Urartu, a major centre of the development of bronze technology, whose influence on Greece is more discernible in the eighth century.

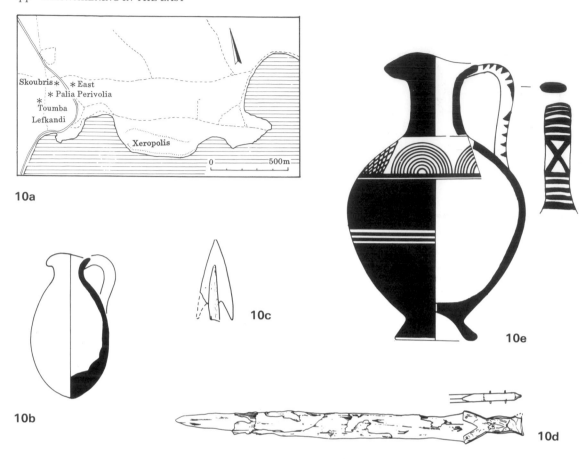

10a

10b

10c

10d

10e

**10** Lefkandi, Euboea, Greece

The modern village of Lefkandi lies on the south-western shore of the island of Euboea, overlooking the Straits of Euripus, the narrow channel which divides the island from Attica and the mainland of Greece. Excavations between 1964 and 1970 revealed a long-lived settlement which had virtually continuous occupation from the end of the Mycenaean period (late Helladic IIIc, *c.* 1200 BC) until the late Geometric period (*c.* 725–700 BC), when the site was abandoned, about the same time that the two nearby cities of Chalkis and Eretria were founded.

The evidence comes from four cemeteries (a)—Toumba, Skoubris, Palia Perivolia, and the East cemetery—and from the settlement on the hill of Xeropolis. No one area has produced a complete sequence—the Sub-Mycenaean, for instance, is not represented anywhere in the admittedly limited settlement excavations, while no graves are known contemporary with the late Geometric occupation. In all 146 burials were excavated, mainly cremations in pits, or pyre burials, or rarely inhumations.

The burials provide a classic sequence comparable with that from Athens. The Sub-Mycenaean graves contain a minimum of trinkets—arc brooches and pins of iron, and one or two gold finger-rings. The Proto-Geometric graves are equally poor, but do contain one object unique in Greece at this period, a small flask (b) perhaps for unguents, which originates from Syria or Palestine (Skoubris 46). No other such traded objects are known in Proto-Geometric Greece, but the technical innovations found in Proto-Geometric pottery show that some contact, however weak, existed with the east.

By the late Proto-Geometric, the end of the tenth century, the gravegoods were becoming richer.

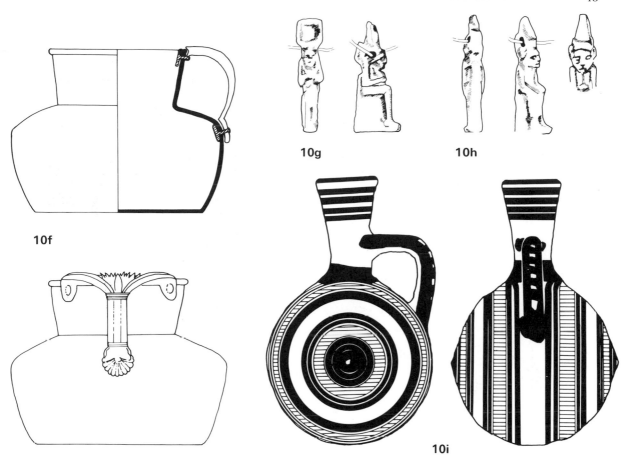

10f

10g

10h

10i

Toumba 26, a man aged 25–35, contained a quiver of arrows with iron tips (c), an iron slash and thrust sword with ivory grip plates (d), and a number of pottery vessels (e).

From the following century imports start becoming more common. From Palia Perivolia 22 comes a flask of Cypriot origin (f), the earliest Cypriot object from Greece in a post-Mycenaean context. Of Phoenician origin in the contemporary grave Toumba 22 was a pendant of Isis in green faience (g) with horns and solar disk, holding the infant Horus, and there are 53 pendants of a lion-headed goddess (h). Bronze too becomes common, like the jug (i) from Toumba 33 with orientalising decoration (the palmette at the end of the handle) of early ninth century date. Gold is not rare, like the ear-rings (j) from Toumba 5 (mid-ninth) decorated with granulation which now reappears in Greece.

The Euboean pottery styles do not show the innovation and experimentation of Athens and Corinth in the Geometric period, and only slowly did more elaborate decoration develop (k). The local styles, however, became widely disseminated, since, as the wealth of traded goods implies, this area was deeply involved in the early overseas settlement and colonisation, both in the east (Al Mina) and the west (Pithekoussai). Burials such as Toumba 36 which belong to this period of the upsurge in trade underline these contacts. The faience scarab with gold setting (l) and the steatite seal (m) are both of Phoenician origin. This child's grave also had a gold sheet diadem and finger-rings, and bronze brooches (n), but it is one of the latest burials from any of the Lefkandi cemeteries.

*Scales: g, h—2:1; j, l, m—1:1; c, i, n—1:2; b, e, f, k— 1:3; d—1:6*

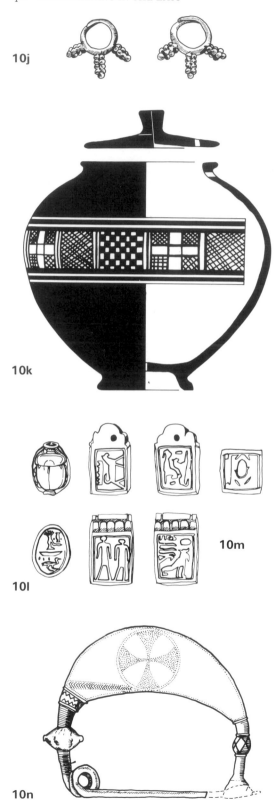

**10j**

**10k**

**10l**

**10m**

**10n**

## Greece and Cyprus in the eighth century

It is during this century that the trade networks developed which were to have such a major effect on Greece and Italy in the formative years of their classical civilisations. We also have greater chronological precision, with objects of Greek origin in contexts which are datable by historical means, notably sherds on Mesopotamian sites, such as the Middle Geometric pottery found at Megiddo, and at Hama in Syria. We also have foundation dates for the colonies which were established towards the end of this period, and, in the case of Syracuse which was founded in 720, the dates are relatively trustworthy, unlike the foundation dates in previous centuries for the Phoenician colonies. For the earlier part of the century, however, it has still been a matter of guesswork, working back from the fixed points. This is especially difficult when looking at the Italian trade network, and it is only in recent years that it has been possible to start to recognise the imports which predate the establishment of the earliest Greek colonies on and around the Italian peninsula. The major development has been the excavation of the early colony at Pithekoussai on the island of Ischia, which was established about a generation before Syracuse, around 750–760 BC. A further assumption is that Greek imports, which are found in early contexts on the Italian mainland, but are absent from the colony of Pithekoussai, predate the establishment of this early colony.

The history of the eastern Mediterranean at this point is dominated by the rise of major empires and their expansion, notably Assyria which starts to encompass the Levantine coast and Cyprus. Following the collapse of the Hittite empire, it is only now that in Turkey new major centralised kingdoms come into existence. One of these, Lydia, with its capital at Gordion, is known mainly from Greek mythological and historical documentation rather than from the archaeology, but the other major kingdom, Urartu, is better understood not only from its own documents (it had adopted a cuneiform script) but also from Assyrian sources. Protected by the mountainous regions of eastern Turkey and Armenia around Lake Van, the kingdom was sufficiently strong to

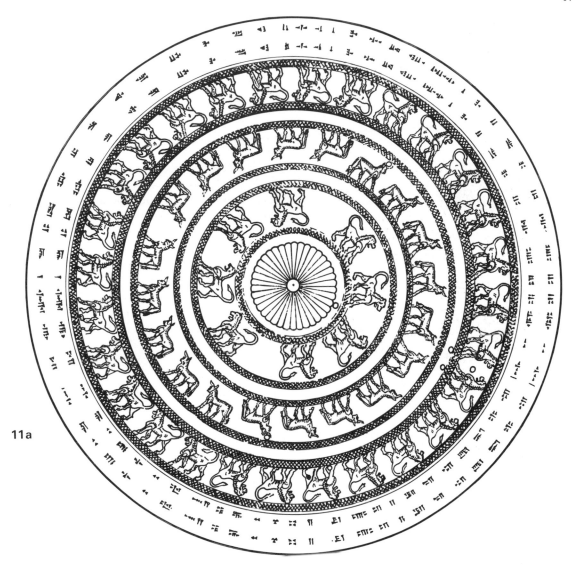

**11a**

11 Bronze work from Urartu

The ancient kingdom of Urartu was centred around Lake Van, in the highland region which extends over modern Armenia and eastern Turkey. It is mentioned in Assyrian sources as early as the thirteenth century BC, but with the collapse of the Hittite empire it gradually rose in importance until, by the eighth century BC, it was able to challenge the power of Assyria, though not with great success. It finally collapsed under the assault of Scythian invaders in the early sixth century.

The working of bronze was highly developed, and a considerable amount has survived, not merely from burials, but from under the destruction levels of the sixth century in temples of towns such as Karmir Blur. In some cases the bronzes are inscribed with the names of rulers whose dates can be fixed with reference to Assyrian sources, giving us a tight chronology for the development of the bronze industry. Asia Minor was certainly one of the sources of inspiration for the developing art of Greece and Italy both in the types of objects made, the technological innovations, and the range of motifs used in the art styles.

The bronze shield from Karmir Blur (*Teishebaini*) (a) comes from the destruction level of the temple. The cuneiform inscription tells us that it was made for the

**11b**

ruler Argishti I (786–764) who dedicated it at the temple in *Erebuni* (Erevan), whence it must have been transferred when the capital was moved. The decoration shows embossed friezes of lions and bulls interspersed with zones of lotus buds.

The bronze cauldrons on tripods also appear as votive offerings in temples, but that from Altintepe (b) comes from a burial dated to about 700 BC. In this case the protomes are of bulls, but gryphons and serpents are also known, or rarely human heads like the winged man and woman from a royal burial at Gordion, capital of Phrygia (c) also dating to around 750–700 BC. It is considered to be an Urartian import.

1c

11c

1c

11c

challenge the supremacy of Assyria. It is possible to correlate the dynasties in the two rival kingdoms, and so date some of the objects which mention the name of Urartian rulers. Urartu is rich in archaeological material, thanks to the extensive excavations by Russian archaeologists working in Armenia, and also because of the exceptional wealth of the finds, due to the eventual destruction of the towns by Scythian raiders in the late seventh and sixth centuries. In some of the sanctuaries, all the votive offerings remain intact in the collapsed debris, and inscriptions show many of these had been in the sanctuaries for 200 years or more.

It is for this reason that we are especially well informed of the bronze technology of the Urartian smiths. We encounter types of vessels and display armour which were to become disseminated right through the Mediterranean area and even into central Europe, demonstrating the process of acculturation and orientalisation which was a significant feature of the early civilisations of Greece and Rome, and in central Europe, of La Tène art. There are the large bronze cauldrons on tripod legs in the form of animal hooves. The shoulders of these cauldrons, and the fixtures for the suspension rings are decorated with elaborate animal or mythological heads. These 'protomes' are commonly in the form of bulls' heads, or gryphons, while a particularly splendid example from one of the royal burials at Gordion is decorated by a siren on one side and a man on the other, both rivetted to the cauldron by means of their outstretched wings. In Urartu itself these objects occasionally occur in tombs, but also in temple contexts on the major sites such as Karmir Blur, and at Toprakale. Perhaps the most spectacular bronze work which is preserved, are the beaten bronze shields which bear concentric decoration formed of friezes of animals, usually lions, but occasionally including cattle, and interspersed with decoration of plant forms such as the lotus bud, which had been a feature of Near Eastern art for many years. Several of these shields bear inscriptions telling us at which temple they were dedicated, and the name of the king who dedicated the shield. In one or two cases we can even detect the transfer of bronze votive offerings from one temple to another, when the capital was transferred from Erebuni (Erevan) to Teishebaini (Karmir Blur). Shields bearing the name of Sarduri the Second can be dated to the eighth century, though other shields of similar character were still being made during the subsequent centuries. The embossed decoration was probably made by laying the bronze sheet on to pitch and punching out the decoration from behind, and then sharpening up the contours of the decoration with a chisel. This form of decoration with animal and especially human friezes, was to be another feature adopted in both Greece and Italy. But not merely was it a transfer of technological information or the simple imitation of prestige forms of metalwork, but also the adoption of ideas, such as the absorption by the Greek and Italian worlds of mythological, half human and half animal,

beasts. We have already mentioned the sirens and gryphons which adorned the tripod cauldrons, and to these may be added such animals as the winged horse (Pegasus of the Greek mythology), and the sphinx (the lion with the human head), though in this case the stylistic associations suggest an origin ultimately in the Egyptian world.

One area to be taken over by the Assyrian empire in the mid to late eighth century was the island of Cyprus, a major source of copper for the Near East. We hear of kings of Cyprus, who were supported by the Assyrian empire as puppet rulers, and of their capital at Salamis just south of Famagusta. Since the collapse of the late Mycenaean civilisation on the island, there is little archaeological information other than isolated finds which can be dated between the eleventh and the eighth centuries BC, and Salamis is no exception. The Bronze Age site here was Enkomi, seemingly destroyed by an earthquake somewhere around 1050 BC. There is a little occupation material from the site of the later Greek and Roman town, which may be datable as early as the ninth century. The earliest evidence we have for the rise of Salamis as an important centre derives from burial evidence, perhaps the burials of the kings themselves. The typical burial rite for rich individuals involved the construction of a subterranean chamber, in poorer cases hewn out of the natural rock, but in the rich burials constructed of high-quality stone masonry, such as had not been seen since the Mycenaean period. The entrance to the underground chamber was approached by a sloping ramp or dromos, which was filled with soil, but which could be reopened when successive burials were placed in the tomb. Some of the poorer burials were certainly in collective tombs, but this is unsure in the case of the rich burials, because in every case the chambers had been emptied out in antiquity, indeed one is still in use as the crypt of a Christian church. The poorer tombs were gathered in a cemetery west of the later town in the area of Cellarka, which remained in use for burial until Hellenistic times. The rich tombs, however, were isolated from the other burials and were scattered across the plain. Though the tombs themselves had been robbed, the entrance dromos had generally been left intact and in this area large numbers of grave-goods were still to be found during the recent excavations.

These graves show the extremely wide connections that an elite group was able to command with imports from Egypt, Assyria, the Levantine coast and the Greek world. The bodies were transported to the tomb on ceremonial wagons drawn by equids (asses?), and the wagon left in the dromos, and the animals slaughtered. In one case one of the animals broke free, and was finally cornered and killed adjacent to the entrance to the tomb. From this same burial, tomb 9, there is a ceremonial seat or throne of wood, inlaid with ivory carvings, for which the closest parallels come from Nimrud, and it may well represent a gift from the Assyrian ruler to his Cypriot subordinate. The decoration includes many of the characteristics which we have noted as being adopted within the Greek art style, mythological beasts such as the sphinx and many of the plant motifs such as the lotus bud, and the palmette. Probably from the Egyptian world come the bronze blinkers found in tomb 79 which bear an embossed sphinx, standing over a reclining figure with negroid characteristics, probably representing the victory of Egypt over the Ethiopians. A cauldron decorated with gryphon protomes may show Urartian connections, though the provenance of these cauldrons is a difficult matter. Tomb 1 contained a range of Greek middle Geometric pottery, the finest available in the east Mediterranean, and it had already achieved a status which was to carry it into the Assyrian world. Three or four of the other tombs also contained Greek imports, and these connections are emphasised by the iron fire dogs in tomb 79, which have their closest parallels at Argos on the Greek mainland. The association of hearth fittings with rich burials recurs in later periods throughout the Mediterranean and Celtic worlds. A bundle of iron rods, one of which was used to bind the others into a pack with a handle, may be a badge of office similar to that borne by the lictors in ancient Rome.

Greek horizons were expanding at this time, not merely geographically, but also in terms of artistic and social development. By around 750 BC

the first colonies or trading entrepôts were established outside the Aegean world. On the Levantine coast Woolley's excavations at the site of Al Mina on the mouth of the river Orontes produced a number of Greek sherds in the lower levels of the town. The quantity suggests a Greek presence, if not an actual Greek trade area with permanent traders, at a site which controlled one of the major trade routes leading from the Mediterranean coast into the Assyrian heartland. The pottery is mainly of Euboean origin, unlike the finds from Cyprus which are mainly of Attic origin. The finds date to about 750 BC, and are contemporary with the trade colony of Pithekoussai on the western coast of Italy. At Pithekoussai we are dealing with a Greek colony, with typical Greek burial rites. Its connections were largely with southern Euboea, and its foundation is traditionally associated with the town of Chalkis. The colony, however, was short-lived, and was soon transferred to the Greek mainland, where the town of Cumae was established towards the end of the century. Excavation at Pithekoussai has demonstrated that metalworking was an important feature of the site, and iron ores were being imported from the island of Elba 200kms to the north, for smelting and the production of iron objects, which previously had been rare on the Italian peninsula. Pithekoussai was also engaged in the manufacture of bronze brooches, both of types current in the north of Italy, and in Greece, producing a fusion of ideas which is typical both in Greek and Etruscan contexts. The siting of Pithekoussai and the Greek presence at Al Mina suggest that the major interest in colonisation at this period was in trade rather than the acquisition of land.

This activity abroad is an indication of the processes that were going on in Greece itself. The major evidence for this external activity is the fine pottery which Greece was producing. Geometric pottery was not only reaching Italy and the Levant, but was also penetrating inland to Mesopotamia. By now numerous centres were producing fine pottery, including the colonies themselves, but the artistic lead was shared alternately by Athens, and by Corinth. Between the early, middle and late Geometric styles there was an

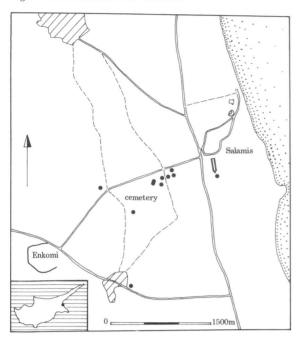

**12a**

## 12 Salamis, Cyprus

The classical city of Salamis lies on the east coast of Cyprus (a), a few kilometres south of Famagusta. Already in the Mycenaean period it was an important centre of trade with the foundation of the town of Enkomi, whose wealth was probably based on the copper resources for which ancient Cyprus was famed. The town survived the demise of the Mycenaean civilisation on mainland Greece, but was itself abandoned somewhere around 1050 BC, perhaps after an earthquake.

Between the demise of Enkomi and the eighth century there is virtually no information—a few settlement finds from the classical city—but at the time of the conquest of the island by the Assyrians Salamis was the capital of the kings of Cyprus, and the series of rich tombs recently excavated presumably belong to the royal family and date to 750–700 BC.

The richer tombs were rock-cut, with a sloping ramp or dromos running down to a chamber constructed of ashlar blocks. The burial took place in the chamber, which was reused for successive burials, but only in the

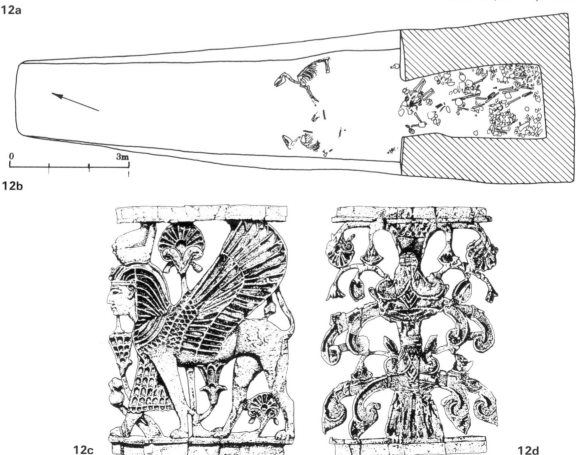

**12b**

**12c**                                                                                    **12d**

case of burial 31 have the contents of the chamber survived intact (b). After each burial the dromos was filled in, covering further offerings and the bodies of the equids (asses?) which had pulled the hearse to the tomb.

The Assyrian connections of Salamis are demonstrated by the carved ivories from a throne found in tomb 79, the closest parallels for which come from Nimrud. One of the supports for the arm-rest (c) shows a sphinx, while the other (d) is decorated with only plant motifs such as palmettes and lotus flowers. A sphinx is also depicted on one of the bronze blinkers (e) from burial 79, in this case overpowering a negro, perhaps signifying an Egyptian triumph over its southern neighbour Ethiopia.

Also from tomb 79 is an example of the bronze cauldrons (f) decorated with protomes, in this case sirens and gryphons. It also contained a pair of iron firedogs (g) and a bundle of twelve iron rods (h).

*Actual sizes: c, d—height 16cm; e—length 19.5cm; f—height of stand and cauldron without protomes 120cm; g—length 115cm; h—length 152cm*

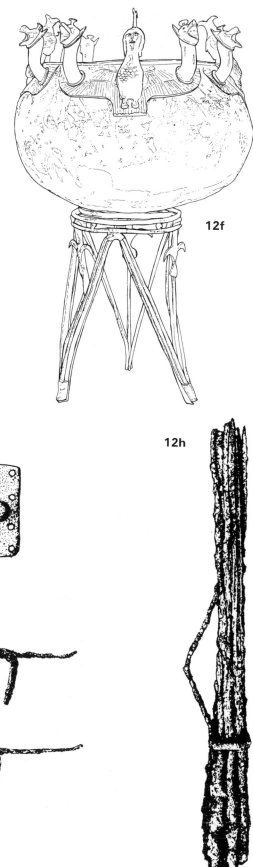

**12f**

**12h**

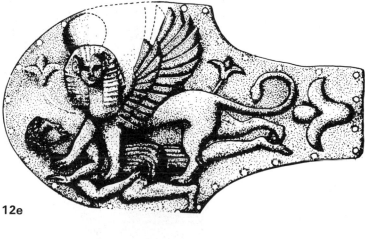

**12e**

**12g**

## 13 Early Greek pottery

After the collapse of the Mycenaean pottery industry, only the most simplified of geometric motifs survived on the painted pottery of the Sub-Mycenaean period. This was the source of the pottery style which was to dominate the Greek world until around 700 BC, and which gives its name to the Geometric period of Greek civilisation.

The Proto-Geometric saw a number of improvements over the Sub-Mycenaean. Firstly there was the appearance of the potter's wheel, secondly a higher standard in the preparation of the clay, and thirdly the introduction of mechanical aids for painting the decoration, notably the use of the compass and of the multiple brush. This allowed a much more careful layout of the design, with concentric circles, and alternating plain and painted bands, producing an austere but pleasing style (a).

The succeeding phases of the early and middle Geometric saw an increasing elaboration of the ornament with more complex patterns based on circles and cross hatched geometrical shapes. The late Geometric bowl from Lefkandi (b), dating to the eighth century, shows how even simple forms such as bowls had developed in distinctive regional styles.

Human and animal figures are only very rarely depicted in the early phases of the Geometric. Before the mid-eighth century, however, some regional styles began to depict both animals and humans, and by the end of the century some of these, such as the jug from Lefkandi (c) depicted full bodied animals, which was

to lead, in around 725 BC, to the orientalising style of Corinth, and later of Athens, heralding the Archaic period.

The most famous group of late Geometric vessels with figures is that from Athens which were first found in the cemeteries such as the Kerameikos outside the Dipylon gate. Many of these are obviously by an individual potter or his workshop, referred to as the 'Dipylon Master'. Typical for the Geometric period, the bodies of both animals and humans are simplified into simple geometric shapes such as triangles, and the limbs are mere matchsticks. The major products are flamboyant funerary vases (d). These themselves often depict funeral scenes with the body lying in state, surrounded by mourners, and with funeral games such as chariot races (e).

**13b**

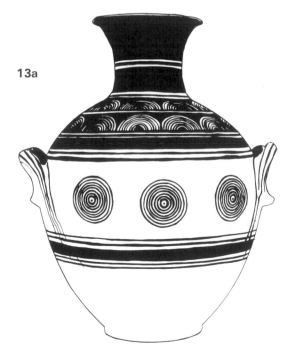

**13a**

**13c**

**13d**

13e

increasing complexity and range in the numbers of motifs employed, and slowly the appearance of animal and human figures in the artistic repertoire, though these too are very much Geometric in style, with triangular bodies, and matchstick legs and arms. The supreme examples of this style are found in Athens, especially in the Dipylon cemetery, on a distinctive group of funerary urns with scenes of shipwrecks, or funeral celebrations, mainly the work of one individual, the Dipylon master. These masterpieces, which were primarily for burial not surprisingly, do not appear far from the source of manufacture, and it is mainly the smaller vessels such as the drinking bowls which formed the bulk of the pottery trade. In the last quarter of the eighth century, however, new innovations appear in the style of pottery painting at Corinth, such as a more full-bodied representation of animals and especially the mythical beasts, which are so characteristic of the orientalising art of Greece and Etruria. Pottery with simple Geometric patterns remained fairly standard for

another century or more, but from now on, starting from Corinth, and spreading to centres such as Athens by about 700 BC, the new more naturalistic orientalising style became dominant, leading directly on to the figured vases of the Archaic and Classical world.

In the production of bronze work the orientalisation of the art style took place considerably earlier than with the pottery. The great problem with the metalwork is that most of it comes from temple sites in deposits derived from the periodic clearing out of the temple. It is very difficult to date individual pieces, and this can only be done in stylistic terms. Crete has also produced some jewellery in early orientalising style, but from collective tombs, which also raises problems of dating. Crete may have been amongst the earliest areas to have adopted the new styles of ornamentation, and from the Idaean cave we possess a series of bronze shields decorated with repoussé ornament reminiscent of the shields we have already encountered from Urartu. The production of bronze shields for votive or ceremonial reasons was very widespread throughout Europe at this period, and there are remarkable inter-regional similarities. The normal form is circular, with bands of embossed ornament, in Scandinavia, central Europe, and Britain usually simply with embossed circles, though occasionally with an inturned 'notch' a feature which is also found in Greek contexts, implying some sort of contact between the Aegean and central and northern Europe. As in Urartu and in Greece, the deposition of these shields in other parts of Europe is associated with some form of votive offering. The stylistic similarity of some of the Cretan shields with those of the Near East suggests the migration of craftsmen from the Near East to Crete and in the gold jewellery we can see the introduction of new techniques of metalwork such as filigree ornamentation. Technical knowledge as well as artistic ideas were passing from one region to another. The Cretan shields possess zones of concentric circles of animals and the Near Eastern mythical beasts, which often appear as the centre piece of the shield. Another favourite form adopted with enthusiasm by the Greek craftsmen is the tripod cauldron, decorated with the protomes of gryphon or human heads. Temple sites such as Olympia have produced these in considerable quantities, and they were used as prizes in games, and as prestige gifts. Human figurines of fairly simple style also start appearing on the temple sites.

This concentration of finds from temple sites leads us on to the temples themselves. Though earlier finds are known from a number of cult sites (indeed some such as the Idaean cave go back to the Mycenaean period), the eighth century sees an upsurge both in the quantity of goods, and in the number of sites which can be documented. By the end of the century, virtually all of the major sites of the Classical period had come into existence. In most cases there is at present no evidence for any building activity and most of them were open air sites, perhaps provided with an altar, but little else. One or two have produced buildings such as the small temple site of Perachora near Corinth, which boasted small rectangular structures by the late eighth century. More

ambitious was the temple of Hera on the island of Samos, where the timber building possessed the colonade structure of the later Classical temple. This preservation may only be due to the flooding of the site, and other temples may be lying hidden or destroyed beneath the podia of later Classical buildings.

Alongside the cult of the gods there was also developing the cult of the heroes who play such a part in the mythology and especially the epic poetry of the Classical world. Burial sites, often of Mycenaean origin, show renewed interest and activity in this period, either in their reuse as burial sites, or in the provision of votive offerings and a shrine. Snodgrass has seen in this the appearance of a new aristocracy and population eager to demonstrate their claims to power in the old order of things. This can also be detected in the genealogies, in which descent from heroes and even gods was claimed by members of the leading families. The importance of family associations is emphasised by the burial of poorer individuals around richer graves in family plots. The existence of richer and poorer cemeteries emphasises the increasing social differentiation which the historical sources might lead us to expect. The importance of inherited as against acquired status is suggested by the increasing wealth of some children's graves, for instance in the 'Plattenbau' cemetery in Athens. Other changes in the intellectual world are less easy to detect but can be surmised from later information. The mythical beasts which we see depicted on the bronze and pottery vessels played a very substantial part in the later mythology of the Greek world: the sphinx in the history of Oedipus at Thebes; or the winged horse Pegasus which transported Jason; or the Chimaera. The epic poetry of Homer perhaps belongs to a slightly earlier date, but now was reaching more permanent form, as writing was adopted from the Phoenician world. Nowhere is perhaps the contrast between Mycenaean and the Early Greek more clearly emphasised than in the nature of the earliest inscriptions that we have in the new script. In contrast to the bureaucratic computations of the Mycenaean scribes, the early inscription on a cup from Pithekoussai dated to around 725 BC states 'this may not be the cup of Croesus, but whoever drinks from it will dream of fair Aphrodite'.

If there are many features of the Classical world in terms of literature, culture, art, language, burial custom that we can already detect in an eighth-century Greece, there is one major aspect which is missing. Centres such as Athens, Corinth and Sparta enjoyed an enormous increase in population, but they still were no more than an agglomeration of people, settled in small communities, and not as yet nucleated into anything that we can recognise as a town or city. There are two ways in which urban sites may have come into existence. One may have been such an increase in population that clusters of smaller centres united into one complex whole, as happened in Athens; secondly the need for defence drew the population into a more defined area around which defences could be built, involving the abandonment of outlying settlements. The latter process might be detected in the abandonment of settlements such as Lefkandi, but defence was more a requisite of the new colonies which were being established in potentially hostile territory on the eastern coast of the Aegean. These colonies may themselves have had a profound effect on the principles of the layout and organisation of the Classical towns of the heartland of Greece. Other than the temples, none of the other institutional buildings associated with the Greek town had yet made its appearance in recognisable form.

## Italy in the eighth century

Phoenician and Greek interaction with the native cultures of Italy is still a problem which is being unravelled as our chronology of events becomes clearer. Only in recent years, with the excavation of Pithekoussai, has a contact period predating the establishment of this colony been identified. Chronologies can now be pushed back, demonstrating more clearly the importance of the native element in the process of acculturation and assimilation of external cultures which lead to the Classical civilisations of the Etruscans and the Romans. But there has unfortunately been considerable bias in the excavation: geographically

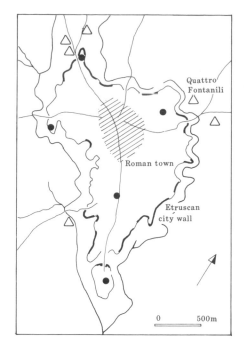

**14a**

work has tended to concentrate on Etruria where the finds are most dazzling, with the result that we know little about the early phases of contact in southern Italy; secondly there has been no concerted plan of campaign of excavation to elucidate the development of settlement patterns, and most especially to tackle the complex problem of the development of the Etruscan towns. Contact with mainland Greece may have continued in some form even in post-Mycenaean times, though it was not far reaching. It only relates to the south eastern part of Italy, and may only have been with the facing parts of Greece, which themselves were not in the mainstream of cultural development. The evidence is slight, but consists of the styles of pottery which are found in this area of Italy, the so-called Iapygian painted wares, which reflect the same trends as in the Greek

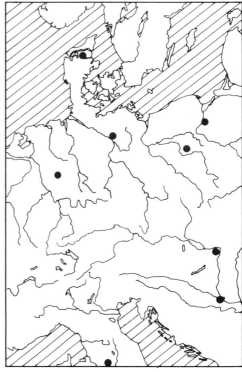

**14b**

**14c**

**14** Veii, Tuscany, Italy

Like many towns of ancient Etruria, the origins of Veii lie in the late Bronze Age, in the century or so either side of 1000 BC. The earliest evidence of occupation is Villanovan, when a cluster of small cemeteries was established around the plateau (a), which may correspond to a number of small villages or hamlets on the plateau itself. There is no evidence for any defensive circuit at this early period, though the defences on the citadel at the southern end have not yet been dated.

Though there is evidence for considerable wealth in the late Bronze Age, mainly from hoard finds and trading contacts with central and northern Europe, this was not translated into differentiation in the wealth of burials, and almost all the burials are cremations in simple urns. Only in the eighth century did this begin to change, to judge from the most systematically excavated cemetery at Quattro Fontanili. Some graves from this period have Euboean Greek bowls of types not found at Pithekoussai, and so presumably predating its foundation.

One of these richer early burials, dating perhaps to 750–730 BC is burial AAI. The cremation was in a bronze urn (b), which was covered by a bronze helmet. Other weapons included a shield, two spearheads and an axe, all of bronze, and a short sword of iron with a bronze scabbard. The grave contained an iron horsebit, bronze razor, bracelets, ear-rings, glass beads, and a faience scarab. The urn is a type which is more commonly found north of the Alps (c), though where these objects were made is unknown.

In the seventh century cremation gave way to inhumation, with graves which are of typical Etruscan type, and there are also above ground chamber tombs. At Quattro Fontanili at least the change-over from Villanovan to Etruscan meant no break in the continuity of the use of the cemetery.

The main defences around the plateau which included a stone built wall, supported front and back by earthen ramps, were not constructed until the end of the fifth century, not long before the period of Roman expansion into southern Etruria. Veii itself fell in 396 BC after ten years of siege, and was the scene of the story of Camillus and the schoolmaster who attempted to hand over his children as hostages to the Romans. Later the town was by-passed by the Roman road system, and gradually declined (see fig 54).

Geometric styles, but the chronology of these wares has yet to be established. More clearly distinguishable is the first wave of imported objects of Greek origin. These avoid the route northwards up the Adriatic, which was not to be opened for another two centuries, but along the south and west coasts of Italy there is a general scatter showing no special concentration even in Etruria. The objects include a few pottery vessels, and occasional bronze vessels, which turn up in rich native burials. The Phoenician element is less clear, as there are no distinctive Phoenician goods distinguishable from those traded by the Greeks. However, by the seventh century we can identify items of North African origin which were certainly coming through the Phoenician networks, and we must assume that some of the early traded goods, such as faience beads and figurines, are of Phoenician rather than of Greek origin. These are especially common in Etruria.

The establishment of Pithekoussai as an entrepôt to develop trade with the nearby coast of Italy marks a major change. It is paralleled by the Phoenician colony of Nora on the island of Sardinia. The fact that more favourable areas for colonisation had been ignored in southern Italy, and Pithekoussai was placed a considerable distance up the west coast, implies that trade was the major element, presumably for the metal resources of Tuscany. However, no attempt was made to establish a colony on the Tuscan mainland itself, unlike the foundation of later colonies in southern Italy, which implies that there was already an organisation in that area sufficiently strong to meet the Greeks and the Phoenicians on equal terms. But it is just this stage in the development of the Villanovan culture and its gradual transformation to the classical Etruscan culture that is one of the most hazy and difficult to understand. Around the plateaux on which the Etruscan towns were later to be founded are clusters of Villanovan cemeteries, which are interpreted as the burial places for individual villages already established on the plateaux. On this model the villages gradually expand until they finally agglomerate into an urban complex which was fortified. Around the plateau of Veii, for instance, several cemeteries are known, and sur-

face fieldwork on the plateau itself has produced several areas with evidence of Villanovan occupation, but the occupation represents no more than a few isolated areas of settlement. This semi-nucleation of settlement suggests some sort of centralised organisation coming into existence, and is similar to that in contemporary Greece. The evidence of hoards shows that the metal industry, especially bronze production, was already highly developed in the late Bronze Age, though there is little to demonstrate this in the burials, which even up into the eighth century contain a single urn, and only rarely one or two bronze trinkets.

During the eighth century gradual changes took place in the burial rite, especially in the cemeteries such as Quattro Fontanili at Veii, where systematic excavation has revealed a cemetery running from early Villanovan to classical Etruscan. To the earlier part of the eighth century belong one or two burials which contain imported Greek vessels of types not found at Pithekoussai, but slowly more and more bronze objects were placed in the graves. From 725 BC onwards, there was an enormous upsurge in interest in funerary rite, including the burial of extremely rich objects in the graves, evidence of an increasing social differentiation, with certain individuals able to obtain exotic goods from the east Mediterranean. In the years before 700 BC and especially just after it we enter the orientalising phase of Etruscan art, but this will be dealt with in the next chapter.

After the foundation of Pithekoussai imported goods show an ever-increasing concentration in Tuscany. In the pre-contact period the Villanovan culture of Tuscany and that of the southern part of the Po valley had shown very close similarities, indeed the culture is named after one of the cemeteries of the city of Bologna. However, with the contact period, there is greater and greater deviation between the two areas, and Bologna remains apart from the orientalising process for a century or more. The same is true of the knowledge of iron working which, though already known on the Italian mainland, is only common in Etruria during the eighth century, and does not spread in any quantity to the north until the following century. Whether there was differential access to the Greek and Phoenician trading markets between the various centres in Tuscany is as yet unclear, though there are hints that it was the maritime cities such as Vulcii, Tarquinia and Volterra controlling river crossings well back from the coastal plain, which developed first. Only later did the inland cities develop in response to the social and economic expansion of their neighbours.

Italy was lagging somewhat behind the Greek and especially the Phoenician worlds, and there is no evidence that by the eighth century the Etruscans had developed as a major maritime power. However, their importance as an industrial power was already established, though their trading links were mainly by land with northern Italy and so on into central Europe, a contact of which they were to make use in subsequent periods. The archaeological record is unequivocal about that much-debated question of the origin of the Etruscans. They were an indigenous people, who were slowly acculturalised under the influence of external trade in much the same way as the Greeks had been in the preceding century. This process of acculturation seems not so much to be a matter of linguistic or cultural origin, as geographical determinism. The areas north of the Apennines, which culturally and linguistically were very close to the Etruscans, were left out of this process, while the Latin-speaking peoples in the immediately adjacent areas to the south, notably around Rome, enjoyed the same development as their Etruscan neighbours.

CHAPTER FOUR

# The Trade Explosion

## Greece in the seventh century

The transition from the Geometric to the Archaic
period of Greek civilisation around 720–700 BC is
defined primarily in terms of art history, especially of pottery styles, with the adoption of
orientalising motifs, first, around 725 BC by
Corinthian potters, by Athenian around 700 BC
and subsequently by some of the more provincial
pottery industries. But this is also a period of
major social and economic change within Greek
society. Writing had already been widely disseminated by the end of the Geometric period, and this
in the seventh century led to the formalisation of
state constitutions, and to the gradual increase of
literary documentation of the processes which
were affecting society. It was also the period of
massive overseas colonisation, which introduced
Greek culture to almost every part of the Mediterranean littoral zone, as well as to the Black Sea.

The Archaic period is that of the *polis*-state—I
hesitate to use the word 'city' state, as not until the
end of the sixth century does the city in the form
that we know it make its appearance in Greece,
but the preceding two centuries did see the
formation of the social and political institutions
which produced it. Locally agglomerations of
population were appearing, usually for reasons of
defence, and already sites such as Lefkandi had
been abandoned, probably at the time of the
foundation of Eretria and Chalkis—though the
island of Euboea, in the process of urbanisation as
in other respects, may have been in advance of the
rest of Greece. The major centres such as Athens
or Corinth were still no more than clusters of small
villages, each with their own cemeteries, and not

until the end of the sixth century was the centre of
Athens laid out with public buildings on a modest
scale.

The Greek state was small. In part we can
invoke geographical determinism—small fertile
plains divided from one another by ranges of hills
or mountains, or islands of modest size.
Communication and access to the political centre
was thus relatively easy on the local scale, but
difficult over larger distances between states—
factors which affected the nature of the social
structure, as all members of the state could
potentially play some part in its running. Not
until the advent of the sea-borne fleet, did a larger
political organisation come into existence and
lead the way to empire.

Where large groupings did exist, they were
either like Thessaly or Macedonia, loose organisations difficult to weld into a unity, or they were
connected with land hunger, a small military elite
holding down a larger territory by force, of which
Sparta is the supreme example. Land in fact seems
to be the key to understanding this period of
Greek history. Both the historical and the archaeological record speak clearly of land-shortage,
though this need not always mean overpopu-
lation. In Attica, for instance, we hear of the
increasing power of an elite land-owning class
who were even forcing fellow citizens into slavery
because of debts. But this centralising process was
tempered by military needs. Effective warfare
could only be conducted by a strong infantry of
hoplite warriors—free citizen soldiers who supplied their own sword, spear, shield, and especially the bronze armour which provided the
weight for massed infantry attacks. In the case of

Athens the quandary was resolved, temporarily at least, by the laws of Solon which released debtors, redistributed land, and extended the citizenship.

Under these crisis circumstances individuals did acquire supreme power, though, as in the case of Solon, it was usually exercised in limiting the power of the land-owning elite and in favour of extending the military basis. But this never led to a centralised power as had existed in the Mycenaean period. The elite may have controlled land, and presumably agricultural production, but industrial production remained separate, indeed was disdained by the aristocracy. Often it remained in the hands of foreign residents, the 'metics' who rarely attained citizenship, a right which was firmly defined in terms of ownership of land. Without control of production, with only partial control of land, total military control was also impossible, and no feudal system could be imposed. This became more true in the period of maritime power when the rowers, themselves free artisans, were able to exert political pressure for democratisation in fifth-century Athens. Military necessity balanced the centralising tendency of power.

This equivocation is reflected in the burial evidence. There is no great sign of ostentation in burial, such as is found in more centralising societies, indeed among the laws of Solon was one limiting expenditure on funerals. The wealthy still displayed themselves, though increasingly during the sixth century this took the form of tombstones and stelae, and was one of the contexts in which sculpture developed with standing male and female youths, the koroi and korai. But even the scale of these was modest in comparison with contemporary Cypriot, Lydian and Etruscan standards.

As in central Europe a few centuries earlier, deliberate destruction of wealth continued, it merely changed its context. Weapons may be unknown in burials excepting a few in peripheral areas, from the beginning of the seventh century, but they start to appear in vast quantities in the shrines. Sometimes they are offerings made by individuals who scratched their names on the objects, but increasingly states would make large offerings, perhaps of several hundred items at a time to celebrate victory in battle. Tripods, cauldrons and other bronze vessels might be directly commissioned for sacrifice, and even heads of kingdoms outside the Greek world, Croesus of Lydia and Psammetichos of Egypt, gave lavish gifts, though at the end of the Archaic period such gifts took on a more architectural and sculptural form.

These foreign gifts reflect the increasing connections of Greece with the outside world, and this too was a product both of land shortage and military expertise. Faced with shortage of land, individuals and communities were left with a number of possibilities. Firstly there was increased agricultural production. This might be achieved by redistribution of land and so of more intensive farming; or by the 'carrot', incentives in the form of desirable products which could be exchanged for surplus; or by the 'stick' of increased social differentiation, with a poor class either forced to work for minimal returns or totally excluded from society. The first and second were the Athenian and Corinthian solutions, the third the Spartan. The second possibility was greater integration of the local economy, whereby different areas could increase their agricultural specialisation, and trade with other specialised groups for necessities which they could only themselves produce inefficiently—the way in which the early Greek states developed suggest this was happening, but it has never been demonstrated archaeologically. Thirdly, there was increased industrial production for goods which could be traded abroad for foodstuffs—again a Corinthian and Athenian solution. Finally, there was emigration. In part this could be an individual choice, and increasingly we encounter Greek traders in foreign ports in the east Mediterranean, artisans setting up business in Etruscan cities, or Greek mercenaries fighting in Egypt, Lydia, Assyria and Persia. But more dramatically parts of, even whole, communities could move and establish themselves elsewhere, and this colonisation movement is the solution which makes the most obvious impact in the archaeological record, and on the development of European civilisation as a whole.

As we have seen, colonisation within the Aegean was already underway as early as the ninth or tenth century, by the early or mid eighth the Euboeans were established at Al Mina, Pithekoussai and perhaps in Cilicia; after 740 this movement became a flood. Firstly it was the south of Italy and Sicily, Naxos around 740, and in 733 Syracuse. By the beginning of the following century some twenty colonies had been established in the west, mainly by states on the Greek mainland. The states on the eastern side of the Aegean, though involved in the westward movement, were increasingly looking to the north, to the coast of Thrace, the Hellespont, and finally to the Black Sea. Colonisation of this area was largely completed by the end of the century, spurred on by the increasing pressures of Lydian, Assyrian and Persian imperial advance on to the Asia Minor coast. By the end of the century, colonisation into the western Mediterranean had extended to the coasts of France and Spain, led by colonists displaced by the Lydians from the town of Phocaea. The Phocaeans were responsible for the major colony in France, near the mouth of the

Rhône at Marseilles, around 600 BC.

Not surprisingly the Euboean states of Eretria and Chalkis, which had initiated the colonial movement to Italy, were the main participants in the first wave of colonisation, which involved the control of their trade route to Cumae through the straits of Messina. But even in the second wave the major states were hardly involved—Corinth founded two or three colonies, Sparta one, while Athens none at all until the end of the sixth century when she attempted to take control of the entrance to the Black Sea. This may in part reflect the success of policies in the homeland, and suggests that colonisation was a matter of necessity rather than of territorial or imperial ambition.

A contrast is often drawn between the earliest 'trade' colonies such as Pithekoussai, and these later colonies which may have been primarily grabbing of land. Possession of land was certainly the key to citizenship in these new colonies as well as in the mother states, so it must have been the

**15** Sites mentioned in chapter 4

ambition of the majority of emigrants. Sites were also chosen for their defensive qualities as often the new land had to be held against native opposition—historical sources record such conflict, and it is detectable archaeologically: when Pithekoussai was abandoned in favour of Cumae on the Italian mainland around 730 BC, the native population who had been trading with the Greeks were expelled, and their cemetery overlain by the new colony. Generally the new colonies also required a good harbour, as contact with the homeland was a required necessity, and only when the colonies themselves established colonies were more inland sites chosen. Trade naturally developed from these ports.

But it is obvious that certain sites were chosen for their trade potential—Marseilles with its relatively poor agricultural land but rich trading hinterland is the obvious example, and the potential of the straits of Messina, the Dardanelles and the Bosphorus were quickly realised. In the Black Sea the most successful colonies controlled river routes into the interior—Olbia on the Dnieper, Panticapaeum on the Bug, and Istros near the Danube. This area was soon to become one of the main sources of grain for the cities of Classical Greece. However, the most important new colony for the development of Greek civilisation and art was purely a trading town, in fact a classic 'port of trade'. Naucratis in the Nile delta was founded by 620 BC, perhaps on the instigation of the Pharaoh Psammetichos I (664–610), partly in gratitude for the assistance of Greek mercenaries in his conquest of Egypt. The port, which was under Greek control, was given a monopoly of Egypt's external trade under Amasis (570–526), and not until the foundation of Alexandria in the fourth century did it lose this position, though it suffered periods of temporary decline.

Unfortunately, the major excavations at Naucratis took place before the advent of scientific techniques, but, both from archaeology and from a description by Herodotus, we know of shrines set up by various states such as Samos which were the recipients of votive offerings for successful voyages. The residential areas are less known, but there was also industrial production of pottery, mainly for local use, and trinkets and figurines of faience which found their way commonly to the eastern Aegean, and as far as Italy and Sicily. It was through Naucratis and the mercenaries that the Greeks were introduced to Egyptian monumental architecture and sculpture, and provided the major source of stimulus for Greek Archaic styles of the sixth century.

The organisation of trade at this period is still shadowy. It seems unlikely that a true merchant class had come into existence, and certainly there is no hint that it ever presented a challenge to those whose wealth lay in more traditional ownership of land. Rather it was in the hands of non-residents, or it was a relatively low-class occupation similar to that of the artisan—as in the case of the mercenary soldier, a means of buying oneself into a respected place in society. Trade may not have had status in the eyes of the Greeks, but it was nonetheless the major cause of social and culture change within the Greek world and among the societies with whom they traded.

## Etruscan civilisation

The transition from 'Villanovan' to 'Etruscan' takes place around 700 BC. It entails no basic change in the settlement pattern. The cluster of villages on the plateaux at Veii and elsewhere continue, and in some areas such as Latium there was a decrease in the number of minor settlements suggesting nucleation was taking place, as well as an overall increase in population size. Cemeteries such as Quattro Fontanili also show complete continuity, though with a gradual change from cremation to inhumation, a phenomenon which starts among the richer burials. The beginnings of Etruscan civilisation are defined by two phenomena, the appearance of very wealthy burials, and by the orientalising objects found in those tombs.

Though both Greece and Etruria were moving towards state formation and urbanisation, the very fact that the Etruscans placed great emphasis on ostentatious burial implies a different social development. The graves of the seventh century include some chamber tombs under large tumuli, with rich gravegoods which might include a chariot, weapons, bronze and silver vessels, gold ornaments, and, increasingly, imported pottery and local fine bucchero and painted wares. Several Etruscan centres have produced these rich burials, Populonia, Vetulonia, Tarquinia, and Caere, and also Palestrina in adjacent Latium. Thus, though there was a tendency for wealth at this early stage to be concentrated in the coastal sites, no one centre had risen to prominence. The limited documentary evidence confirms the archaeology. We hear of individual 'city' states rather than a centralised Etruscan state, though as in Greece these city states joined together in leagues against common foes, and by the sixth and fifth centuries they were strong enough to challenge Greek and Carthaginian supremacy in battle.

We also hear of kings in the early stages of development, and in this Rome was no exception, though as in Greece kingship soon turned into oligarchy controlled by the land-owning class. But it is unclear what made kingship possible in Etruria and not in Greece. The military constraints of the need for a citizen army may not have been present; or the new elite may have interested itself more in other spheres of the economy, perhaps with greater control of mineral production, or again—and more likely—it may have taken a more active interest in trade. However, by the time we know more of Roman society (which closely resembled that of the Etruscans) the elite senatorial class were strictly land-owners, while trade and industry were the realm of the Equites, who, despite their wealth, were debarred from senatorial office.

The imported goods from the rich graves are likely to have come both through the Phoenician and the Greek trade networks. Of north African or Near Eastern origin are the silver plates with embossed scenes of a shipwreck, and of marching warriors from the rich burials at Palestrina. The figures have a strong Egyptian flavour. Certainly Egyptian is a faience vessel with the cartouche of the Pharaoh Bocchoris from a grave in Tarquinia. Several cauldrons with protomes are known, mainly of oriental rather than Greek origin. That from the Regolini-Galassi tomb at Caere has a stand of beaten bronze, embossed with friezes of sphinxes and other mythical beasts. The same

tomb produced a gold brooch with embossed lion and a lotus bud pattern in filigree ornament. These objects most likely came through the Greek network, and Greek pottery, especially Corinthian and later Athenian fine wares became increasingly common.

As in Greece, local production was stimulated both by the style of the imported objects, and by the arrival of foreign craftsmen, though the latter are easier to identify in the sixth and fifth centuries, when we can even name one or two of the Greek potters who settled in Etruria. The potter's wheel was introduced, and stimulated local fine ware production, notably the plain bucchero wares for local use and export. Greek geometric styles were also imitated. The metal-working industry was profoundly affected, with the introduction of new techniques such as granulation and filigree. By the end of the century, sophisticated bronze vessels were being produced, such as the beaked flagons which appear so commonly north of the Alps. How this industry was organised we cannot guess without archaeological excavation in the developing proto-urban centres.

One other introduction must be mentioned, the adoption of the Greek alphabet, that of Megara which had been involved in the foundation of colonies such as Syracuse. Unfortunately the briefest of inscriptions appear in the Etruscan world, and no literature survives to compare with that of Greece. One object deserves special note, an inscription on a gold brooch from Palestrina. It is written in Latin—the earliest example known—and it demonstrates that the orientalising process was not only affecting the Etruscans, but neighbouring Latium as well, including Rome. We are not looking at a process which was ethnically determined, rather at a socio-economic acculturisation which could cross linguistic boundaries.

## Situla Art

The impact of the foundation of the Greek colonies in Sicily and southern Italy upon the natives is little understood. At several sites such as Cumae the natives were physically ousted, but

**16a**

## 16 The orientalising period in Italy

At the end of the eighth and beginning of the seventh centuries the burial rite in Etruria and adjacent parts of Latium underwent fundamental changes. Instead of burial in flat cremation cemeteries, as in the previous late Bronze Age, the richer members of society constructed elaborate stone and earth structures above ground, covering chambers in which successive members of the same family could be buried. Cremation gradually gave way to inhumation.

The trend already noted at Veii for an increase in gravegoods (fig 14) now went much further, with vehicles such as chariots included, and a wealth of local and imported goods, including many in precious metals. The burials from Palestrina (Praeneste) in northern Latium are fairly typical. The imported objects include a gilt silver cauldron (a) decorated with a frieze of marching warriors, and protomes in the form of serpents heads. A silver bowl is also likely to be Syrian in origin (b), and shows battle scenes, processions and hunting scenes, the whole enclosed by an entwined snake. The gold brooch (c) is local, and is inscribed with the earliest known Latin inscription, *Manios med fhe fhaked Numasioi*/*Manius me fecit Numasio*, 'Manius made me for Numasius'.

*Actual size: b—diameter 19cm*

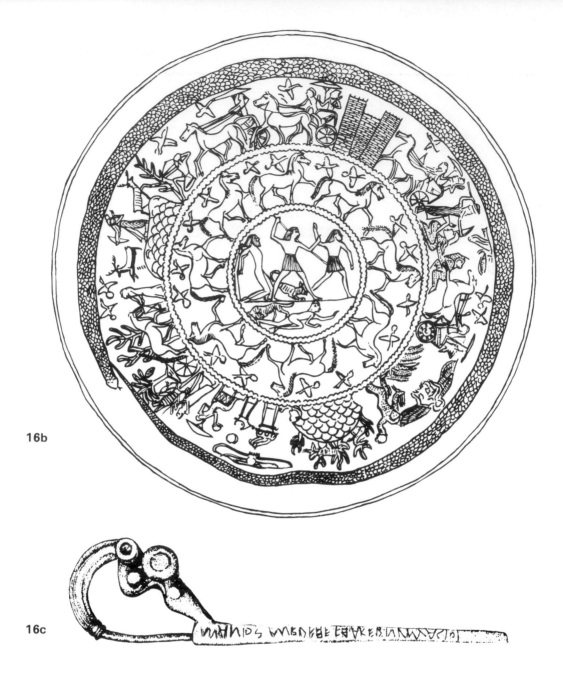

**16b**

**16c**

elsewhere the literary sources suggest greater collaboration, at least initially, and doubtless every colony had a native element, though numbers and status might vary. Generally the coastal plains were taken over by the Greeks, or, in western Sicily, by the Carthaginians, but the natives survived inland. In the immediate hinterlands some trade and interaction occurred— Greek pottery turns up in native graves and settlements. In more distant areas, however, impact may have been minimal. In the Biferno valley on the Adriatic coast, for instance, surface survey suggests that fine imported wares did not arrive until as late as the fourth or third centuries BC.

Even north of the Appenines and in the Po Valley, areas which had shared the same Villanovan tradition with Etruria, in the seventh century saw a virtual rupture of contact. From Bologna, objects in orientalising style, with the

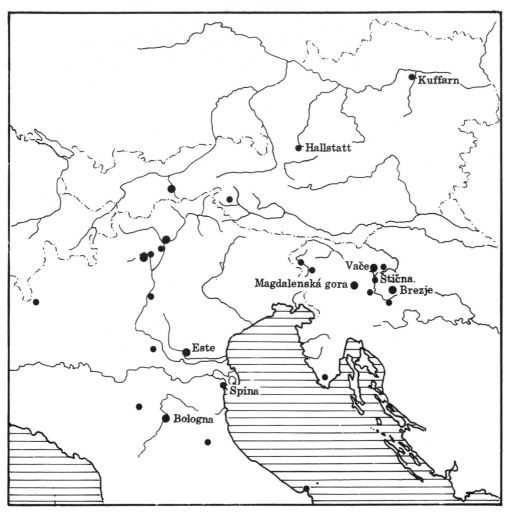

**17a**

### 17  Situla Art

new techniques of manufacture such as filigree ornament, only occur as very rare imports, and though there is an increase in wealth in the burials, especially of bronze and iron work, the basic Villanovan tradition continues, with none of the exotic elements of Etruria proper. In other respects, however, the processes that took place in northern Italy very much resemble those of Etruria. We find the same concentrations of cemeteries around centres such as Bologna, and north of the Po valley, at Este, implying that some sort of central organisation was coming into existence.

The orientalising process in this area was retarded by about a century and, when finally the new art styles appeared, they showed very strong

Northern Italy received the influence of the Orientalising Art styles of the Mediterranean at second-hand through Etruria. There was already a well-established tradition for producing beaten bronze metalwork in the form of buckets, and the new ideas of figured ornament were readily adopted, firstly in the form of friezes of browsing animals, and by about 625 BC with human figures in scenes taken from local life. The earliest bucket decorated in this style is the Benvenuti situla from Este (b, c).

In the extensive use of bosses it is still archaic in character, following on the geometric motifs which had long been established on Urnfield metalwork (e.g. fig 14), but it already has most of the characteristic scenes of Situla Art. In the top frieze there is the party scene with boxers and drinking. The vessels depicted include a situla, a ribbed bucket, and a bronze cup, all types made locally, and found in graves in Este. The middle frieze has browsing animals and mythical beasts, the lowest frieze the procession of warriors, in this case with captives and a chariot.

By the following century this art style was well established in the eastern Alps and Slovenia (a), and in the fifth century it reached as far north as Kuffarn on the Danube in Austria. By about 500 BC it was fully developed, as on the situla in Providence Museum, Rhode Island (d) which perhaps comes from the Certosa cemetery at Bologna. This too has three friezes, with the top one again the party scene, with people playing musical instruments. The middle scene is of soldiers, now more obviously bearing local weapons and armour. The third scene is again of animals.

Other workshops, in Slovenia for instance, had their own distinctive characteristics, such as the greater use of the punch as infill on the clothing and the animals,

but the scenes were closely similar—mythical beasts, marching soldiers, chariot races, processions, parties, boxing matches, and erotic scenes as on the belt plate from Brezje in Yugoslavia (e). By the end of the fourth century, however, Situla Art was in decline, and situlae like that from the Arnoaldi cemetery in Bologna are more roughly finished. Imported Greek goods were taking their place as the prestige goods in burials, and by the fourth century only a few plaques on ritual sites continued the tradition.

*Scales: b—1:4; c—1:3; d—1:2*

**17e**

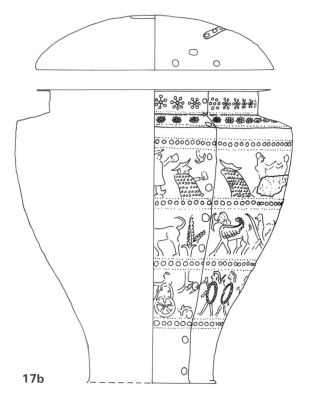

**17b**

native influence, mixed with oriental ideas gleaned entirely from Etruria rather than directly from the Phoenician and Greek worlds. The best indicators of this process are highly decorated bronze buckets, known by the Latin term *situlae*, which give their name to Situla Art. It is distributed over a wide area of northern Italy, especially from Bologna, Este, and extending into Austria, where examples are known from the Hallstatt cemetery, and from Kuffarn on the Danube, and into Yugoslavia, at Magdalenská Gora, and Vače. In all areas it first appears around 650–600 BC, and finally disappears around 400 BC.

The bronze situla itself is of central European Urnfield origin. Plain beaten bronze buckets had been made in Hungary and adjacent areas from about 1000 BC onwards, and were frequently copied in pottery. In northern Italy these buckets

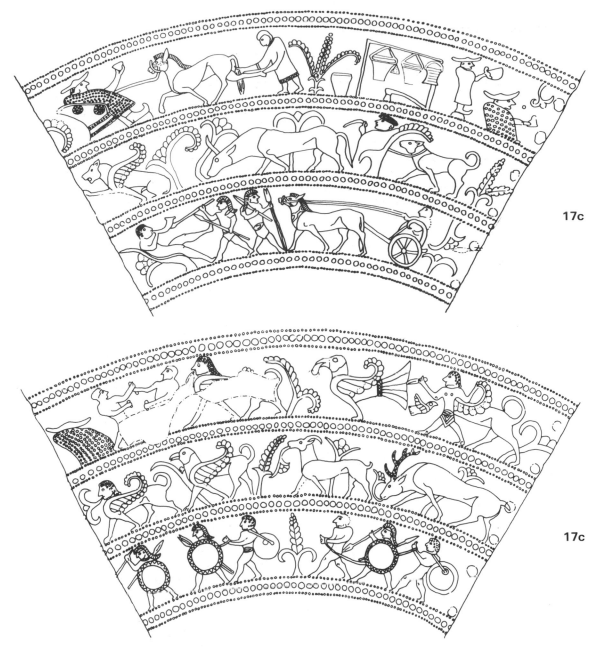

**17c**

**17c**

had occasionally been decorated with embossed geometric designs, such as meanders, and similar designs occur on some of the pottery with decoration made by inserting bronze nails. The earliest examples we have of Situla Art come from Este, and include a bronze lid decorated with a frieze of browsing animals, which have foliage coming from their mouths, a peculiarly Etruscan trait, common in Situla Art. The earliest decorated situla is also from Este, from the Benvenuti cemetery, dated to about 625 BC. It shows many early features, including a predilection for embossed decoration, where full-bodied and incised decoration was used later on. But it also possesses fully developed characteristics of Situla Art, namely the friezes on which party scenes are depicted, with the guests sitting around in chairs or sleeping, wearing their broad-rimmed hats. There is the boxing scene, a frieze of animals, some browsing, but also with mythical beasts such

**17d**

as the sphinx. The bronze situla seems to be used in a party context, and in some scenes we see the situlae themselves depicted either hanging on stands, or being carried to the party.

For the following century we have no further examples of situlae (Situla Art in the narrow sense) but we do have various other items such as lids and sword sheaths which bear either embossed decoration, or incised decoration (Situla Art in the widest sense), showing that the tradition for producing decorated items continued and that it is pure chance that no actual situlae have survived in the archaeological record. Possibly contemporary with Benvenuti are a number of finds from Austria, from the burials at Klein Klein where some bucket-like vessels bear simple embossed decoration and include some motifs of situla art, for instance the boxers. But these objects also include many things which do not appear on Situla Art, and lack the typical friezes. They also possess purely local scenes, such as fish, or herds of animals such as goats, and there is no sign of the orientalising styles of further south. It suggests the local tradition for decorating these vessels is as important as the orientalising influence of Etruria.

The next situla proper, from the Certosa cemetery at Bologna, is datable to somewhere before 500 BC, and shows Situla Art in its fully developed form. Though the scenes are taken from local life, including the party scenes, a ceremonial procession, and rows of warriors, there is already an indication that the style had developed a traditional way of depicting things, which is deviating from the normal daily life. Some of the bronze vessels pictured on the situla are archaic, and depict types which were in use a century or more beforehand, for example a bronze bucket with bird's head attachments which is being carried by two individuals. The frieze of marching warriors, bearing shields, spears and helmets of local type, is now fully developed, but it derives ultimately from the Egyptian tradition, via the imported silver vessels in Etruscan contexts such as those from the Palestrina burials. We also have mythical beasts, some with another touching Etruscan trait, animals with human legs and other bits of bodies hanging from their jowls.

Certosa has four friezes, but more usual is three: the warriors, the party scene, and the beasts. This is found on the presumably contemporary situla (possibly even made by the same individual) which is now in the museum at Providence, Rhode Island, but which also possibly originates from the Certosa cemetery at Bologna. This particular situla bears an inscription on the rim, demonstrating that in this area too writing was becoming known.

Contemporary with these situlae in northern Italy are the finds from Yugoslavia, such as the Vače situla. This shows the standard scenes of mythical beasts, the party with the boxing scene, the frieze of warriors, and also with racing vehicles, which appear on several situlae. However, the style of decoration is different from the Italian examples, with a greater love of infilling using a square toothed punch. This is especially used to decorate the clothing, and also to give texture to the hides of the animals. Otherwise the standard techniques are used, with punching out from behind presumably against a pitch base, and then with incised decoration sharpening up the profiles of the individuals. It is this use of the punch, that gives the Situla Art its individualistic character with, for instance, the very large noses and puffy faces of the individuals. In Yugoslavia too the art is not confined to the buckets, but appears on such other items as belt ornaments. There are also erotic scenes on the situlae, most often individuals lying on beds, and on the belt fitting from Brezje women sitting on chairs, and the men kneeling before them.

The period around 500 BC represents the high point in Situla Art. Although there are very fine specimens of a later date, the examples from northern Italy belonging to the middle and later fifth century show signs of being more roughly finished, or with the scenes less clearly depicted. These will be dealt with in a later section.

## Central and western Europe in the seventh century

The period known as Hallstatt C in central Europe coincides more or less with the eighth century. As the terminology implies, it in many ways represents a simple continuity from the preceding Urnfield period (Hallstatt A and B). But in central more than western Europe there are hints of changes taking place that were to reach fruition in the sixth century—changes in technology, burial rite and social structure, though the cause of these changes is not immediately apparent in the archaeological record.

One technological change is obvious—the adoption of a developed iron working technology. Rare iron objects had appeared before, but the seventh century marks the watershed, with iron becoming, if not common, sufficiently normal to excite no comment at least in the areas immediately north of the Alps. On the other hand, bronze was not entirely ousted from use in weapons and tools for which iron was more suitable. In central Europe, swords of bronze and iron are equally common. In the Atlantic zone and Scandinavia, bronze swords far exceed iron in quantity, and everywhere bronze was probably still the main material for agricultural tools. Initially the new technology probably had little impact on levels of agricultural production.

There are two possible reasons for a gradual transition from bronze to iron. Firstly iron was still primarily a prestige material. The majority of finds are derived from rich burials. They include horse fittings and knives, but the most startling objects are long iron swords (over a metre in length) named after the Bavarian burial of Mindelheim. These swords were elite weapons, with large wooden pommels sometimes decorated with gold overlay. More than anything else they show that iron working was now mastered in central Europe. Their distribution is essentially the Alps, Czechoslovakia, southern Germany and eastern France, with outliers in Scandinavia and Britain.

The second limiting factor was disseminating the expertise to the new class of blacksmiths. Who were the people who took up iron smithing, and how did they acquire their knowledge? In part the iron tools themselves provide an answer. The hoard from Llyn Fawr in south Wales includes, alongside a range of local bronze socketed axes, sickles and horsegear, an iron Mindelheim sword, an iron spear, and two iron sickles. The sword could be an import but the sickles are certainly

not, as they are iron versions of the bronze sickles, themselves a type peculiar to Britain. In other words we have a blacksmith making imitations of local bronze objects. Sporadic socketed iron axes are known—a type easy to make by casting bronze, whereas with iron a shaft-hole type is easier to forge. The Mindelheim sword is also known in a cast bronze form. Though its immediate typological antecedents are unknown, it is in the tradition of leaf-shaped late Bronze Age swords. The elaborate ribbing is easy to cast in bronze, difficult to forge in iron. The earliest blacksmiths of Temperate Europe thus seem to be trained bronzesmiths changing over to a new metal. Within the eighth century, iron working spread very quickly, but only a small number of individuals, especially in the Atlantic and Baltic areas, were producing a limited range of objects, mainly prestige. Bronze still provided the bulk of metal goods—an interesting contrast with Proto-Geometric Greece, where bronze virtually disappeared.

The widespread distribution of the Mindelheim sword, and its contemporary, the Gündlingen type, also raises problems of interpretation. They are the first types to have an almost pan-European distribution since the Erbenheim and Hemigkofen types at the beginning of the late Bronze Age. To what extent is this a trade in prestige goods from a small number of production centres, to what extent adoption of a type by numerous regional workshops? The Mindelheim, at least the iron form, represents a technological breakthrough (as had the earlier leaf-shaped forms), but this can hardly be claimed for the Gündlingen. Further the Gündlingen seems to be an Atlantic type, probably a British invention, but not uncommon in central Europe, including several from the Hallstatt cemetery itself. This hardly tallies with the traditional diffusionist model which sees central Europe as the source of all major developments in the late Hallstatt period. These sword types were accompanied by scabbards whose elaborate chapes show a variety of distinctive forms, which have disjointed distributions over the same wide areas as the swords. Whatever the mechanism, contact was extensive.

What the breakthrough was that carried iron

**18 Hallstatt**

The modern town of Hallstatt lies in central Austria, overlooking the Hallstatter See, and surrounded by mountains. Above the town lie the salt mines which were its only source of wealth in medieval and modern times, when tourism began to take over. The earliest recorded finds date back to the seventeenth century with observations by the miners of earlier 'heathen' workings. Even the body of a miner was found preserved in the salt, and a plaque records that he was buried near the church, but not in consecrated ground because it was thought 'he was not a good catholic'. Recent excavations by Barth and a reconsideration of the tool typology coupled with C14 dates has suggested three phases of mining (a).

The earliest phase starts in the late Bronze Age with the opening of the northern mines, using techniques already developed in the eastern Alps for the extraction of copper. This was abandoned, perhaps deliberately sealed off, around 800 BC. Around 700 the mines were re-opened, and this time concentrated in the southern area. Work continued until around 400 when the mines were again abandoned, perhaps as a

result of a landslide. To this period belongs the famous cemetery which gives its name to the Hallstatt period. Finally the western mines were opened in the late La Tène, and a settlement established higher up the valley at Dammwiese.

Sporadic excavations began on the cemetery in the 1830s, but systematic excavation started under the local Burgermeister J. G. Ramsauer in 1846, and he continued to excavate until 1863 with a level of recording virtually unparalleled at the time. We possess plans and sections of many of the graves, and many of the grave groups can still be reliably reconstructed, though unfortunately he tended to discard pottery. More recent excavations before the last war concentrated on the La Tène phase of the cemetery, but unfortunately are largely unpublished.

The earliest graves belong to the very end of Hallstatt B, but the majority date to Hallstatt C and D. The richest of the early graves are typified by the long swords of bronze or iron. The Mindelheim type (b) can be of bronze or iron, and where preserved they have elaborate hat-shaped pommels, in one case overlaid with gold sheet (c). Contemporary is the

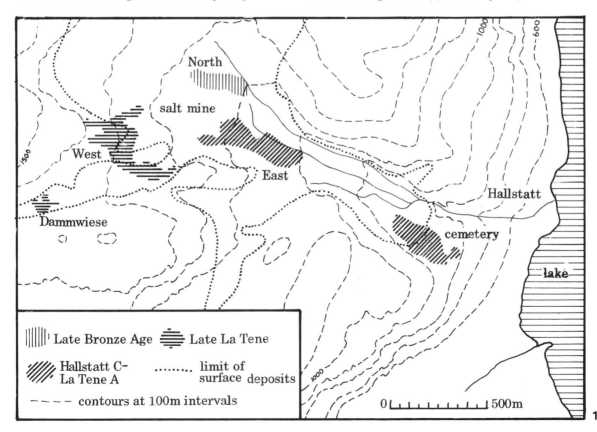

Late Bronze Age    Late La Tene
Hallstatt C-La Tene A    limit of surface deposits
contours at 100m intervals    0 —— 500m

**18a**

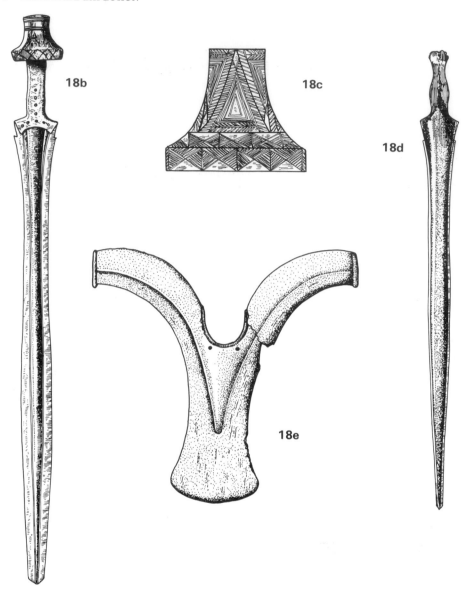

18b

18c

18d

18e

Gündlingen sword type (d), generally shorter, and always of bronze but with similar pommels. These tend to have elaborate chapes (e) likewise of bronze. Both sword types, and the various forms of chape have very extensive distributions throughout central, western and northern Europe (g). They represent the end of the slash and thrust sword tradition in Europe.

In Hallstatt D the swords were replaced by daggers (f) (D for daggers, C for swords!) and that from burial 696 is clearly a prestige weapon with its iron blade inlaid with gold ring-and-dot motifs. The Hallstatt cemetery is still one of the wealthiest known of this period. The graves contain numerous bronze vessels, some probably imports from northern Italy, ceremonial axes, bronze helmets, as well as the usual range of brooches, pins and other personal items.

*Scales: b, d—1:3; c, e, f—1:2*

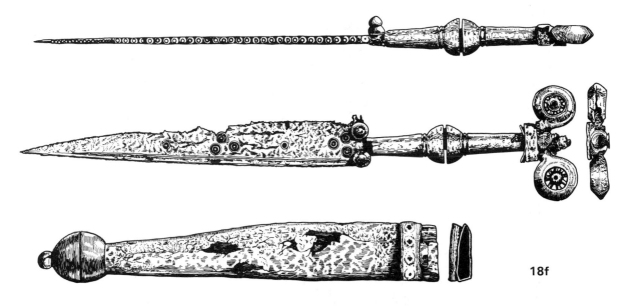

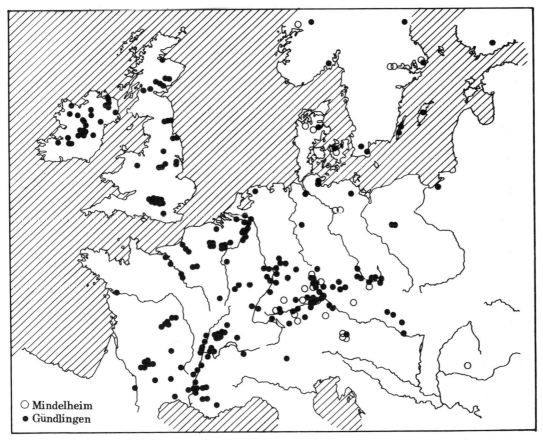

18f

○ Mindelheim
● Gündlingen

18g

technology through Europe is still unclear. As it follows on so soon after central and northern Italy, it is tempting to see a causal relationship, a diffusion of iron working from Greece via the old Urnfield network into central Europe. The trade in metals and salt would suggest the east Alpine region as the area of contact and the density of early finds here and in adjacent areas lends support to this view. Alternatively Romania and the Balkans have been suggested. Central European contacts certainly existed, as the iron sword of Romanian type from Pécs-Jakobhegy in Hungary demonstrates. A third source might have been through Greek contacts with southern France, where the Hallstatt C iron dagger from the Cayla-de-Mailhac is not in the central European tradition, though this area forms part of the old Urnfield network.

One reason for our limited knowledge of the advance of iron working is the disappearance of hoards. This is mainly true of central Europe in the eighth century, but it is followed by Scandinavia and the Atlantic coast in the seventh, due perhaps to the longer survival of major bronze production in those areas. Bronze by no means disappears, it just changes its role, with increasing emphasis on personal ornaments (pins, brooches, belt fittings), bronze-sheet vessels and harness ornaments; so there were still plenty of bronze objects to be hoarded. Hoarding does in fact sporadically reappear in the Iron Age, mainly of gold, silver (torcs and coins) and iron currency bars, and in Britain of bronze harness fittings in the first century AD, but these exceptions rather highlight the contrast with the Bronze Age.

Hoarding and the provision of gravegoods have on occasion been linked in a negative way—the more in the graves, the less in the hoards or river finds—as though these may be alternative ways in which wealth was ostentatiously discarded or destroyed for social purposes. Hallstatt C conforms with the pattern. In central Europe hoards disappear, but gravegoods rise rapidly in importance. It may only be the provision of a sword and 'sceptre' in an otherwise normal Urnfield context, as at Platěnice in northern Bohemia, but more normally a tumulus was constructed over the richer graves covering a timber-lined chamber. In addition to swords and an increasing range of personal ornaments and pottery vessels, harness equipment and often a complete wagon are included. These latter suggest we are dealing with increasing social differentiation with ostentatious emphasis on individuals. Inhumation in part replaces cremation for the richer burials, reflecting similar trends in contemporary Etruria.

The settlement pattern shows little difference from that of the late Bronze Age; if anything, there is more emphasis on open village and farm settlements, as hillforts are virtually unknown. With the one or two exceptions discussed below, there is no concentration of wealth, and each group of tumuli large enough to relate to a village size settlement contains burials in wooden chambers, with sword, horsegear, and possibly a wagon, suggesting small-scale chiefdoms. There is little evidence for industrial production—the metalwork indicates specialists but whether any were full-time is unclear. Pottery was also a prestige item: large plates, bowls and storage jars, with a rich range of incised, stamped, incrusted and painted wares, have been found from southern Poland to central France, but not on the Baltic or Atlantic coasts.

One of the two exceptional cemeteries is Hradenín in western Bohemia. It was only in use for about a century, but the 128 burials excavated included many in wooden chambers, several with complete or fragmentary wagons. A peculiarity of these Bohemian wagons is a wooden yoke decorated with bronze studs forming geometric patterns. Hradenín lies on the löss soils typical of northern Bohemia, and possesses no special raw resources, defensive situation or any other obvious reason for this concentration. Unlike the centres of Hallstatt D its richest burials are no richer than others in the region; it is only the number that is peculiar, and may indicate a concentration for cult purposes. It does however suggest that in Bohemia, and probably elsewhere, there were larger tribal groupings which at present we cannot define archaeologically.

The second site is easier to explain; it is the salt-producing site of Hallstatt itself. The Urnfield period mines had been abandoned, perhaps deliberately closed down, but at the end of the eighth century new mines were opened. Heart-shaped blocks of rock salt were extracted, for export not only to central Europe but also to northern Italy, presumably transported on foot over the Alps, as in the Middle Ages. The trade contacts are indicated by the rich range of grave-goods found in the cemetery adjacent to the mines, which includes not only the standard range of Hallstatt metalwork such as Mindelheim and Gündlingen swords, but also bronze vessels of Italian type such as a bucket lid decorated with Situla Art. Wagon burials are unknown, not surprisingly in this rugged terrain, but the concentrations of other wealth indicators in certain graves make this the wealthiest cemetery in central and western Europe.

Copper mining must also have continued in the eastern Alps, but it is neither concentrated, nor easy to demonstrate. It is, however, the best explanation of the wealth of certain burials in some of the minor Austrian valleys, such as the burials from Klein Klein which include swords, bronze helmets, a bronze cuirass, and bronze vessels decorated in a local version of Situla Art.

Perhaps connected with this trade in raw materials, at some time in Hallstatt C a new settlement pattern appears, on the eastern fringes of the Alps in western Hungary, and on the main route between northern Italy and the Hungarian Plain in Slovenia. The dominant settlement type is the hillfort. Little is known of the hillforts themselves, but clustered around them are large numbers of barrows. Rich central burials in timber-lined graves do not occur (though Pécs-Jakobhegy in Hungary is the exception), rather, barrows seem to have been set up as corporate cemeteries by lineages or some other social grouping. If some burials have more gravegoods— bronze helmets, swords, decorated situlae—they have no special siting in the barrows. All indications are that the hillforts themselves were centres of production. The Slovenian sites possess iron ores; bronze and amber were being imported, and there is a wealth of person ornaments (bracelets, brooches etc.) in even the poorer burials. Glass was also being produced, not only for beads, but occasionally small vessels. Fine pottery imitates the cordoned styles in the north

Italian centres such as Este, while the famous decorated pottery from the Hungarian site of Sopron-Burgstall shows the more domestic crafts like weaving. The pottery, especially the outstanding examples of Situla Art from Magdalen-ská Gora and Vače, confirm this group's Italian contacts; peculiar bronze fittings from harness decorated with animal ornaments are to be connected with the nomad pastoralists who were establishing themselves on the Hungarian Plain especially in the sixth century (the Slovenian sites continue in occupation well into the fifth century, but the Hungarian sites were abandoned earlier). The distribution of the latter sites (Pécs, Sopron) suggest they may have been regional tribal centres; the Slovenian sites, however, are densely distributed with fairly small territories, and each tribal grouping probably possessed several centres.

The internal processes in Hallstatt C are still something of a mystery. If we are right in identifying increased social differentiation, it is difficult to identify its cause. The one major change, iron working, might decrease rather than increase trade with the availability of more localised resources. There is no clear indicator of pressure on resources, and, if trade expanded, it was an internal process not connected with Mediterranean developments. Contact over the Alps continued, but it was with northern Italy rather than the developing classical civilisations. Greek finds are unknown north of the Alps, and only four or five objects appear in the orientalising style of Etruria, such as the bowl and censer both from the same burial at Appenwihr near Kastenwald on the middle Rhine. These too are likely to have come through the north Italian contacts rather than directly from Etruria.

In the Atlantic and Scandinavian zones, Mediterranean influences were even less, though they are none the less detectable in certain types of prestige bronze work. Most obvious are the circular bronze shields with concentric ribbing. These, as experimental work has demonstrated, were not functional, as the bronze sheeting of which they were made splits on impact from a blow from a sword; moreover leather examples are known, and were more efficacious. Clearly the

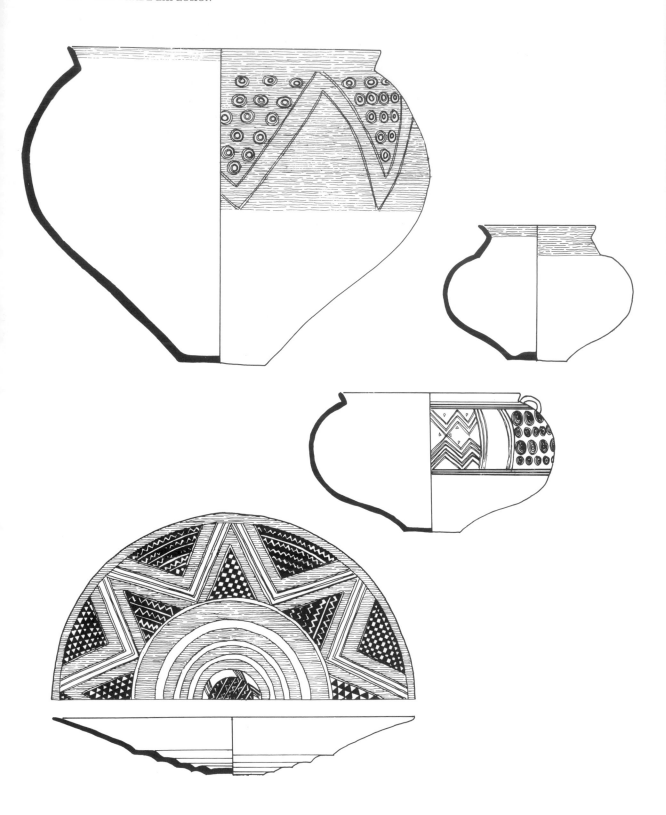

**19** Hallstatt pottery

During the late Bronze Age in central and western Europe a tradition had been developing for fine pottery apparently associated with feasting and drinking. This tradition reached its climax in the Hallstatt Iron Age, with a rich array of highly decorated pots found in an area which encompasses southern Poland, Czechoslovakia, Austria, southern and central Germany, Switzerland, and eastern and central France. The detailed chronologies have yet to be established, so we do not know where the styles originated, but they were current throughout Hallstatt C and D over most of this zone.

There was a considerable range of decorative techniques used, which appear in various combinations—red paint, black graphite paint, incision and stamp—sometimes used in their own right, sometimes merely as keying for white inlay. The patterns were almost entirely geometric (those from Sopron are the exception, fig 20), but especially in the eastern areas peculiar symbols are included whose meaning is now unknown. Generally, however, we encounter lozenges, triangles and chequer patterns in bewildering combinations.

It is clear that there was a number of local and regional traditions, but no studies are yet available of fabrics or decorative features to define these workshops or establish how widely pots were traded. In some areas of Bavaria for instance, decoration was mainly formed using graphite paint, in others there was a tradition for incised decoration, while in Baden-Württemberg, the incised, stamped and painted 'Alb-Salem' wares of Hallstatt C were replaced in Hallstatt D by red painted wares on white slip, perhaps made at centres such as the Heuneburg.

The forms included large plates, in which often the whole of the interior is decorated, tall jars with decoration on the body, or shallow bowls. They are especially common in the burials, and the richer burials may have sets of several vessels with different ranges of decoration. The examples illustrated here come from the burial at Mindelheim, Bavaria, whence came the original of the sword type of Hallstatt C.

*Scale: 1:4*

bronze versions were for display, and are often found in riverine deposits, reminiscent of their ritual function in the Greek and Urartian contexts. The peculiarity of these shields, which betray Mediterranean contacts, is the 'V' or 'U' notch in the ribbing, a non-functional feature which is found in Scandinavia, Britain, southern Spain, Etruria and Crete. The date of these shields is a problem, as they are usually isolated finds, but the seventh century is most likely. Seventh-century bronze cauldrons in Britain also betray similarities to contemporary types in Etruria, and in this case it must be diffusion of technical knowledge through the west Mediterranean and Atlantic routes.

## Hallstatt D 600–475 BC

For the Hallstatt cemetery, indeed for much of the east Alpine area, the beginning of Hallstatt D brought no obvious changes other than a gradual evolution of brooch and other artefact types. The newly established salt-mining centre on the Dürrnberg bei Hallein did not as yet present a threat to the pre-eminence of Hallstatt. The Slovenian forts too continued, as did trade contacts between both areas and northern Italy. The Hungarian Plain however suffered one of its periodic incursions of nomads from the Russian steppes, in this case Scythian groups with their distinctive art forms and burial rites such as the inclusion of horses with the dead—a custom which is never found in vehicle burials in central and western Europe. Southern Poland too seems to have suffered, and nomad incursions have been blamed for the disappearance and abandonment of the Lausitz forts such as Biskupin which had been established in the late Bronze Age; however the more likely explanation is localised over-exploitation of the land. Distinctive Scythian artefacts have been found as far west as Vettersfelde near Berlin.

How late the hillforts on the fringe of the Hungarian Plain—Pécs-Jakobhegy and Sopron-Burgstall—survived is unclear, but they do not all seem to continue into Hallstatt D. In Czechoslovakia rich burials disappear, but here, as in other areas Hallstatt D was a period of hillforts. One,

Závist just south of Prague seems pre-eminent. At its centre on the so-called 'Akropolis' lay a cult site with a large free-standing altar which has been compared with contemporary Greek sites. The defences enclosed a massive area and contained a large population, but its layout and economy have still to be elucidated. Its size and siting at the natural centre of Bohemia imply that here at least the process of state formation was well advanced.

Surprisingly Greek and Etruscan imports are totally unknown in this area during Hallstatt D, but they are also rare in the parts of northern Italy with which central Europe was trading. The Adriatic was closed to Greek traders until the end of the period. The furthest north Greek goods penetrated was Trebeniště in southern Yugoslavia. The most famous find is a large crater, smaller than that from Vix, but still of immense size. This area shows links with the Alpine area, and perhaps acted as an intermediary for the importation of metals into Greece.

This lack of direct contact between Greece proper and the adjacent regions of Europe, which must have supplied it with raw materials, is all the more surprising when we compare it with the western Hallstatt area where contact between Greek and barbarian was both direct and extensive. Two major factors brought this about. One was the foundation of Marseilles near the mouth of the Rhône, and the establishment of the trading network inland; the second was the evolution of a markedly hierarchical society in south-west Germany and eastern France which became the recipient of this trade.

Four explanations can be put forward to explain this social development. The first, indicated by the German nomenclature—*Fürsten, Adel*—to describe the rich burials, implies a feudal society along medieval lines in which the basis of power is the control of land. This has never been argued in detail, but the distribution of sites, the apparent availability of land, and the relative simplicity of the society make it unlikely. Neither is control of production of a key resource likely, as the major sites are not in areas rich in minerals. Military control imposed from outside in the form of an invasion from the east has been put forward, but central European society was not noticeably more hierarchical than that on the Rhine in Hallstatt C, and markedly less so in Hallstatt D.

The final, and most likely, suggestion is control of external trade. Three of the richest sites (the Heuneburg on the upper Danube; Asperg on the Neckar at Stuttgart; and Mont Lassois on the Seine) all lie on headwaters of rivers leading away from the Rhône–Saône route. The fourth rich site, the Britzgyberg, lies on the Befort gap controlling the route from the Rhône/Doubs on to the upper Rhine. Mediterranean imports are virtually confined to these four centres and to two or three other defended sites.

In Hallstatt C Mediterranean goods were already reaching this area from Etruria, passing along the old Urnfield network over the Alps, as the Appenwihr tumulus demonstrates, and this may have already accelerated the process of social differentiation. Hallstatt D, because of the very fast development of brooch typologies can be subdivided virtually into generations (Hallstatt D1, 2 and 3), allowing us to define the sites where we can first detect change. Already in Hallstatt D1, change was visible, with the construction of a huge burial mound—the largest in prehistoric Europe—the Magdalenenberg near Villingen in the Black Forest. Unfortunately the central burial in its timber chamber had been robbed, so we possess no exotic goods, other than a belt-fitting of Iberian origin from a secondary grave. The tumulus was subsequently used as a cemetery for individuals presumably belonging to the same social grouping (clan, lineage, etc) as the primary individual. None of these burials was of the 'chieftain' rank, but neither were they poor: daggers, spears and personal ornaments are abundant. Nearby is a contemporary hillfort, but excavation has been too limited to demonstrate its nature.

The primacy of this site was short-lived, but by Hallstatt D2 Asperg and the Heuneburg had become centres of 'complex chiefdoms.' Within a 5–10km radius of a central defended site is a cluster of rich burials, characterised by massive mounds, timber-lined graves, wagons, gold objects, bronze vessels, and imported Mediterranean goods. Around Asperg, there is Eberdingen–Hochdorf belonging to D1–2, the

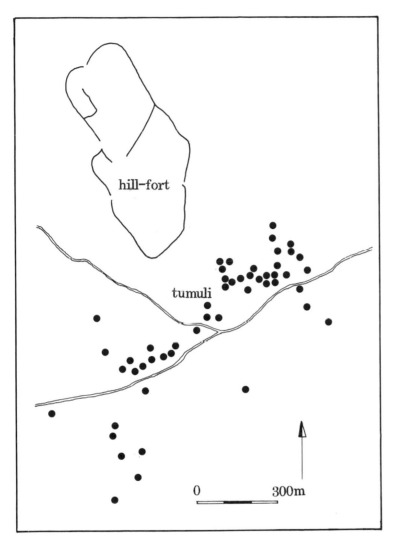

**20a**

**20** Hallstatt sites in Slovenia and Hungary

The pattern of settlement, of nucleated defended settlements surrounded by their cemeteries, typical of parts of northern Italy in the seventh and sixth centuries (e.g. Este), is also found in Slovenia and eastern and southern Hungary. In Slovenia there is a concentration of sites controlling the route from Italy to the Hungarian Plain, and the north Italian connection is supported by the similarity of the Situla Art, brooch and pottery styles. Stična (a) is fairly typical. Little is known about what went on in the hillfort, we only know it was occupied in Hallstatt C, but the tumuli have been extensively excavated.

Unlike central European graves, there is no rich central burial, and the graves in the mound seem to belong to some related family group, but no studies have yet been made of the human remains to test this hypothesis.

The hillforts around Sopron fall into a similar pattern. They lie in a poor highland area overlooking a fertile plain, but the relationship of their short-lived occupation to surrounding areas is unknown. The most famous finds from the tumuli around the Burgstall at Sopron are the stamped pots, which include a depiction (b) of a number of women engaged in weaving.

**20b**

Grafenbühl, Römerhügel and Bad Cannstatt of D3 and Klein Aspergle La Tène A. The richest burials from the Heuneburg belong to D1 and D2, Talhau, and the Hohmichele, second only to the Magdalenenberg in size. The Mont Lassois burials, Vix and St Colombe both belong to D3.

By Hallstatt D3, if not earlier, it is clear that the main source of the exotic Mediterranean goods was Marseilles, though finds such as a sherd of Este pottery from the Heuneburg show that the cross-Alpine connections with northern Italy still continued. Two of the main classes of imports point to southern France. Firstly there are wine amphorae with a distinctive micaceous fabric which were manufactured in the Marseilles region itself. Secondly Attic black figure ware, of which several hundred sherds have been found at Mont Lassois, and more rarely at the Britzgyberg and the Heuneberg, is virtually unknown in northern Italy, but is relatively common in southern France. We must assume that the bronze tripods, beaked flagons (even Etruscan), the silk and other items also came up the Rhône/Doubs.

The trade seems to have been in the hands of Greeks. The huge crater from Vix is unlikely to have been transported whole. The figures which run round the frieze have Greek letters scratched on them which correspond to letters on the body of the vessel, but which were concealed when the figures were soldered on. It would probably have needed a Greek craftsman to assemble the pieces. There is also the Phase III wall construction of the Heuneburg defences. This was built of sun-dried bricks on a limestone footing; a type of construction known in the Mediterranean, but unparalleled in central Europe. It was also furnished with hollow rectangular bastions allowing crossfire against attackers, a technique of defence equally without central European parallels. It contrasts with the normal earth-and-timber 'box ramparts' found at the Heuneburg and elsewhere. Its construction must have been supervised by someone familiar with Greek techniques, most likely an actual Greek. Though the wall was repaired and added to sometime after its construction, and though it survived longer than the indigenous techniques, the experiment was not repeated. Thus there is positive evidence for Greeks north of the Alps, probably as part of trading caravans.

The nature of the traded goods themselves also suggests the same conclusion. The objects are by no means 'beads for the natives', or the sorts of

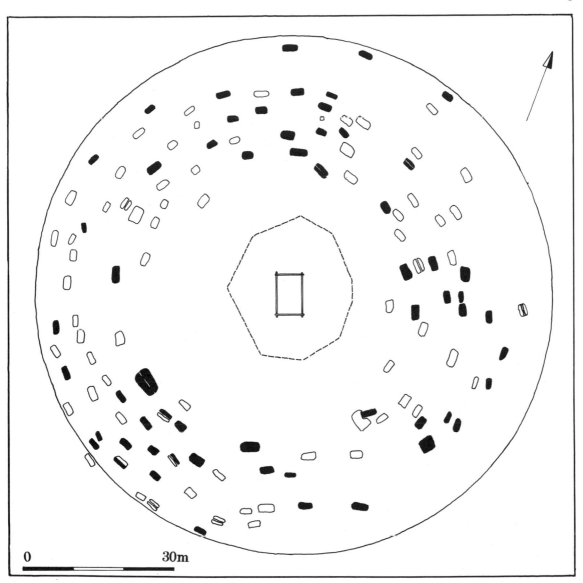

**21a**

**21** The Magdalenenberg, Baden-Württemberg, Germany

Near the town of Villingen in the Black Forest lies the largest prehistoric burial mound in Europe. Over 100m in diameter and 16m high, the recent excavations have demonstrated that it belongs to the early part of Hallstatt D. The central burial in a wooden chamber had already been robbed before it was excavated earlier this century.

The latest excavations have produced 127 secondary burials arranged in a circle around the central burial (a) (male graves are depicted in black). None of

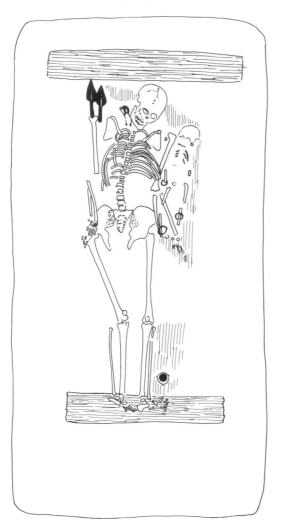

**21b**

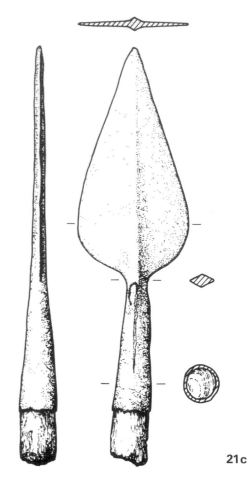

**21c**

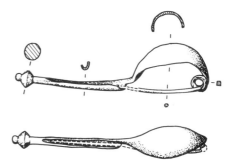

**21d**

these graves belongs to the richest classes of the Hallstatt burials (i.e. there are no chambers, vehicles, or other rich gravegoods), but the richest are by no means poor. The better furnished male graves may have spears (b, c) or a dagger, brooches (d) and pottery. Both men and women were buried on wooden biers. Typical female gravegoods (g) may include earrings, hair-rings (h), hair-pins (i), torcs (e), and bracelets, some of large proportions made from schist or bronze sheet (f) and worn on the forearms. Even young children may have gravegoods, like the young girl with anklets buried with the man in burial 93 (b, right).

*Scale: 1 : 2*

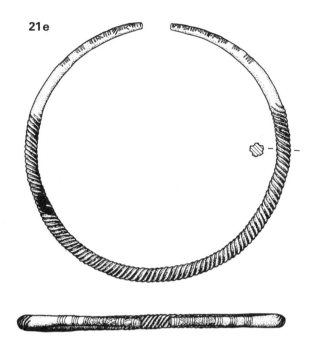

21e

21g

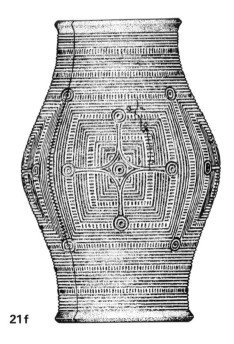

21f

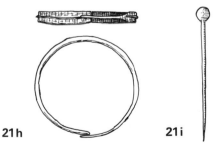

21h

21i

22a

## 22 The Heuneburg, Baden-Württemberg

The most extensively excavated of the major centres of Hallstatt D is the Heuneburg, which overlooks the upper reaches of the Danube (a). The hillfort itself is fairly small enclosing some 3.2ha, but there was also occupation outside, at least in the early phases, and the distribution of the rich tumuli around the site, suggests there should be other areas of settlement in the vicinity (b).

The hillfort had already been occupied in the late Bronze Age, but had then been abandoned during Hallstatt C. During the sixth and the beginning of the fifth centuries it was rebuilt on a number of occasions, usually with a box rampart, a wall of timber back and front, with the middle divided by cross-timbers into chambers which were filled with stone and earth. But in one phase, period III, a different construction was used, of bricks dried in the sun, and laid on a limestone foundation (c). This was not the only feature unique to central Europe at this time, the rampart was provided with bastions, square projecting towers which allowed cross-fire against anyone attacking the wall (d). These are all features found in the Mediterranean world, and were perhaps introduced by a Greek. Towards the end of its life the wall was patched up using the same techniques, but, despite the fact that the knowledge of the construction technique had not been lost, and although it seems to have shown considerable resistance to the climate (it survived longer than any of the other ramparts), the experiment was not repeated.

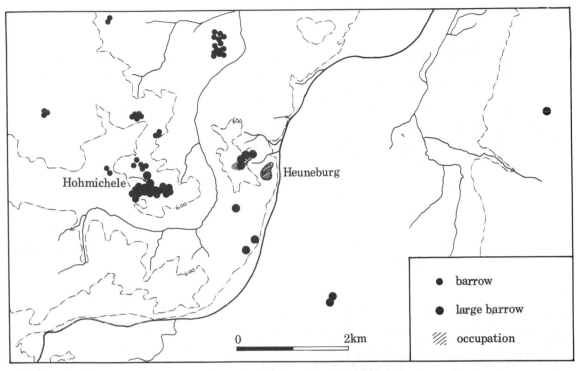

**22b**

**22c**

**22d**

Excavations have been largely confined to the southeast corner (e) where there is a deep build-up of deposits. The buildings consisted mainly of workshops (f) with traces of hearths, ovens and four-post structures which may have been chimneys. The area seems to have been completely cleared every decade or so, and reconstructed, though in some cases there was continuity of the same industry on the same plot of ground. Bronze was certainly worked, and one find included the mould for the face at the base of a handle from an Etruscan-style jug. Bronze was also worked in the extra-mural settlement where moulds for bracelets have been found.

This external occupation area was later replaced by an elaborate wooden building, and this in turn covered by a tumulus with a timber chamber, one of a group of four. These, like other surrounding tumuli, produced bronze vessels and other luxury items during the nineteenth century. The only intact burial of the rich class excavated under modern conditions is from the Hohmichele (g), after the Magdalenenberg, the largest prehistoric burial mound in Europe. The primary burial had a wagon and timber chamber, but had been robbed, and most of the other burials contained only weapons or ornaments, like the secondary burials in the Magdalenenberg. Each time there was a burial, the mound was increased in size. Burial VI (h), however, survived and had a wooden chamber and a wagon, as well as a quiver with arrows, a bow, bronze harness equipment and vessels, and traces of textiles. Among these were threads of silk, the earliest recorded occurrence in Europe.

**22e**

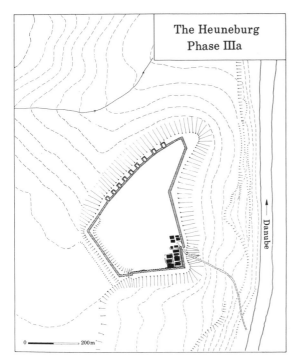

The Heuneburg
Phase IIIa

Danube

0 ——— 200 m

**22f**

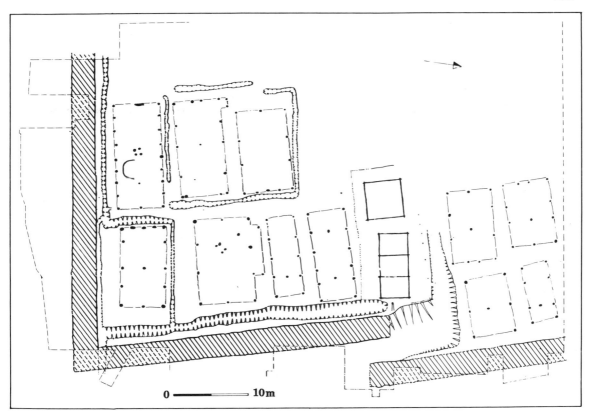

0 ——— 10 m

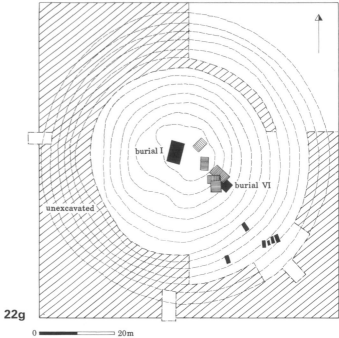

**22g**

0 ▬▬▬ 20m

**22h**

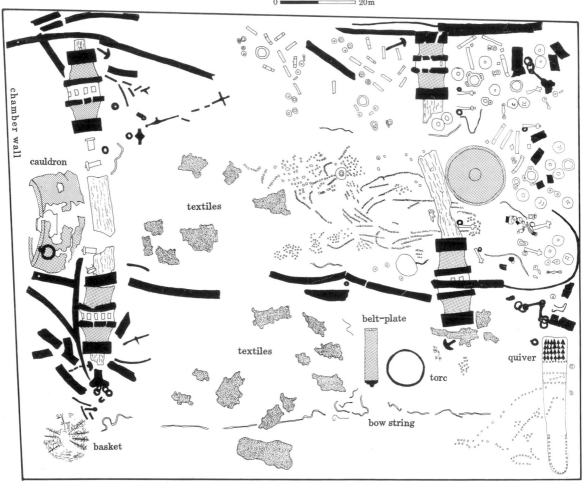

chamber wall

cauldron

textiles

textiles

belt-plate

torc

quiver

bow string

basket

0 ▬▬▬▬▬▬ 1 m

**23** Eberdingen-Hochdorf, Ludwigsburg, Baden-Württemberg, West Germany

This is the most recently discovered of the rich burials of Hallstatt D, being excavated in 1978–9 by J. Biel. It is the earliest of the burials in the Asperg complex, dating to the end of D1. It lies on a hill 10km away, but still visible, from the Hohenasperg. The mound itself was 57m in diameter, built of turf and löss, revetted by a three phase stone wall and timber posts. The central burial was in a pit containing a structure 7.5 by 7.4 by 2m high built of oak logs. Within this was a chamber 4.7m square. The pit was covered by 50 tonnes of stone which had protected the burial from tomb robbers.

In terms of Mediterranean imports it is not rich, a bronze cauldron on a wooden stand being the only definitely Greek piece and this had been repaired, by the replacement of one of the three lions which decorated the rim. The cauldron contained a gold bowl, perhaps a ladle, and traces of honey extract, presumably mead. There were nine drinking horns with gold fittings. They were hung on the wall, which was draped with textiles pinned together with 20 bronze brooches.

There were also nine bronze plates, and three dishes laid on top of the wagon, with an iron axe, a knife and a spear. The wagon was partly plated with iron sheets, and had an elaborate yoke, but this has not yet been published. There was also the usual complement of horse harness fittings.

The most spectacular object was a bronze sofa or bed (it is too low to sit on comfortably). It was 3m long with traces of upholstery. The back was decorated with scenes of warriors standing on wagons, and three pairs of warriors with swords and shields, apparently dancing. It was supported on eight castors (b) in the form of women with inlaid eyes and iron ear-rings, and punched decoration representing their jewellery.

The body of a 40-year-old man was laid on this sofa. He had a conical 'coolie' hat of birch bark like that worn by the Hirschlanden statue, or depicted in Situla Art. Like Hirschlanden he also had a torc of gold, and a belt plate, and a dagger, both overlaid with gold. His shoes were overlain with gold and his bracelet and two brooches were also of gold. Around him were traces of textiles, leather and feathers. He also had a quiver of arrows.

Some of the objects were made especially for the burial, and the debris from this was buried in three pits in the mound. It included half-finished brooches, and a piece of gold. The gold objects certainly made in

**23a**

**23b**

this workshop were the brooches, the belt and shoe fittings, the sheath and the bracelet which were linked by the use of the same decorative punches. The nine drinking horns also formed a group from the same workshop, but the torc and the ladle came from other sources.

Though there was nothing to compare with the Vix crater, in other respects it is a richer burial, especially in terms of the local objects. The gold is richer—about 500gm as against 480 in Vix. It also pushes back the date of the Asperg complex almost as early as the Heuneburg.

small items that would travel 'down-the-line'. They are luxuries of the highest quality. Tripod cauldrons were objects which might be prizes in prestigious games, gifts to temples, and 'diplomatic gifts' given by cities to other cities or individuals. The Vix crater is without equal within or outside the Greek world in terms of both size and quality of craftsmanship, and can only have been the diplomatic gift of a city such as Marseilles to an individual of royal status. The Vix diadem or torc of solid gold falls into the same category. The trade is 'administered' at a high level, and 'directed' at the chiefly centres.

The best parallel for this situation in the ethnographic record is in west Africa, as seen in the trade between the royal courts, such as Dahomey and Congo, and white traders on the coast. Trade was directly controlled by the native rulers, who held a carefully guarded monopoly. All goods must pass through them, as their position rested on an ability to give prestigious gifts to their supporters. A hierarchical system of tribute, extracted, by force if need be, through kinship or client networks, provided the chiefs with the necessary surplus with which to trade. Production of certain prestige native goods might also be controlled to maintain the lower parts of the social hierarchy. However, there is a number of differences between the west African and the Hallstatt systems: the transport of goods seems to be entirely in Greek rather than native hands, and the main good traded in west Africa was firearms which allowed the dominant chiefs further to assert their control over less privileged neighbours.

What went back in return for these goods? We have no archaeological material from Temperate Europe in Mediterranean contexts, nor are exports mentioned until a much later date. As the Hallstatt centres were not themselves in areas of mineral production, we must assume that they were at the ends of routes extending down the river systems of the Seine, Rhine and Danube. Of the metals, iron was probably too bulky in raw form, but gold, copper and tin are likely possibilities. Amber, animal pelts and other products of the northern forests are further possibilities, and of course slaves for the labour-intensive production methods of the ancient world.

Internal production may also have been controlled. Of the major centres only the Heuneburg settlement has been excavated to any great extent. Bronze bracelet moulds have been found in the open settlement just outside the fort, beneath the later burial mounds at Talhau. Bronze workshops also occur in the south-east corner of the fort in several phases, and one unstratified find includes a mould for casting a bronze beaked flagon-handle, decorated with a Silenus head. Pottery was almost certainly produced, but the installations have not been found. Black wheel-turned pottery is virtually entirely confined to the major defended sites—Mont Lassois, the Heuneburg, and a secondary site at Breisach on the Rhine. The potter's wheel was a new innovation

**24** Vix, Burgundy, France

Mont Lassois is more prolific in imported Mediterranean pottery than the Heuneburg, with several hundred sherds of Massaliote amphorae, Attic black-figure vessels, etc. But we know little about the structures on the site or the nature of the defences. The majority of the brooches seem to belong to Hallstatt D3.

Of the rich tumuli which lie around it, that at St Colombe a few kilometres to the south has produced a cauldron on a tripod, decorated with gryphon protomes. At the foot of Mont Lassois is the mound of Vix, a cairn 42m in diameter and 6m high. In the wooden chamber (a) there was a dismantled wagon whose wheels had been leant against the wall. The corpse of a woman in her mid-thirties lay on the body of the wagon, defined by a series of bronze fittings. The woman had a number of brooches of Hallstatt D3 date

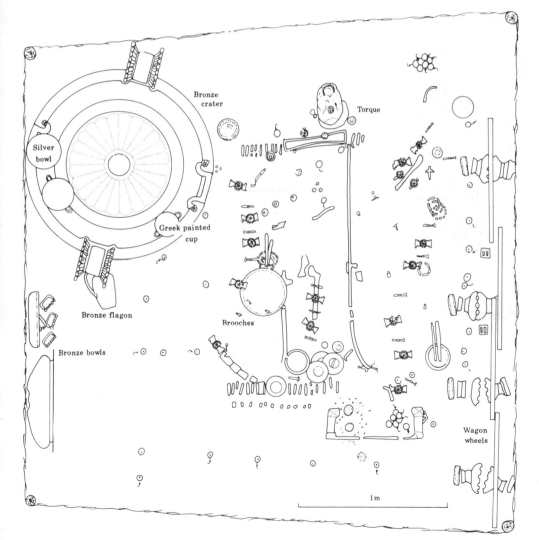

Silver bowl

Bronze crater

Torque

Greek painted cup

Bronze flagon

Brooches

Bronze bowls

Wagon wheels

1 m

**24a**

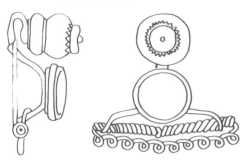

**24b**

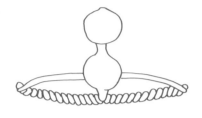

**24c**

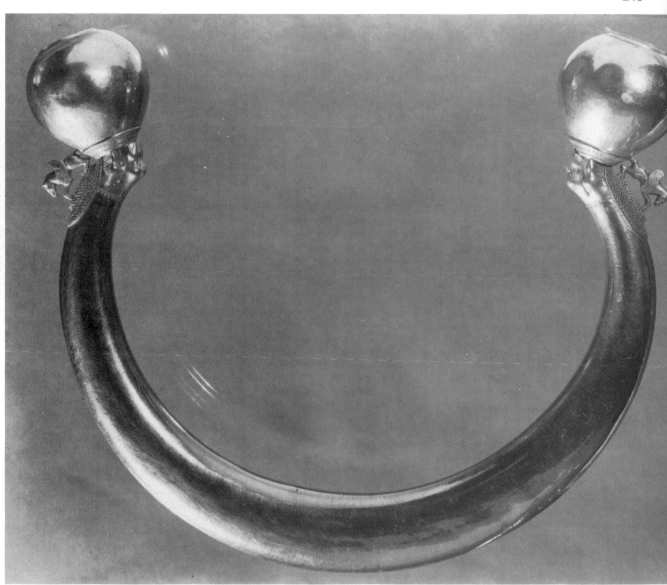

**24d**

(b) and she was wearing a gold ornament originally interpreted as a diadem, but more likely to be a torc (c). It was of solid gold, weighing 480gm, and was decorated with winged horses. It is probably from a Mediterranean workshop.

There were also three Etruscan bronze vessels, two bowls and a beaked flagon, and an Attic black-figure ware dish (d), all dating the burial to the end of the sixth century. The most impressive vessel was a bronze crater for mixing wine (e). It was 1.64m high, surmounted by a strainer decorated with a standing figure of a woman. The elaborate handles are in the form of gorgons, and the frieze around the neck is of armed hoplites and charioteers. These had been soldered on, the positions of each figure being marked by a Greek letter found also on the backs of the figures. This hints that the vessel was put together after it was transported to central France. The precise origin of the crater is unknown, both Tarentum and Sparta have been suggested. In size and quality it has no peer.

CRATÈRE en BRONZE

• TRAVAIL GREC •
FIN DU VI° SIÈCLE avant J.C.

HAUTEUR 1·64
POIDS 208 kg

of Hallstatt D north of the Alps. The majority of pottery was still made by hand, though the painted Alb-Salem wares of Hallstatt C, and earlier Hallstatt D, and their successors continued to retain their prestige, and some seem to have been manufactured at the Heuneburg. Coral certainly and possibly gold were also being worked there, but these belong to the relatively prestigious class of finds.

Outside the Heuneburg information on production is minimal. Schist bracelets and armlets were made somewhere in southern Germany, but not centrally, and they occur in the medium-rich burials, but not the richest, so they were not among the high-prestige goods. Painted pottery is concentrated on some of the minor hillforts and control of production by minor chiefs is implied. The evidence for social organisation however is derived from burials rather than settlements, and we must suspend judgement until more settlement archaeology has been performed.

The gravegoods from burials do support the idea of a centralised, hierarchical, complex chiefdom. We can detect several levels of status even within the chiefly class. At the top are burials such as Vix, Eberdingen–Hochdorf, and the Hohmichele. It is the presence of imported objects which especially define this group—bronze and silver vessels, Greek pottery and silk. The only Mediterranean import that occurs outside this group is coral, which was used as the inlay on local brooches. Gold, mainly in the form of sheet torcs, bowls and drinking horns, is also largely restricted to the richest. At a lower level are timber-lined graves with wagons or harness fittings, local pottery and bronzes. Spatially in Hallstatt D2 and D3 these rich burials seems to conform to the 'tribute' distribution pattern mentioned in Chapter 1. The richest burials are not all immediately around the centre, but do cluster within a few kilometres. The less rich burials are found more widely scattered, in what we must assume to be the tributary territories of each centre.

Below the chiefly class there is a further series of rich graves which lack the chambers and wagons, but possess metal goods of status: in the case of a man, an iron dagger in an elaborate bronze sheath, a spear, and one or two ornaments; in that

of a woman, a set of bronze brooches and bracelets, lignite bracelets or armlets, and perhaps anklets. These individuals may have their own tumuli (female primary burials at Mühlacker, male at Mauenheim), but they almost all contain less rich secondary burials. The poorest, often children, may be cremations accompanied by a single pot.

In the area around Asperg this symbolisation of wealth in terms of gravegoods is cross-cut by other statuses. There are differences, especially among females, which are connected with age, and possibly marital status. Mature women tend to have three brooches on the shoulder, young women and children usually only one or two, with glass beads and amulets of various kinds. Occasionally older women have similar gravegoods to those of the children, which may signify that they are unmarried.

Most cemeteries produce the poorer burials, but they differ in how rich the richest burials are. Mauenheim contains a couple of burials with timber-lined chambers, possibly with complete wagons, but no exotic items. Mühlacker has males and females with daggers and brooches, but nothing richer; while Hirschlanden, despite its pretensions of a stone figure wearing torc and dagger, has no wealthy burials either. The position of each settlement in the social hierarchy seems clearly symbolised in its burials.

The society I have described is confined to eastern France and southern Germany. These extremes of wealth, the ostentatious concentration of power are features which are not found, or are only weakly reflected, in neighbouring societies, either before or after. It represents a new phenomenon, a society in Temperate Europe which was utterly dependent on relations with the Mediterranean world. At some time early in the fifth century the systems collapsed. The centres were abandoned, the rich burials disappeared, and the trade on which they depended broke down. In Temperate Europe, the Heuneburg, which in its combination of 'central-place functions'—political power, trade, production— might warrant the status of 'urban', was not to be equalled for four hundred years.

However, the trade did not necessarily cause

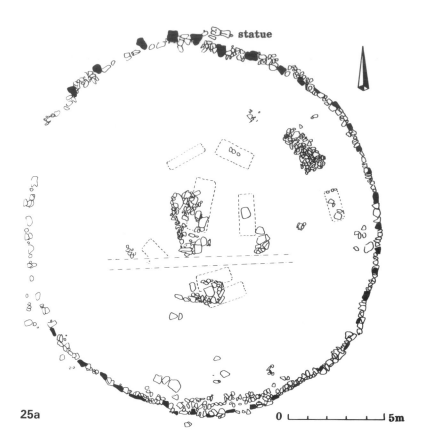

statue

25a                                    0 ⌞_ ⌞_ ⌞_ ⌞_ ⌞_ ⌟ 5m

## 25 Hirschlanden, Baden-Württemberg

The tumulus of Hirschlanden represents the lower status level of cemeteries in Hallstatt D. There is no timber-lined grave, wagon, horse equipment, goldwork, or imported luxury items. The graves are those of men and women of middling status, buried with personal ornaments such as brooches and bracelets, and the occasional spear. It thus represents the vast majority of cemeteries in the Asperg area of influence.

The mound itself is small (a) with two levels of inhumations, presumably from a small family group, and covering the latter part of Hallstatt D, and possibly the very beginning of La Tène A. In all there were some 16 inhumations. What makes Hirschlanden special is the presence of a stone statue (c) which was found lying at the foot of the mound, but which probably originally stood on top of it (b). Several other barrows are known in Baden-Württemberg with carved stones standing on them, but this is the only one with a naturalistic human figure.

The statue is that of a naked ithyphallic man. On his head he has a hat or helmet, and around his neck a torc like the gold examples which occur in the richer graves in the Asperg complex. Around his waist is a belt, into which is thrust a typical Hallstatt D dagger. The sculpting has been compared to Archaic Greek statues, but we know little of any indigenous traditions, for instance in wood, and it is difficult to explain the mechanics of how such ideas might have travelled—unlike pottery and metalwork, statues were not being traded, and this is a case of the Mediterranean connection being wrongly invoked.

*Actual size : c—height 1.5m*

**25b**

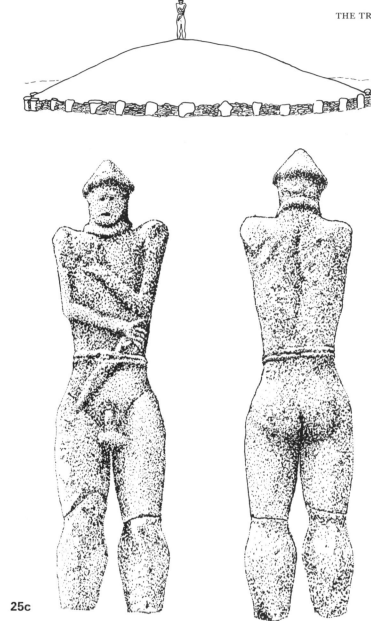

**25c**

such centralisation. The route by which the traded goods reached both the Rhine and the upper Seine lead through the valley of the Saône. This area is by no means devoid of imported goods, but they are not confined to special central sites. In fact there are several open settlements as well as hillforts which have produced imports such as Greek pottery and multicoloured glass vessels. Rich burials occur with imports, but again they are not concentrated around one site, nor yet are they as rich as those of the Heuneburg, Asperg or Mont Lassois. These three sites may be the most spectacular, but they are not the norm, rather an eccentric extreme, and other adjacent areas of eastern France, Switzerland and parts of the Rhineland have a rather different settlement pattern and social organisation which we still perceive but dimly.

Outside this core area of contact, obvious evidence of classical influence is rare. Occasional Greek vessels found their way further north and east—such as the Attic sherd from the Kemmelberg in southern Belgium. This is the only site outside the core area which shows any concentration of power. Exceptionally fine painted and incised pottery is virtually unknown on surrounding sites, and there is also a gold ornament. The rich burials, indeed burials of any kind, are absent and this lack of ostentatious burial monuments implies that it is of a different nature from the other Hallstatt D centres. It is a complete outlier, and nowhere in the area between is there any sign of similar centralisation.

Status burials do occur, for instance in Champagne (Les Jogasses) and on the Mosel (Bell-im-Hunsrück) but these are only wagon burials with none of the exotic or indigenous prestige goods, such as gold objects. The occurrence of this evidence for increasing social differentiation in fringe areas, which was to become more marked in the succeeding La Tène A, is presumably connected with the trade routes emanating from the core area, but physical evidence is difficult to demonstrate. Pottery painted in styles reminiscent of those of Vix occur elsewhere in the Paris Basin; a brooch identical to examples in the Vix burial has been found in Bohemia, but even brooches generally failed to spread out of the core areas.

One fashion which was more widespread, from Britain to Austria, was the change from swords to daggers. It had appeared earlier in parts of Spain and southern France, and was to survive long in Italy in the form of the Roman *gladius* which was ideally suited to formation battles rather than individual fighting with the sword. The blades were universally of iron, but the hilts may be of bronze, and gold inlay is not unknown. They do not appear in the richest group of burials (in which weapons generally are rare, and may, like the bow and arrows in the Hohmichele, be for hunting), but they are clearly status symbols. But to what extent these short swords imply formation fighting, or are merely insignia of office is a matter of debate. The major fighting weapon was still the spear, the only weapon in many 'warrior' graves, supplemented by the axe in the eastern Alps.

This was also the age of the hillforts, though the idea did not spread onto the north European Plain. In the hilly areas of Czechoslovakia, central Germany, France and Britain, hillfort building reached a new peak. Defences were constructed with vertical timber fronts, backed by timber lacing or box structures filled with rock and soil. Exceptions like the Kemmelberg, or the Johannisberg in Thuringia, were centres of industry and population, but generally the role of the hillforts in Hallstatt society is little understood. The houses within are usually simple, and include four-post structures interpreted as granaries. But they were neither the residences of an elite or of a large population—industry was sited elsewhere, and the economy was still essentially based on farms and small hamlets.

Hallstatt D represents a new, if short-lived departure from the previous pattern. For the first time a powerful group of individuals had become entirely dependent on the Mediterranean cities for its power. But adjacent areas, though certainly within the trade network emanating from the core area, and undergoing social differentiation, show little specific evidence of how the trade between core and periphery was organised and what was being traded. When the external trade collapsed, so did the core; the periphery survived and even prospered.

# CHAPTER FIVE

# The Tide Turns, 500-250 BC

For historians of the Greek world, the fifth century is the pinnacle, the classical phase of the classical world. Yet strangely, rather than seeing the peak of interrelationship between Greece and the developing Celtic world, the decades after 500 BC saw trade diminishing. What contact there was seems to have been stimulated from north of the Alps, culminating in the invasions of Galli, Celtae and Galatae into Italy, Greece and Asia Minor. A new phase of interaction had been reached.

## The classical world of Greece

With the rise of democratic Athens, the interests of the prehistorian, the classical archaeologist, and the classical historian diverge even more markedly, and comparison between the archaeological data in different areas becomes more difficult. Traditionally the classical archaeologist has concerned himself in Greece with art history—with the development of vase painting, sculpture, and architecture, especially that of temples. These are developments which mark Greece apart from its neighbours, especially to the north. They represent the uniqueness of Hellenic experience, the essence of Greek civilisation, while that which Greece had in common with other societies—peasant agriculture, the process and impact of urbanisation, economic and social evolution—have either only recently become matters of concern, or are approached through the more informative written sources rather than from archaeology.

The relationship between artistic development, economic and social change, and physical remains are none the less obvious. Aeschylus and his contemporaries took the enactments of myth held at religious festivals and turned them into theatre, while Sophocles and Eurypides turned them into dramatic tragedy. But this development was only possible within the social and economic climate that prevailed in fifth-century Athens, and it received its physical expression in the construction of prestigious theatres. From this time onwards the theatre was part of the Greek concept of what urban life should be, and the cultural amenities a city should offer.

The theatre was not the only feature of the new urbanism. Gymnasia and baths offered physical recreation; sophists—less easy to identify archaeologically—provided the intellectual training for the wealthier citizens. The rural shrines of Olympia, Delphi and Dodona which encouraged pan-Hellenic unity, may have flowered, but religious observance also flourished in the towns, from small family shrines to the major state cults whose temples became a matter of civic pride. Assembly halls served the developing needs of political, administrative and judiciary functions that the cities increasingly took upon themselves. The divide between town and country had become irrevocably institutionalised.

By the fourth century, when Greek philosophers began to discuss the nature of the city, these features were taken for granted. The Agora at Athens had merely been an open space within the developing city of Athens. By the sixth century, and especially in the fifth, it became the official assembly place in which the citizen body could discuss political and fiscal matters. But it may also have witnessed another revolution which receives no mention in the literature—the

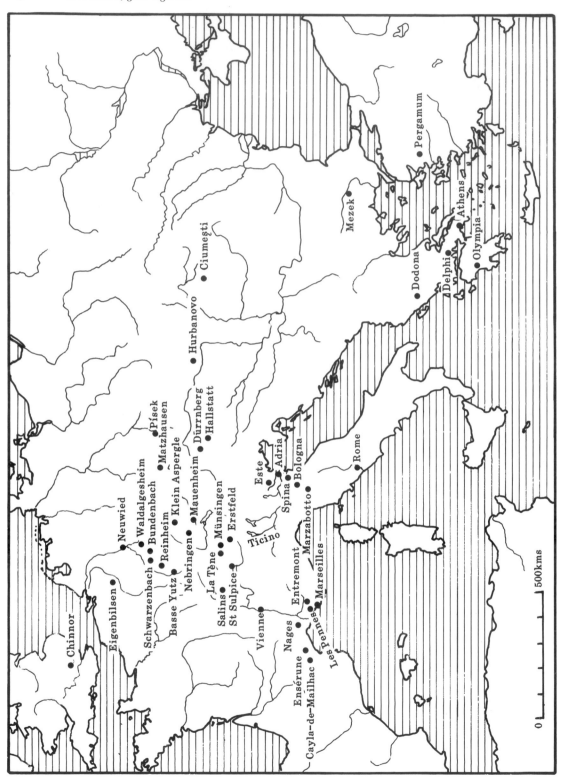

26  Sites mentioned in chapter 5

**27**  The development of Athens

It was the defensive possibilities of the Acropolis that
led to the earliest development of the city. The hill-top
had been given defences in the late Mycenaean period,
and may have even boasted a palace. The subsequent
early history of the city is largely derived from burial
evidence. In the Sub-Mycenaean and Proto-
Geometric periods (a), Attica is one of the few areas
which may even have increased its population, and the
burials show a concentration around the Acropolis at
Athens, as though defence was a major factor in the
settlement pattern.

The succeeding Geometric period (b) suggests no
great change in the pattern, merely a gradual increase
in the population size, and increasing social
differentiation. The wealthiest burials in Attica tend to
be concentrated at Athens, suggesting it was
developing a dominant social and economic role. By
the time we start having documentary evidence in the
seventh and sixth centuries, virtually all of Attica was
united under the leadership of Athens.

In the latter part of the eighth century the numbers of
burials increase rapidly, suggesting a steep rise in
population, but it is not until the Archaic period,
mainly the sixth century, that we start to obtain
archaeological evidence for public buildings such as
temples on the Acropolis. At what point in time we
can start talking of a town or city at Athens is unclear,
probably the seventh–sixth century. However it was
only after the destruction by the Persian army in 480
that the city started taking on the form which we know
from the classical sources (c).

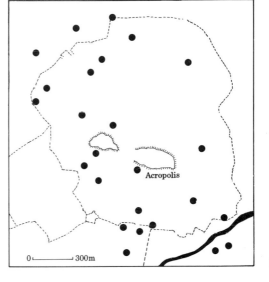

**27b**

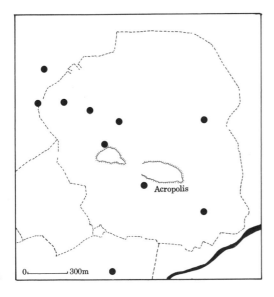

**27a**

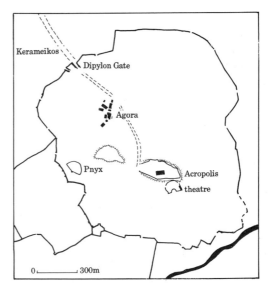

**27c**

appearance of a new exchange mechanism, market exchange employing low-value coinage.

The concept of some valued material acting as a standard against which the value of other objects could be measured was nothing new— gold and silver by weight, corn by volume had served this function in Mesopotamia for hundreds of years. At the beginning of the first millennium small hoards of lumps of scrap metal, which could be cut up to the required weight, are not uncommon. But the major step of producing a small ingot of precious metal of known weight and purity, and stamping it with a design to indicate its value, and who stood as surety for its value, was an innovation of the seventh century BC in Asia Minor, traditionally the kingdom of Croesus, Lydia. These earliest coins were of gold, and their use was clearly limited to specific types of transaction of a political or prestige nature—the payment of tribute, gift exchange, dowries, and the like.

By the sixth century the idea had been adopted in the Greek world, but it is still a problem who actually produced these coins. The earliest coins at Athens, the so-called *Wappenmünze*, bear, as their German name implies, designs which have been interpreted as the insignia of leading families who may have issued them privately. During the fifth century, coin production was certainly taken over by the Athenian state, with the striking of a characteristic drachma, portraying the head of Athene on the obverse and her owl on the reverse, made from the silver produced in the state mines at Laurion. Clearly these were designed for state functions—payments to soldiers and sailors serving in the armed forces—and for state building projects—temples, public buildings, triremes for the fleet.

By the end of the fifth century this system was found not to be sufficiently flexible. Jurors, workmen, and others engaged in part-time activities on behalf of the state required smaller payments, and so lower-value coins such as the obol appeared. It became worthwhile for the state to expend time producing small silver and bronze coins. But rapidly these acquired a use beyond that originally intended. Not only could they be used for state/individual relationships, they could also be used for transactions between private individuals, and unlike most previous forms of exchange, which relied on the pre-existence of a personal relationship, this form of exchange could be entirely impersonal, between two strangers who would mutually accept the coin at its face value as a medium of exchange. The retail market had been born, and open spaces such as the Agora could become the market place where town and country could meet to exchange goods.

By the fourth century when Aristotle came to discuss economics for the first time, much of the new order was already accepted, but the full concept of the market economy, in which 'supply' and 'demand' caused fluctuating prices, had not yet arrived. Some traces of the older order still survived. One of the factors which Aristotle considered important in fixing price was the status of the individual with whom one was trading, a throw-back to the concept of 'gift exchange' with relatives and trading partners.

Athens provides a clear-cut picture of another economic change that occurred in the fifth century. The Greek towns had relied on trade to obtain basic raw materials such as metals, ivory, marble, but for food they had generally been self-sufficient. When the population outgrew the land available, the remedy was colonisation, the typical feature of the seventh and sixth centuries. With the fifth century the main period of colonisation ended, and presumably the increasing population was absorbed at home by the expansion of trade and industry. No longer were all the trading cities self-sufficient in grain; increasingly they relied on the importation of grain, especially from the Greek colonies on the Black Sea. Despite the consequences of major military losses, especially the abortive Sicilian campaign, and despite the effects of the plague which ravaged the city, both of which depleted its population, Athens was only forced to capitulate in the Peloponesian War when Sparta managed to defeat the Athenian fleet and close the Dardanelles to her grain ships. Athens at least, and doubtless others of the Greek cities, relied on external food sources to feed her population.

One other fundamental change can be seen in fifth-century Greece. The city state is considered

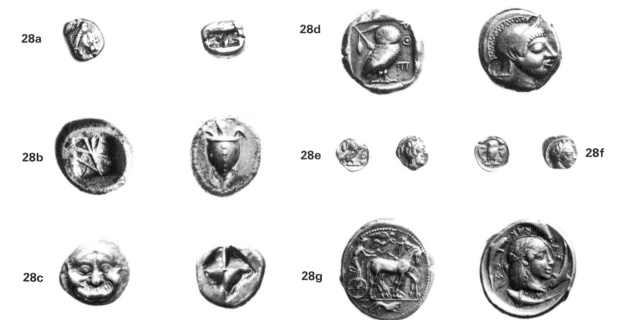

## 28 Early Greek coinage

Coinage first appears in Asia Minor, in the eastern Greek cities such as Ephesus, some time around 650–600 BC. Who issued the coins, and what for is unclear, but one bears the inscription 'I am the badge of Phanes', and shows a stag, while others have symbols such as heads of seals, lions, gryphons and the like. They may be the marks of individual moneyers. Coinage was soon adopted by the kingdom of Lydia, whose king, Croesus, put his name on some of the coins, suggesting a more centralised control. The earliest Lydian coins (a) like the early Greek, were of electrum (an alloy of gold and silver), but later it produced gold and silver coins as well. Silver soon became the normal metal in the Greek world.

In the western Aegean, the trading island of Aegina was probably the first to adopt coinage, not long after 600 BC and here distinctive coins, with a turtle or tortoise on the obverse (b) were widely distributed in the sixth century, finally reaching as far as Sicily in the west and Afghanistan in the east.

Athens did not mint coins until the second half of the sixth century, and as in the east Aegean, the earliest show a variety of 'heraldic' devices (Wappenmünzen) such as a gorgon's head (c), an amphora, a horse, a beetle, knucklebones, etc. These coins enjoyed only a limited circulation in central Greece. The circumstances of their minting is unknown—again they may be the symbols of private moneyers or officials under the tyrant Peisistratos.

Some time in the last quarter of the sixth century a new, uniform and presumably centralised coinage appears in Athens, with the head of Athene on the obverse and on the reverse the symbols of the city, the owl and olive branch, with the name of Athens (d). These were to remain the standard type, with only stylistic changes to their design, for over 200 years, well into the third century. The discovery of the silver mines at Laurion added prestige and quantity to these official state coins, and they became widely disseminated throughout the Mediterranean.

The normal coin was the tetradrachm, but as the fifth century advanced, the requirements for state payments to private individuals for services necessitated lower denominations such as the obol (e) and the one and a half obol (f), resulting in the first coinage capable of use for relatively small transactions in the market place. Athens adhered to silver coinage into the fourth century, but elsewhere, starting in southern Italy and Sicily, bronze coinage started to make its appearance.

The majority of coins produced by the Greek cities was, however, intended for local use, presumably for the payment of taxes, tribute, etc., but also for prestige activities. Certainly the products of cities such as Syracuse (g) in the fourth century were meant for display, as they still rank artistically among the finest coins ever minted.

the norm for the organisation of Greek society. This had been largely true of the sixth century, the exceptions being the *ethnoi*, in which the population remained essentially rural, or, as in Boeotia, where no one city achieved political dominance. The *polis* organisation was still considered the ideal by Greek philosophers of the fourth century, but already larger organisations were coming into existence. Generally they started as 'leagues' of cities uniting against a common foe, but the largest, the Delian League headed by Athens to free Greek cities from Persian control, was, step by step through the fifth century, changed into a maritime empire controlled by Athens to whom the members sent tribute. Passing through Spartan, then Theban control, the process was to culminate in the vast Macedonian Empire of Philip and Alexander. A similar process is detectable in Italy—the kingdom of Dionysos of Syracuse, or the Etruscan conquest of northern Italy. The concept of empire, built on a combination of alliances and of military force had appeared in Europe.

## The classical world of Italy

This picture of developments in the Greek world is largely derived from written sources. When we turn to Italy, especially Etruria, we must rely almost entirely on archaeology. The Greeks we know from their literature, their art, and their public buildings; the Etruscans from their tombs. The one common denominator in which we might make a direct comparison, the development of cities and settlement history, is denied us, because the archaeology has concentrated on the unique traits of these two civilisations rather than on what they shared in common. Though, through Rome, the Etruscans may have left Europe a legacy almost as important as that of Greece, we know little of it, as their history has been written, or rather ignored, by their enemies.

At present the picture we can draw of the classical Etruscan town is largely negative: it lacked the theatre, the monumental temples, and probably some of the other refinements that Greeks thought essential. Administrative buildings presumably existed, as there is plentiful evidence of centralised control, not only for the essential features such as defensive walls. Drainage was one aspect at which the Etruscans excelled—though it is the rural underground drains for fields we know best, the *cunicula* cut for several kilometres through solid limestone. The evidence for similar work in an urban context comes from Rome—the great sewer, the Cloaca Maxima, was built in the sixth century, allowing settlement to spread from the hills into the intervening valley where the forum was later to develop.

Regular street layout on a grid pattern had also been introduced by the fifth century, at least on new foundations such as Marzabotto. Road construction, which was to be such a major feature of the Roman Empire, had its ancestry in Etruria. Considerable efforts were made to improve communication between the cities and the countryside, with the digging of cuttings to reduce slopes. Each centre possessed its network of roads, but inter-city communications were less developed.

## Northern Italy and southern France

The Po valley underwent major changes at the end of the sixth, and at the beginning of the fifth centuries. Two factors contributed towards this. Firstly there was the opening up of the Adriatic to Greek influence. Precisely what had caused the avoidance of this area earlier is unclear. The copper resources of the eastern Alps might have made the head of the Adriatic as attractive as Etruria in the eighth century, and the land hunger of the seventh century, which saw the colonisation of Sicily and southern Italy, failed to affect the Adriatic coasts north of Apulia, though eventually colonies were established on the Dalmatian coast.

The major events were the establishment of Adria to control the routes into Austria and Yugoslavia, and the foundation of Spina near the mouth of the Po. Who was responsible is unclear, but the wealth of both Etruscan and Greek wares from Spina suggest a very cosmopolitan society. Though best known for its rich burials with high-quality Attic red-figure wares, the deserted settlement of Spina shows up from the air as a series of

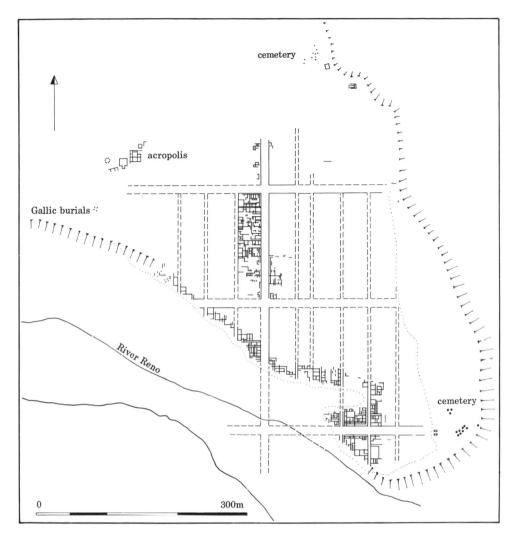

cemetery

acropolis

Gallic burials

River Reno

cemetery

0         300m

**29** The Etruscan town

Most of the major Etruscan towns were like Veii (fig 14). They show signs of gradual organic growth starting as a cluster of small villages and cemeteries on and around a defensible plateau. However, usually it was not until the seventh or sixth century that occupation coalesced, and defences and other urban amenities such as streets and drains started to be constructed. It is assumed that in these cases layout tended to be irregular, dictated by the topography.

The conscious desire for orderly planning is usually only visible when new cemeteries were laid out, but from the sixth–fifth centuries new settlements and colonies started to be founded which show considerable organisation. The best known of these are the port of Spina on the Adriatic, and the colony of Marzabotto (a) which controlled the north–south route along the river Reno across the Apennines, from

Etruria to Bologna and the Po valley.

The initial occupation on the site belongs to the end of the sixth century, but it was early in the following century that the town was formally laid out. The street system was rectilinear, with major roads 15m in width, minor ones 5m wide. Not all the area within the defences was finally occupied, but there were extensive industrial areas given over to metalworking and pottery production. Some of this area has been eroded by the river. The 'Acropolis' like the rest of the site was not in a defensive position, but it had a concentration of public buildings. This is one site in northern Italy where we have evidence for the Gallic colonisation of the fifth–fourth centuries. There are several graves with La Tène ornaments, and the site has given its name to one of the typical brooch types of La Tène A. The town had been abandoned by the third century BC.

**30a**

**30** Entremont, Bouches-du-Rhône, France

From the seventh or sixth century BC we see in southern France the development of a large number of defended hill-top towns and villages. Many are agricultural, and it appears that the population was entirely nucleated. Most produce evidence of trade contact with the Greek colonies such as Marseilles on the coast.

Entremont is a relatively late foundation. The earliest phase has not yet been located, but sculptures from it were used in building the second phase. This consisted of a drystone wall with projecting bastions, built in the third century BC. The town expanded quickly, and a second wall, also third century, was built, now enclosing an area of 3.5ha (a).

The interior was laid out on a fairly regular grid parallel with the walls. The houses were all built of drystone walling. Some, especially in the lower town, show evidence of involvement in agriculture—finds of sickles, etc., and many have presses for olive oil. The buildings in the upper part have larger storage facilities, though it is not yet clear whether this is of social significance. Many of the houses have storage jars set in their floors for the storage of valuables, and four have produced hoards of silver coins.

A consistent feature of the sites around the Rhône mouth is the presence of a shrine, in the case of Entremont, built between the bastions of the inner defences. The cult shows a concern with the human head, and at Entremont skulls were nailed on the wall. One had a javelin head in it, so presumably it was that of an enemy killed in battle. There are also sculptures sometimes depicting piles of human heads (b).

The Saluvii who occupied Entremont were anti-Roman, and the site was destroyed at the time of the conquest of Provence 125–120 BC. From the excavations there are ballista bolts and bullets from catapults. Though there was some re-occupation, the site was rapidly abandoned in favour of the new colony founded at Aix-en-Provence.

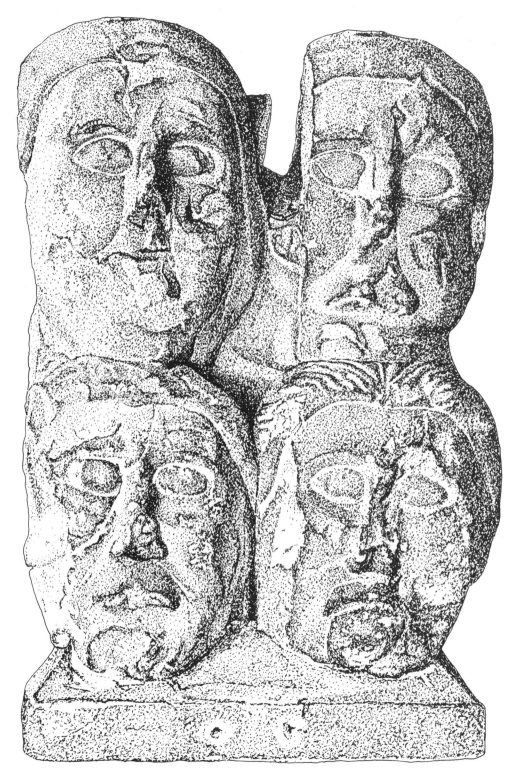

**30b**

rectangular blocks separated by a system of canals, reminiscent of its medieval successor, Venice.

The second factor was the physical expansion of Etruscan power north of the Apennines into the Po valley. This information comes from the historical sources. The archaeology is ambiguous. We have no evidence of the foundation of colonies, except Marzabotto controlling one of the trans-Apennine routes, and Spina. On the other hand, Etruscan goods became more common, and the distancing in material culture, which had become apparent between Etruria and Bologna in the seventh century, started to diminish. Etruscan-style personal ornaments and bronze vessels as well as Greek and Etruscan fine pottery appeared in the graves. Situla Art still continued, but its gradual decline in quality and its final disappearance at the end of the fifth century are likely to be due to its loss of prestige against the imported luxury goods. The Arnoaldi grave, the latest from Bologna to produce a situla, contains an Attic red-figure ware vessel datable to about 425, but the situla itself shows neither the wealth of scenes nor the same artistic skill, while its warriors bear Gallic style long shields, reminding us that immigration was also taking place from north of the Alps. Este remained more conservative, though here too the standard of Situla Art, characterised by two situlae from the Boldu Dolfin cemetery, dropped. Etruscan objects may be rare in the graves, but one belt-plate in Situla Art style shows a woman pouring out wine from an Etruscan beaked flagon for a man reclining on a couch, rather than sitting upright on a chair as was the local custom.

Control of the cross-Alpine routes was one objective of the Etruscan advance, and one group prospered, the inhabitants of the Ticino valley controlling the Simplon Pass into Switzerland. Little is known of the late Hallstatt conditions, but from the fifth century there is a rich array of funerary evidence containing a wealth of beaked flagons and other Etruscan items. This group seems to have acted as the middlemen between Etruria and the new La Tène centre of wealth on the Mosel in western Germany.

If northern Italy flourished, southern France seems to have been in decline, at least in terms of trade contact with Greece and Etruria. Attic red-figure ware is not uncommon, but it is rarer in comparison to the black-figure wares of the previous century. Marseilles had lost much of her trade with her hinterland. Between the end of the sixth and the start of the second century, virtually no imported goods penetrated further up the Rhône than Vienne; all other finds north of the Alps seem to have gone through the Alpine Passes.

The hill country between the southern edge of the central massif and the Mediterranean coast of France is, between the sixth and the first centuries BC, a bewildering kaleidoscope of small defended hill-top towns, rarely more than four or five hectares in size, the vast majority of them unexcavated. Many show some form of contact with the Greek colonies, as black- and red-figure Attic wares, and later campanian black-gloss wares are by no means uncommon. Though this trade can be demonstrated, and though we can understand some of the cultural processes going on, the nature of this society and its economic basis is still far from clear. The density of the hillforts suggests that the population was entirely nucleated within them, and limited field survey has so far failed to locate minor open settlements.

The forts show a wide spectrum of development from very sophisticated sites indistinguishable from Greek colonies to small defended native villages. This variety is neither connected with chronological development, or proximity to major sites such as Marseilles. At one extreme, St Blaise, with its organised streets, ashlar stone defences and profusion of imported pottery, is almost indistinguishable from a Greek colony. But the religion practised at one of its temples is local and certainly not Greek. Entremont, though late in the period we are discussing, also has classical pretensions: limestone walls defended by bastions, a rectilinear layout to its streets, and mosaic pavements in its shrine. At the opposite end of the spectrum is Les Pennes, a village on a spur defended by a cross-bank, showing no sign of an ordered layout, and only rare imported objects.

It is the religious cults of these sites at the mouth of the Rhône which have excited most interest. A number of them have produced stone sculptures, some like the frieze of heads from Nages, or the horses from Roquepertuse inspired by Greek sculpture. But the majority is by no means Greek. The Tarasque from Noves is a mythical beast with its paws perched on severed human heads, while a human limb hangs from its jowl, like animals in Situla Art. Piles of sculpted human heads are a feature of the Entremont shrine, where human skulls from the shrine had obviously been nailed to the wall. The entrance to Roquepertuse has hollowed-out niches for human skulls, while a vulture sits above the doorway. Fortunately this particular cult is without parallel elsewhere in Europe!

Similar sites, though lacking the grisly religion, occur further west. The hillfort of Ensèrune demonstrates the complex cultural nature of its inhabitants—the burials produce local, Attic and Iberian pottery. Introduced in the second century, the coinage bears mainly Iberian inscriptions, while one grave slab commemorates in Greek lettering a man with a Gallic name. Many of the sites start in the sixth–fifth centuries, but one at least, the Cayla-de-Mailhac, originated in the Urnfield period, and continued to the Roman conquest. Like its north Italian counterparts, it is surrounded by cemeteries, which show signs of ever increasing social differentiation—wealthy burials are by no means uncommon, often chambered tombs under barrows. Finds include two carts, a La Tène bronze beaked flagon, Attic dishes, swords, brooches and pottery. The pattern is one of increasing Greek influence, and increasing wealth, connected doubtless with the expanding trade which ran over the Carcasonne gap to the Garenne and western France.

The reasons for the changing shifts in trade from southern France to northern Italy may, in part, lie in a greater emphasis on the Black Sea trade; partly in the opening up of the Adriatic; and partly in military conflict in the west Mediterranean—the defeat of the joint Etruscan and Greek fleet by the Phoenicians in the naval battle of Himera. Though this might explain the Etruscan interest in northern Italy, Marseilles was by no means cut off from trade with mainland Greece; but the volume of that trade may well have decreased.

## Orientalising in central Europe–La Tène A

The reorientation of trade in the central and western Mediterranean was matched by changes in central Europe, though which was cause and which effect is unclear. Dependent as they were on long-distance trade, the chieftains of Hallstatt D are not likely to have halted the trade. It seems most likely that the route from Marseilles, vulnerable at all times, was finally broken soon after 500 BC. The Camp du Château at Salins, near the confluence of Doubs and Saône, which had produced Attic black-figure ware, also had some fragments of red-figure ware, but further north the line is broken. Neither Mont Lassois, the Britzgyberg or the Heuneburg have produced red-figure ware, or early La Tène brooches, and all must have been abandoned soon after 500 BC.

Of the centres only Asperg may have survived. We know nothing of the hillfort as it is overlain by a medieval castle, so the date of its abandonment is unknown. But one of the rich burials, Klein Aspergle only 1.5 kms from the fort of Hohenasperg, belongs to La Tène A, and contains a red-figure bowl dated to about 430. Like Eberdingen-Hochdorf it contains drinking horns overlain in gold, and this might argue for continuity from the Hallstatt D chieftain burials. Alternatively the burial may be an outlier to the main concentration of rich burials on the central Rhine and Mosel.

With the disappearance of the Heuneburg the upper Danube seems to have undergone some form of state collapse. Exotic goods disappear entirely from the area, and even poorer burials become rare, suggesting that there may have been depopulation as well. One or two of the Hallstatt D cemeteries contain objects which might normally be dated to La Tène A, but they were soon abandoned. Only Mauenheim/Bargen has richer burials—two timber-lined chambers beneath tumuli, both unfortunately robbed, but nowhere is there anything remotely comparable with the richer burials of the Heuneburg.

Trade with the classical world continued, indeed geographically the imported goods are more widely spread than ever before. But the organisation, the motivation and the orientation of the trade have changed. The big centres have disappeared, trade seems to be over the Alps, and the movement of goods is probably in Celtic rather than Greek hands. Gone are the diplomatic gifts (only one tripod cauldron is known); rather the trade goods are beaked flagons, two handled *stamnoi*, and red-figure ware cups, though more exotic items do occur such as silk from Altrier in Luxembourg and a gold headband from Schwarzenbach.

The centre of this trade is on the ranges of hills either side of the lower Mosel, the Eifel to the north, and the Hunsrück to the south. The area has a good sequence of burials extending back into the late Bronze Age, but not until the end of Hallstatt D did certain individuals receive special treatment, such as the provision of a bronze situla or more rarely a four-wheeled wagon. With the beginning of La Tène A there is no change in burial rite (extended inhumation under a stone cairn), only evidence of increasing wealth in the gravegoods, and a new range of objects decorated in early La Tène Art style. Burials with two-wheeled chariots, or Greek and Etruscan vessels are relatively common, and a few are very rich, especially female graves such as Reinheim and Waldalgesheim with their gold torcs, bracelets and armlets, though none have the wealth of Vix, or Eberdingen-Hochdorf of the previous century.

There are other dissimilarities. Though wealth is concentrated on the Mosel, there is no one centre that stands out, no concentration around one hillfort. Cemeteries rarely contain more than two rich burials, and they are often separated from the more usual burials of women with bronze jewellery, or men with a spear or, exceptionally, a sword. Contemporary hillforts are known, but they do not play the central role that the Heuneburg had. Befort in Luxembourg is merely a defended farmstead; Bundenbach contains many small rectangular or square structures of unknown·function, but has produced little in the way of finds. The majority of the population, especially the wealthy, seem to have lived in open settlements in the valleys, though only at Theley have we traces of such a settlement adjacent to the rich tumulus burials.

Neither are the burials on obvious trade routes, nor on the richest agricultural land; rather some are in distinctly marginal areas. However, their distribution does show a marked correlation with that of iron ores, notably with haematite which is the most easily smelted. Power may thus have been based upon control of production of iron, and perhaps also copper, though this does not mean that these were the materials that were being exchanged for the exotic imports. Control of the local economy would have given access to other more tradeable materials such as gold.

All the evidence points to northern Italy, and specifically the Ticino valley, as the source of these exotic imports. Though the Greek and Etruscan types found in the Hunsrück-Eifel are also found in southern France, they are more common in northern Italy. Styles of pottery, especially rich geometric burnished decoration, is similar in the Hunsrück and in the Ticino. La Tène style brooches and other objects occur in northern Italy, but not at the mouth of the Rhône. The mechanics of this trade route are not easy to understand. It is some form of 'directed trade' which by-passes the intervening areas. There are burials from Switzerland belonging to La Tène A,

**31** The Hunsrück-Eifel, West Germany

Before flowing into the Rhine at Koblenz, the Mosel runs through a highland area, with the Eifel range to the north and the Hunsrück to the south. Agriculturally this is not a rich area, and before the introduction of the vine in the Roman period, its wealth was based on the exploitation of mineral resources, especially copper, gold and iron.

In La Tène A it rises to importance with an exceptional concentration of rich graves unparalleled elsewhere in central Europe at this time. Though not as ostentatious as the burials of Hallstatt D, the richest have personal ornaments such as gold torcs and bracelets, two-wheeled vehicles, and a range of imported Mediterranean goods. The most common of these are the two-handled Etruscan vessels, called *stamnoi* (a) and beaked flagons of Etruscan origin (b), though recent work has demonstrated that it is not always easy to distinguish imports from local copies. The distribution of the flagons suggests they were coming over the Alps from northern Italy (c).

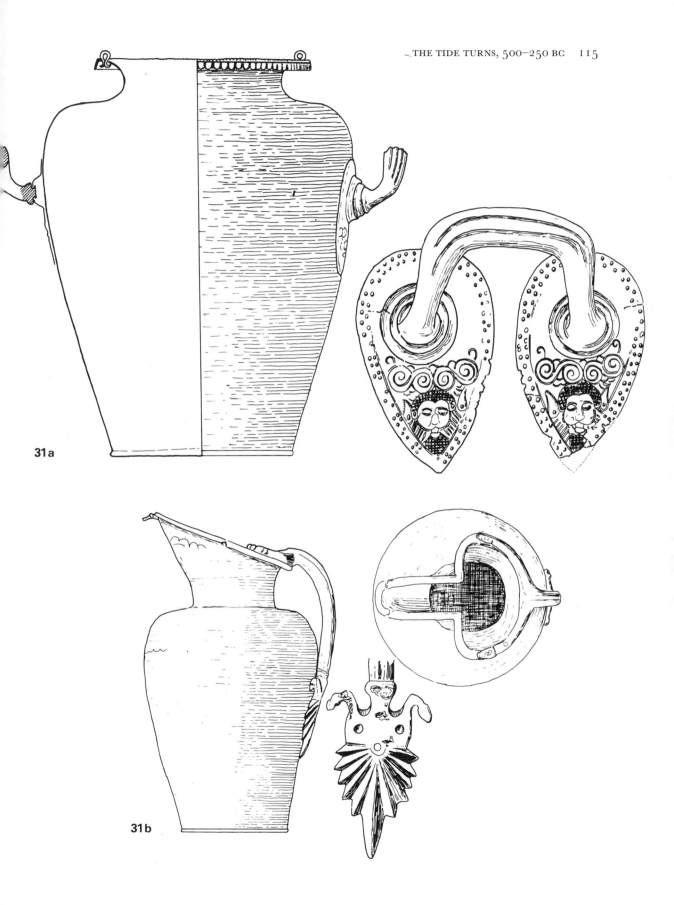

31a

31b

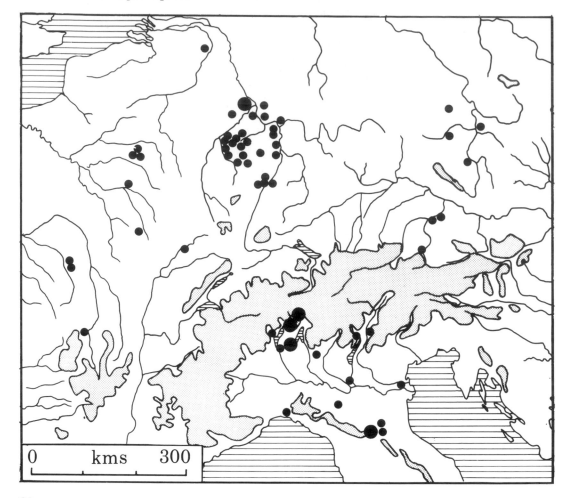

0    kms    300

**31c**

Driehaus has pointed out that there is a close correlation in the Hunsrück between the distribution of the richest burials and the occurrence of haematite iron ores (d), the most easily worked of the local iron sources, and this has now been documented more closely in a number of cases, for instance at Schwarzenbach (e). In this case there is also a contemporary hillfort, Otzenhausen, though the rich burials are in the valley below the fort, and more likely related to an undiscovered open settlement. Otzenhausen was subsequently abandoned in the middle phases of La Tène, but was refortified in the late La Tène with a *murus gallicus* rampart.

The Hunsrück-Eifel has been seen as the homeland of the 'Celts' by earlier writers, but continuity such as we have from Hallstatt D to early La Tène can now be demonstrated for other areas such as Bohemia. It was certainly one of the main areas where La Tène Art was developing, and it is exceptional in both the number of masterpieces it has produced, and the range of motifs which were employed. By historical times the area was occupied by the tribe of the Treveri who were Celtic speaking, and in the first century BC it again shows a concentration of rich burials. Eventually the Roman town named after the tribe, the modern Trier, was to become one of the capitals of the Roman Empire.

*Scales: a, b—1 : 4, details 1 : 2*

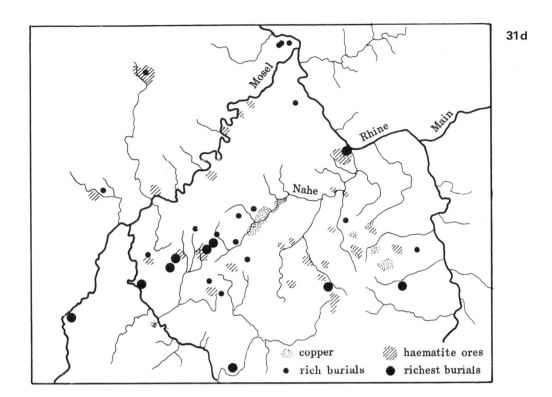

31d

31e

copper     haematite ores

• rich burials     ● richest burials

Mosel

Rhine

Main

Nahe

Otzenhausen

Schwarzenbach

0     2km

for instance the earliest phase at Münsingen. But exotic items are confined here to the fairly ubiquitous amber beads and coral inlays. None of the burials is notably wealthy—no gold, timber-lined chambers or chariots—and the society does not seem particularly differentiated. The same is true for the upper Danube and upper Rhine; the two chamber burials at Bargen already mentioned are the sole exceptions.

Wells has suggested that the exotic goods may have been needed on the Mosel for some social function such as bride purchase. Aspiring young men were accordingly forced to travel to northern Italy and work for the goods; in other words, labour was the commodity which was exchanged for the trade goods. However, we have evidence for once of goods travelling in the opposite direction; for instance the La Tène sword from a grave at 'Cá Morta'. More indicative is the hoard find from Erstfeld in Switzerland; three gold bracelets and four gold torcs found under a boulder on one of the passes over the Alps. These objects are without parallel in Switzerland, but such is their similarity to some of the Hunsrück grave-finds that it has been suggested that they were made by the same craftsman. A more likely interpretation is of a direct trading relationship, through trading partners, with individuals travelling down from the Mosel to the Ticino, and from the Ticino perhaps to the Po valley, or even directly to Etruria—the route that had taken the Etruscan bronzes to Kastenwald a couple of centuries earlier.

The Hunsrück-Eifel was not the only recipient of Mediterranean goods. In lesser quantities they were reaching Belgium, Champagne and central Germany, and in these cases it seems likely that they travelled via the Mosel. Champagne style pottery turns up in the Hunsrück-Eifel, but not vice versa. Champagne was an essentially agricultural area with not over-rich chalk soils, so what it traded in return is not clear. In La Tène A it supported a dense population, and almost every parish possesses an Iron Age cemetery. Though imports (beaked flagons and Attic red-figure ware) are rare, local goods suggest a hierarchical society. Chariots are relatively common in graves, with swords, spears (usually a pike and two throwing spears), bronze helmets, and elaborate bronze harness and chariot fittings. Female graves, however, do not produce the wealth of gold found in the Hunsrück-Eifel. Bronze torcs and bracelets are the norm, while normal male burials usually have only a spear, and rarely a sword. Belgium and eastern France have a more intermediate place. Rich burials are rare, but they may contain gold like the horn mount from Eigenbilsen, or exceptionally fine local goods like the Basse Yutz flagons; and both these burials contain Mediterranean imports.

The pattern as we observe it may be explained by two processes. Firstly, by intra-regional trade around a core area. In the case of the Mosel, the Hunsrück forms the core, with a peripheral area embracing the central Rhine, Belgium and parts of eastern France. Chieftains in the peripheral areas may have obtained their goods either by trading with the core, or by participating sporadically in the inter-regional trade. Secondly by inter-regional trade between core areas: Ticino with Etruria; Hunsrück with Ticino; Champagne with Hunsrück; Thames valley with Champagne. In the latter case the link is suggested not by imported goods but by the similarity of the indigenous finds, La Tène brooches, pottery styles, and most specifically the iron daggers from the Thames. Mediterranean goods may have been reaching Britain—no find has yet been authenticated—but decoration on pottery from Chinnor in the Chilterns seems to be imitating the handles on Greek *stamnoi*.

One commodity involved in this inter-regional trade was salt. The mines at Hallstatt continued in production into La Tène A, though generally the burials are not as wealthy as in previous periods. One contained a bronze strainer, a spear, and a La Tène sword whose scabbard is decorated in late Situla Art style. But by the end of the fifth century the Hallstatt mines were closed, occasioned by a rock fall which covered part of the cemetery area. But already it was being eclipsed by a new centre, the Dürrnberg bei Hallein, south of Salzburg. Wealthy burials are by no means uncommon: chambered tombs under tumuli, including two cart burials, a La Tène bronze beaked flagon, Attic dishes, swords, brooches and

**32** The Erstfeld hoard

The gold torc illustrated is one of four discovered under a rock near the town of Erstfeld, Kt Uri, Switzerland in 1962. Also in the hoard were three armlets, two of which clearly pair with two of the torcs. The decoration is in Early Style La Tène Art, and all the closest parallels are to be found on the Mosel and central Rhine, in the area of the Hunsrück-Eifel. Indeed some specialists have gone as far as to suggest the craftsman who made these torcs was also responsible for some of the Rhineland grave finds, such as the Dürkheim bracelet. The objects, both in their quality and in the use of gold, are without parallel among contemporary Swiss finds, and Erstfeld itself is not in one of the major areas of Iron Age settlement. It does however lie on one of the major routes to Italy, which crosses via the St Gotthard Pass, and so may be connected with the trade between the central Rhine and northern Italy, which was taking Etruscan goods north of the Alps.

The torc illustrates the use of fantasy in early La Tène Art. On either side at the top there are double-headed figures, one with a simple human head, the other human, but with a horn and pointed ears. These surmount an abstract design from which protrude two animal heads, one possibly a bearded goat, the other perhaps a bovid. On the main body of the torc, where it borders the ornament, there are elaborate palmettes.

*Actual size: diameter 14.5cm*

pottery. The stamped pottery styles link the Dürrnberg with Bohemia to the north; the zoomorphic 'mask' brooches also with Bohemia, but more specifically with northern Bavaria and Thuringia; the metalwork styles with the Hunsrück-Eifel. Though individually the graves do not match the richest graves of La Tène A, collectively-they make the Dürrnberg the wealthiest site of its period.

The association of the rich burials of La Tène A and raw resources is reiterated in Bohemia. All the graves with imports occur in the south or west, rather than on the agriculturally rich areas of the löss soils. The tumuli at Písek with their beaked flagons overlook the valley of the Otava, the main source of gold in Bohemia. These imports in Austria and Bohemia may have reached the area directly from northern Italy, independently of the Hunsrück-Eifel. The best evidence is the continuation of Situla Art in La Tène contexts—the Hallstatt scabbard, the animals incised on the pottery *Linsenflasche* from Matzhausen in Bavaria—while the finest of the late situlae comes from a rich early La Tène burial at Kuffarn on the Danube in Lower Austria. Another area that may have had direct Mediterranean contacts is the Berry on the western side of the central Massif in France. There is a concentration of imported flagons around where Bourges was to be established in the late La Tène and the quickest route would have been from southern France over the Carcasonne gap. But the Bituriges are specifically mentioned as having north Italian contacts, and a story preserved by Livy relates how they were involved in the Gallic invasion of northern Italy at the end of the fifth century.

In terms of art history the century 500–400 BC is the period of orientalising. At the end of Hallstatt D bronze-smiths on the Heuneburg were imitating Etruscan flagons, but during La Tène A the flagons take on a distinctively central European look; those from Basse Yutz and the Dürrnberg bear little relationship to the classical types other than in their basic functional shape. The drinking horns from Klein Aspergle, with their ram's-head terminals, imitate Persian types, but the majority of this first experimental stage (Jacobsthal's 'Early Style') is found on purely central European

33a

33b

**33** La Tène pottery

The potter's wheel first made its appearance north of the Alps during Hallstatt D, probably early in the sixth century, but its use seems largely confined to the major centres—the Heuneburg, Mont Lassois, and Breisach. In the following century during La Tène A it was in use in the Hunsrück-Eifel. As the vessels from Dienstweiler show (a) these pots followed the tradition of Hallstatt D, and represent some sort of continuity. However, it still formed only a minority of even the fine pottery in this area. Like the two vessels from Horath (b) the majority was still hand-made, and burnished with elaborate decoration. Further west in Champagne, where there was a long tradition for fine pottery, the wheel was still unknown. In the burials we encounter fine angular vessels with simple geometric patterns like those from the cemetery of Les Jogasses (c).

Wheel-turned pottery also appeared in central Europe during La Tène A, but with a different tradition, and a range of forms derived from the local preceding Hallstatt D. The main products were flasks (d) known as *Linsenflaschen*, and bowls or cups (e), the Braubach bowl. The examples illustrated come from the salt production site of the Dürrnberg bei Hallein in Austria. Typically these bowls have stamped decoration in star-shaped patterns on the interior, and occasionally the more elaborate curved motifs of early La Tène Art. The *Linsenflasche* is less commonly decorated, though that from Matzhausen in Bavaria (f) bears animals in late Situla Art. Initially the distribution of the bowls was largely limited to Bohemia, Austria, Bavaria and adjacent areas, but in La Tène B the tradition spread to western Germany including the Hunsrück-Eifel, and also to the east into Hungary and Romania, though it was already dying out in its homeland.

*Scales: d—1:3; c (cup), e—1:2; rest—1:4*

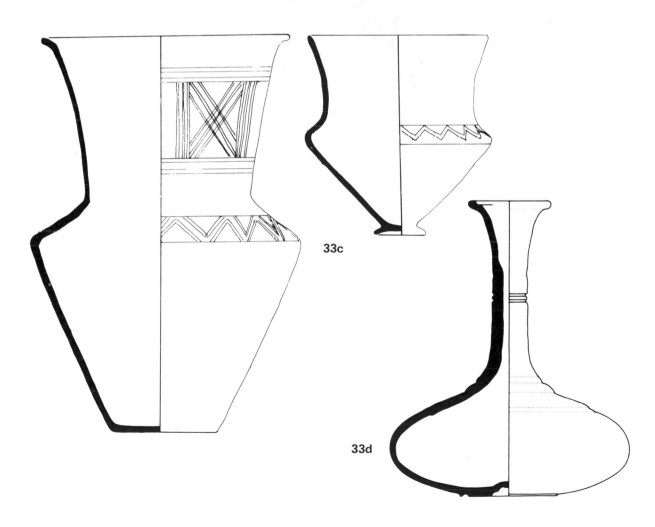

33c

33d

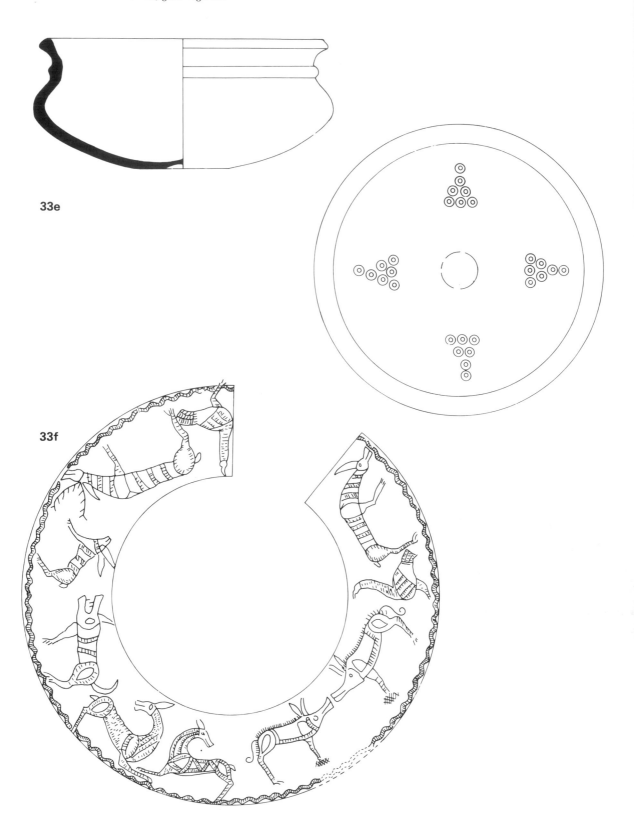

**33e**

**33f**

style objects—torcs, bracelets, belt fittings, spouted flagons, and wagon fittings.

Like the Greeks and Etruscans before them, La Tène craftsmen took over the rich repertoire of art motifs which emanated from the Near East: palmettes, lotus flowers, lyre patterns, human faces, mythical beasts. But whereas in the classical civilisations this had led on either to tight stylised friezes of floral patterns, or to the naturalistic art of the sculpture and vase painting, north of the Alps a few artists of outstanding genius transformed the plant forms into a dynamic, intricate abstract art, adorned with human masks, sometimes deliberately masquerading as a floral pattern.

The centre of the innovation was the Hunsrück-Eifel. Here metalwork was the main medium for the new art style, and the range of motifs—floral, geometric and human—was more varied than elsewhere. Most of the great masterpieces come from the Mosel burials—Reinheim, Schwarzenbach, Basse Yutz. In Bavaria and Bohemia cast brooches in bird or human form were a great speciality, but in Bohemia the art is more geometric, and especially appears stamped on pottery bowls. This stamped decoration is found on drinking bowls (Braubach bowls) and small flasks (*Linsenflaschen*) which commonly appear in graves, and are probably connected with some form of drinking ceremonial. In Champagne too, and on the Thames, the art style is more geometric; harness fittings, scabbards and brooches are the main objects decorated. The compass was used to produce complex interlinking circle motifs, and the sizes of the different circles suggest that the principles of the ratios of the radius used in Greek architecture were also being employed.

La Tène A marks one of the high points of interaction between the cultures north and south of the Alps. The information flow is still essentially from south-east to north-west, but, if my interpretations are correct, this period does mark a profound change. No longer is central Europe simply a source of raw materials for the neighbouring civilisations to exploit; the stimulus for trade is now coming from central Europe rather than from the south. Briefly, the tide has turned.

**34a**

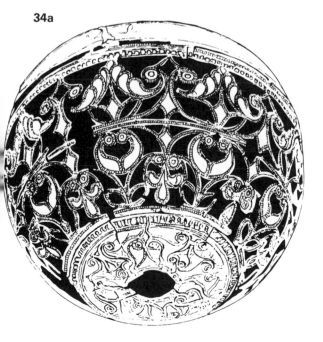

### 34  Early Style La Tène Art

The orientalising process in the art of central Europe had taken its first steps during Hallstatt D, with the initial imitations of classical goods such as beaked flagons. However, it was in the fifth century that a number of craftsmen moved beyond slavish copying to produce a new abstract style, which art historians name after the site of La Tène.

The gold bowl from Schwarzenbach (a) demonstrates how one master craftsman achieved this new style. The original motif is the classical frieze of alternating lotus flower and palmette linked at the base by a tendril (b). On the gold drinking horn overlay from Eigenbilsen (c) this motif is simplified to a three-leaf palmette, and on the Schwarzenbach bowl (d) the palmette is turned upside down and the lotus flower virtually becomes two petals with sepals. On the bowl these motifs are used purely as geometric motifs,

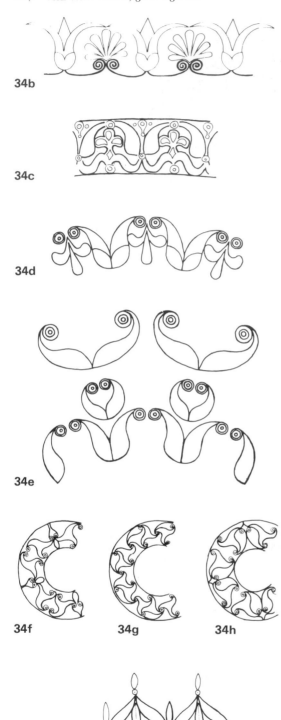

34b

34c

34d

34e

34f    34g    34h

34i

sometimes the sepals alone, sometimes the petals alone. In (e) we can see how the lotus flower is divided into two lobes which can be split apart at the base and joined with the neighbouring flower (e, middle) and then split apart at the top (e, upper).

In (f), from the base of the bowl, the simplified lotus flower alternates with a lyre pattern to which it is linked by a tendril. The space between them is a triskele, another common pattern in La Tène Art. On two disks from the Schwarzenbach burial this process is taken further. In (g) two triskeles are linked with a leaf to form a dynamic running pattern, in (h) a lyre pattern is flanked by triskeles, and each motif is linked by a palmette now so simplified that it looks like a human face with a large nose, a favourite visual pun throughout the history of this art style. In (i), taken from the Reinheim bronze flagon, the lower frieze consists of alternating lotus buds and split lotus buds similar to those in (e). However, this can be read differently as a four-leafed whirligig, most easily seen on the bottom left-hand corner of this drawing.

From neither the Heuneburg nor Mont Lassois is there evidence, either from the settlement or the burial evidence, that the centres survived into La Tène A. Asperg may have done so, however, from the evidence of one burial, that of Klein Aspergle which is situated at the foot of the hill. It was a tumulus covering two chamber burials, of which only one survived intact when excavated in 1879. It contained one Attic red-figure ware vessel, and a plain bowl, a ribbed Italic bucket, a bronze Etruscan stamnos and a bronze cauldron. Of local origin are a beaked flagon, the gold mounts from two drinking horns with rams head terminals, and a number of gold fittings, some of which had coral inlay.

The red-figure vessel (figs j, k) is by the Amphitrite potter, and dates to around 450–430 BC. It had been broken in antiquity, and it has been repaired and embellished using strips of gold attached with bronze rivets. The other Greek vessel was similarly decorated around the rim. This is in Early Style La Tène Art, with palmettes, and leaf patterns similar to those on the Schwarzenbach bowl (a).

*Actual size: j, k—diameter, with handles, 22cm*

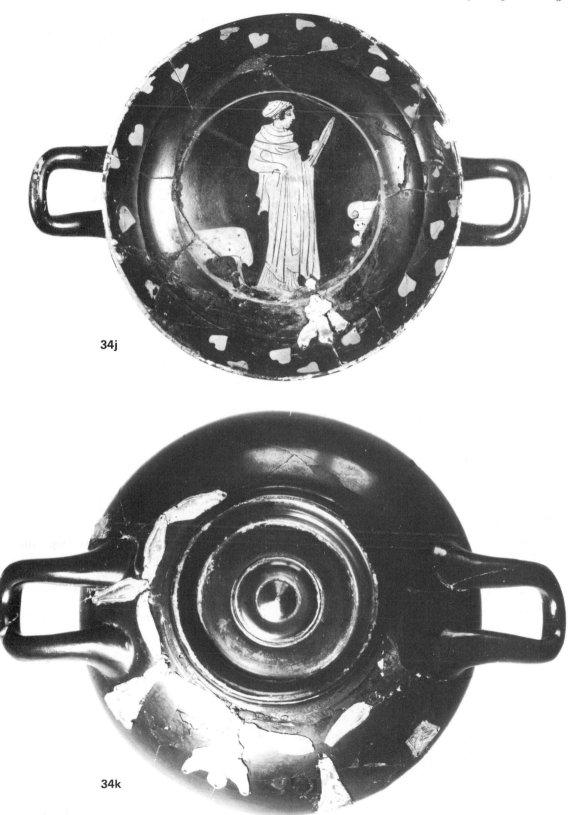

34j

34k

## La Tène B–C—the age of migration

From about 400 BC the tide of influence turned completely. In 390 BC Gauls, who had already overrun northern Italy and broken the power of the Etruscans, attacked and sacked the city of Rome. In 279 the Galatae attacked the Greek sanctuary at Delphi; in 270 a group of Galatae were settled around Ankara in Asia Minor. There can be no doubt that they were of central European origin. The depiction of the weapons on the monument at Pergamum, celebrating their defeat, shows types of shields and swords familiar in La Tène contexts, and as late as the fourth century AD St Jerome remarked that the Galatians of Asia Minor spoke a language similar to that of the Treveri, the inhabitants of the Hunsrück-Eifel.

The picture drawn a generation ago was of the Celts, bearers of La Tène culture and art originating on the central Rhine-Mosel, and after 400 spreading east into central Europe and west into northern France and Britain. This view can no longer be accepted. Firstly, objects such as brooches and scabbards of typical La Tène A type are found as far apart as Wales and Slovakia, and one supposedly typical La Tène type, the stamped pottery, had its origin in Bohemia, and spread from there to the central Rhine—the opposite of what the 'invasion hypothesis' demands. Secondly, in many areas supposedly colonised during La Tène B, we can demonstrate complete continuity in settlement patterns and pottery styles from the Hallstatt period. This is true for both southern England and western Czechoslovakia. The correlation between 'peoples' and material culture is of dubious validity, and the concept of a 'Culture' may not be particularly useful in this particular case to explain the processes that were going on.

In cases where we know the reasons for mass migration, be it military or peaceful, the precise causes are not usually of a kind that we can demonstrate archaeologically—the political pressures in Norway in the tenth century that led to the colonisation of Iceland and Greenland, the Irish potato famine of the nineteenth century. So we are forced back to more general statements. Societies seem particularly vulnerable when they are in the early stages of 'state formation'. Interaction by trade, or external military pressures can lead to the establishment of short-lived states which are able to support high densities of population for a while, but do not necessarily bring about the fundamental political, social and economic changes which can induce a stable situation. At the beginning of the period of Celtic migration, Temperate Europe was in precisely that situation. At the end of Hallstatt D the Heuneburg and Mont Lassois disappeared, apparently leading to depopulation of those areas. The same may have happened in the Hunsrück-Eifel and Champagne early in the fourth century, at the beginning of La Tène B. At the end of the migrations, a new order had appeared, with tribal states, often with power based in urban centres. Migration is perhaps an alternative to urbanisation.

In the classical historical sources two explanations of the Gallic invasion of Italy are found. One is greed for the wealth of the classical civilisations, the other is population pressure. In fact the two may be intimately connected. Trade for luxury goods encouraged social differentiation, and that encouraged increased production and greater specialisation. If the trade stopped the whole system could collapse, leading to sections of the population with no means of supporting themselves, other than to move. Areas such as Champagne would have been particularly vulnerable, where high, specialised populations did exist. The evidence from the burials of La Tène B generally suggest less social differentiation, though we are hampered by the fact that La Tène B–C cemeteries tend to come from different areas from those of La Tène A; so direct comparison is difficult.

The Hunsrück-Eifel area is typical. In one area, the Neuwied Basin, no less than 237 burials are known belonging to Hallstatt D, 290 to La Tène A, both periods of about 100 years, but for the 300 years of La Tène B–C only 44 burials. The problem is whether there was a genuine change in the social order with the disappearance of trade in La Tène B, or merely a change in burial rite with wealth not symbolised in the funerary rite, so imported luxuries do not appear in the archaeological record. The latest rich burial is the woman from Waldalgesheim, with wagon, gold torc, bracelets, armlet and an Italian bucket. There is no other rich burial in the area until late in La Tène C; by La Tène D rich burials are back again with imported Italian bronze vessels after a gap of over 300 years. In Bohemia and northern Bavaria the absence of burials is almost absolute. The one exception is the Dürrnberg bei Hallein where burials continue, but the richest class of burial is no longer found.

The archaeology of this period is largely found on the lighter agricultural soils, on the löss, gravels and sands. It is dominated again by burial evidence, cemeteries of inhumations, or occasionally by cremations with no sign of a tumulus. The men are buried with their weapons—usually a spear, more rarely a shield and sword. The women have their jewellery—bronze anklets, bracelets, brooches and torcs. Gold is rare and confined to small items such as finger-rings. Except in peripheral areas, such as northern Italy, the Balkans or north-western France, burials with vehicles, exotic imports or large gold objects are unknown. The gravegoods suggest that this is a 'ranked' society, with higher status indicated by complete sets of weapons or jewellery, while many graves contain only one or two items, or nothing at all.

In comparison with the cemeteries of La Tène A where up to 200 burials may be found, those of La Tène B–C are small (30–40 graves); or, if they are large like the famous cemetery at Münsingen, south of Berne in Switzerland, it is because they are long-lived. The Münsingen cemetery served a village of about 30 inhabitants. In areas such as Bohemia where we have settlement evidence, there is nothing larger than a village, hillforts are unknown, and there is no great difference in wealth between one settlement and the next.

We know little of production. The Dürrnberg shows that specialised sites could still exist. The quality of metal and pottery production remained high, but it seems likely that each village would have supported one or two specialists at the most, and were linked with one another in localised trade systems. Iron was traded around in the form of currency bars, hinting at decentralised produc-

tion of finished objects. Inter-regional trade is not easy to identify. Some Swiss-style brooches inlaid with coral reached southern France, but really we know nothing of how trade was organised and to what extent it existed.

Trade with areas outside the La Tène zone was limited. Amber still continued to be imported from the north, and occurs as beads in children's and female graves. The Waldalgesheim bucket, presumed to be from southern Italy is almost unique. One other example is known north of the Alps, surprisingly from Denmark. Otherwise there are two glass beads in the form of human faces from the Swiss cemetery at St Sulpice, which are of possible Phoenician origin. This is the sum total of imports for La Tène B, except for coral. This had always been an exception. In Hallstatt D it was the only import to occur outside the rich graves, and its importation, presumably over the Alps, was unaffected by the trade decline of La Tène B. It was being worked on the settlement of Aulnat in central France, and even reached as far as northern England. Its main use was as an inlay on the foot and bow of brooches.

The cross-Alpine contacts also caused the spread of the new style of La Tène Art. The 'Early Style' had been experimental with a number of regional variants. With La Tène B one style became both dominant and widespread, and influenced many of the subsequent developments as well. It is named after the rich burial from Waldalgesheim, which not only contains outstanding examples of the new style on the torc, bracelets and wagon fittings, but also demonstrates the source of the new style. On the handle attachment of the Italian bucket there is a delicate design of vine tendrils, leaves, buds and flowers, all of which motifs appear in the Waldalgesheim style. As in the Early Style, the La Tène artists have taken this formal layout, and transformed it into a dynamic arrangement of geometric patterns in which the branches cross over, forming sometimes pure patterns, at others hints of stylised human faces, or deliberate imbalance to give the designs more movement.

This masterly and exciting new style in its pure form is found in Germany, Switzerland and northern Italy, and close derivatives in Britain

35a

**35 Waldalgesheim, Kreuznach, West Germany**
There is considerable disagreement about both the date and nature of the Waldalgesheim burial. It was unscientifically excavated in the 1860s, though it is recorded that the finds under the cairn of stones came from different depths. This has led some to suggest it was a double burial, the lower male with a wagon and a 'coffee pot', the upper female with the majority of the goldwork, but it seems more likely that it is in fact one female burial. Various dates have been suggested on the basis of the occurrence in it of an imported bucket from southern Italy, for which dates between 390–325 BC have been suggested. All agree, however, that it is the latest of the Hunsrück-Eifel group of rich burials.

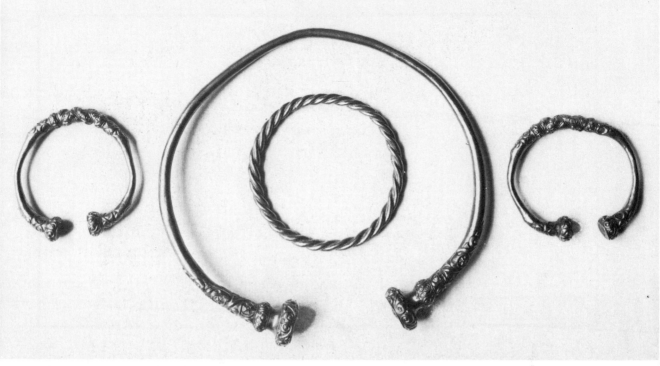

**35b**

**35c**

The oldest object in the grave is the 'coffee pot' (a), which is in Jacobsthal's Early Style, and it finds its closest parallels in early La Tène burials dating before 400 BC. However it was certainly old when buried, and it was heavily worn on the body where it would have been supported during pouring.

The gold torc and bracelets (b, c) which are typical of female gravegoods are decorated in the new Waldalgesheim Style (see fig 39), though in terms of the craftsmanship it is the plain twisted ring which shows the highest quality. The bronze wagon fittings too are in Waldalgesheim Style, though they are the product of a different craftsman or workshop from the gold jewellery.

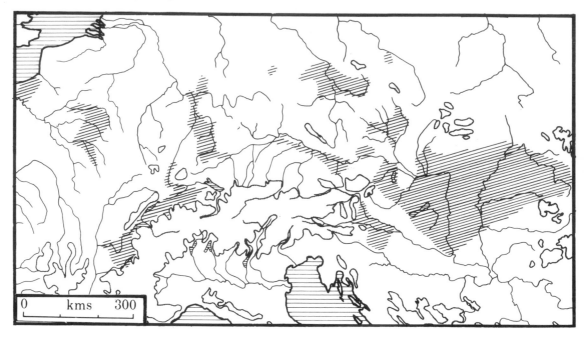

**36a**

### 36 La Tène flat inhumation cemeteries

From about 400 BC the most common burial rite in central and western Europe is extended inhumation in small cemeteries. Though this was not the only rite— there are areas such as the Hunsrück-Eifel which have produced virtually no burials of this period—the burials show remarkable homogeneity over considerable areas (a). There are differences in orientation, or the prevalence of cremation for instance, which is more common in the east, and more common in La Tène C than B, but the types of gravegoods cover a limited range of objects.

The men (b, d) are accompanied by their weapons, mainly sword, spear and shield, though many male graves have only brooches or nothing at all. Especially in central Europe they may be given a pig or a goose, and a knife with which to cut it up. Only very rarely do more exotic items appear such as a helmet or corselet. Usually the men have one or two iron brooches, only rarely an armlet. Pottery is virtually unknown in areas such as Switzerland, and limited to two or three vessels elsewhere.

The women (c, e) are buried with their jewellery— two, three or more bronze brooches are not uncommon, even up to twenty or thirty as at Dietikon in Switzerland (f). Armlets, bracelets, anklets and, more rarely, torcs and finger-rings readily distinguish female graves. Some women, and especially children, may have beads and amulettes. Decoration where it occurs is in La Tène Art style.

The rite appears in Switzerland, eastern France and western Germany as early as La Tène A, if not Hallstatt D, and spreads to central Europe during La Tène B. It starts to die out during La Tène C, and had totally disappeared by La Tène D around 100 BC.

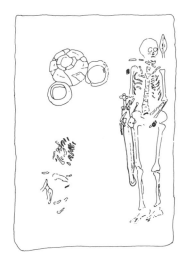

**36b**

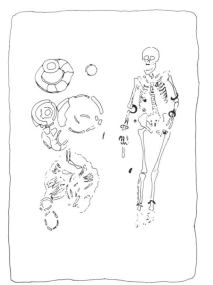

**36c**

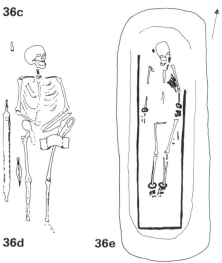

**36d**        **36e**

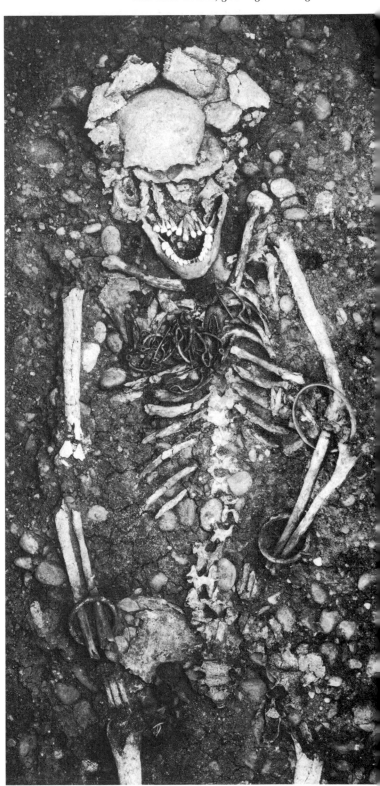

**36f**

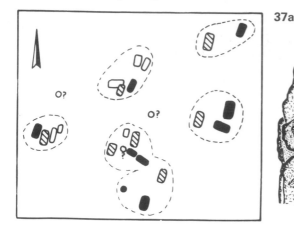

**37a**

**37b**    **37c**

## 37 Nebringen, Baden-Württemberg

In certain ways the La Tène cemetery of Nebringen is typical of the flat inhumation cemeteries. It is small, with about 27 burials (a). It is also relatively short-lived, belonging to the century or so after 400 BC, La Tène B. Assuming it is the only cemetery of the community, this suggests a small hamlet or farming settlement of about two or three nuclear families. The burials are in clusters of about four or five bodies, usually consisting of a male (black), a female (cross-hatched) and some children (open), leading the excavator, Krämer, to suggest that these were family groupings. Lorenz, however, has pointed out that it is difficult to reconcile the age and relative date of the male and female pairs in the groups with the interpretation that they are husband and wife, and he has suggested there may be a more irregular grouping into male, female, and child zones of burial.

In one respect the cemetery is atypical, in its relative wealth of gravegoods for this period. No less than six of the male burials have swords, and four have spears as well, and one has the rare addition of a helmet. Two of the women and one of the men possess another rarity, a gold finger-ring. Burial 5 (b–g) includes the standard set of three weapons, sword, spear and shield, found in the richer graves of this period. The rattle is most commonly found in warrior contexts.

The women's gravegoods, in contrast, are usually of bronze. In burial 23 this included the regular brooches (i), bracelet (j), and anklets (k). In southern Germany at this period the torc was still in fashion, and the Nebringen examples, all of bronze, have red glass inlay on them (h).

*Scales: b, c, d, e—1 : 3; f, g—2 : 3; h, i, j, k—3 : 4*

**37d**

**37e**

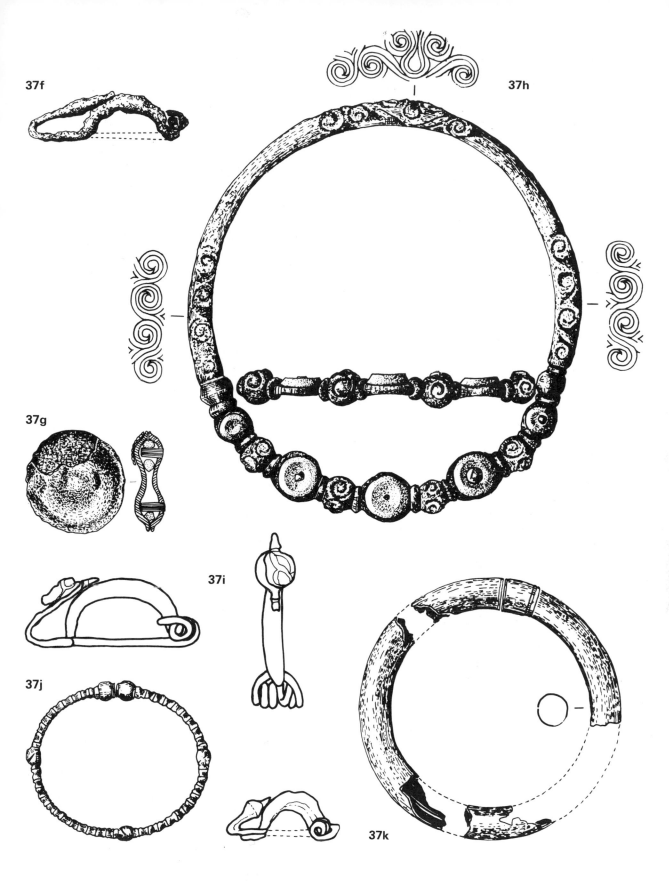

37f

37h

37g

37i

37j

37k

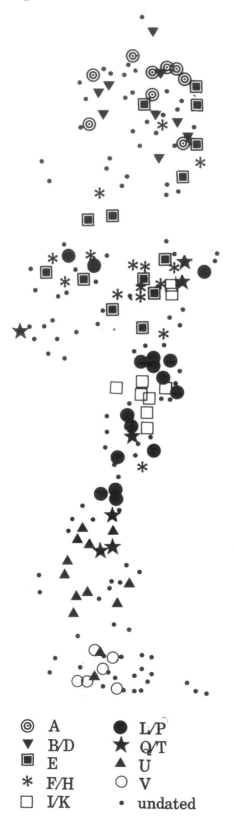

a

## 38 Münsingen, Switzerland

After Hallstatt, Münsingen, just south of Berne, is the most famous Iron Age cemetery in Temperate Europe. Not merely is it one of the best documented, it is also the key to the chronology of the early and middle La Tène from Romania to Britain, and northern Italy to Scandinavia. Part of its importance lies in its unusual longevity. It starts in La Tène A, around 450 BC and continues nearly to the end of La Tène C, around 100 BC. Secondly, it is relatively wealthy, with a number of good associations of different brooch types, and other objects.

Thirdly, its topographical layout is unusual. It lies on a narrow spur of land, which meant that it could only expand in a linear direction along the spur. Thus all the early graves are at one end, and the late ones at the other, and each period in between is largely confined to restricted zones in the area between (a). This 'horizontal stratigraphy' has made it possible to test out theories on the typological development of brooch types, and place them in a relative sequence. As these types are often very widely distributed, it provides us with a working hypothesis for the chronologies in less favoured areas of Europe, though caution is needed, as some features that disappear early at Münsingen can survive one or two centuries longer elsewhere.

In a series of studies, F. R. Hodson has applied various statistical techniques to the sequence, and subdivided the period into about twenty sub-phases, in detail probably only relevant to Münsingen and a few neighbouring cemeteries. With the development of more powerful computers in the 1960s, he was able to compare individual brooches with one another in terms of a number of their characteristics ('attributes'), including shape and decoration, though these methods were still too complex for more than a small group to be studied at one time. Once individual types had been defined, it was possible to use the computer to work out the approximate order of the graves on the basis of the different types associated with one another in each grave. Many graves, however, had insufficient gravegoods for them to be assigned to a period.

The earliest La Tène brooch type typical of Phase A is the 'Marzabotto' type (b), with short high-arched bow and foot bent back parallel to the pin. In Phase B the main type has a pointed bow, with foot bent up towards the bow (c). These two types are typical of La Tène A and the very beginning of La Tène B1 in the Reinecke system, as is a third type, the 'Certosa' with button foot (d) commonly found in northern Italy, though it survived later, as this example from Phase E demonstrates.

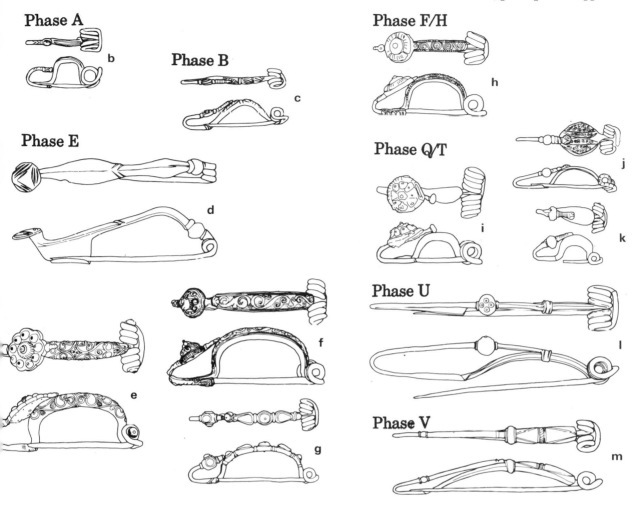

In Phase E the foot is at an angle of 45 degrees to the pin, and touches the top of the bow, which is now long and flattened (e, f, g). The first two are of the 'Münsingen' type with an elaborate decorated rosette on the foot, often inlaid with imported coral, and the bows are decorated with ornament derived from Waldalgesheim Style. The brooch from Phase F/H (h), though still of Münsingen type, shows a tendency for the bow to become shorter and high-arched again, as in the brooches from Phase Q/T (i, j, k) which all come from the same grave. These equate with La Tène B2. Two have a profiled knob on the foot, the characteristic of the Dux type which runs parallel with the Münsingen type throughout La Tène B.

The characteristic feature of brooches of La Tène C is that the foot is strapped on to the bow, and there is also a tendency for the bow and foot to be elongated. These features appear in Phase U (l) and the final phase at Münsingen, V (m). In the earlier brooches the decorative knob on the foot is still important, but this gradually disappears until it is merely a slight moulding (m). The last brooch type, the 'Mötschwyl' or 'Moravian' type, is important chronologically as it is the earliest type to turn up on oppida in central Europe.

*Scale: brooches all 1 : 2*

**39a**

**39b**

**39d**

**39** Later La Tène Art

The experimental period of La Tène Art continued into the fourth century, until the trade on which the inspiration depended dried up. The final major phase of imitation and adaptation of the Mediterranean styles occurs with the development of the Waldalgesheim Style around the middle of the fourth century. One of the sources of the inspiration is also provided by the Waldalgesheim grave—a bucket of southern Italian origin found in the grave (a).

However, the commonly accepted view that we can actually see a 'Waldalgesheim Master' developing his style as he produced the objects in the grave is no longer acceptable. Firstly, a recent study of the grave by Driehaus suggests there were no less than three artists involved in the production, of varying abilities, but all of them decorating in Waldalgesheim Style. The bracelets showed a certain amount of wear, the torc none, and it was of lesser quality.

The second problem is that finds of Waldalgesheim Style are widely distributed, and include examples from Switzerland and Italy. It seems unlikely that individual objects were traded quite so widely. The influence that the style had from Britain to Hungary shows that a number of craftsmen adopted it, but it is still difficult to talk about individual workshops and craftsmen.

The Style saw a number of innovations. The original Italian motif was based upon a vine pattern, and we see the tendrils, flowers, and buds entering the La Tène artists' repertoire. The stalks are allowed to intertwine, producing figures of eight patterns (b, c), the former with a deliberate pun on a human face. It also allowed the development of asymmetrical motifs (d). Other motifs not found on the Waldalgesheim bucket also appear, like the lyre patterns on the torc (c), but the star-shaped flower in this case is directly taken from the bucket.

La Tène Art developed in two main directions after this. On cast objects such as torcs there was a tendency towards a greater emphasis on three dimensions with strongly profiled scrolls, Jacobsthal's 'Plastic Style'. On flat surfaces, incised ornament dominated, and this is especially developed on sword sheaths, which led Jacobsthal to refer to 'Sword Style'. This has many regional variations. One of the most exciting, and closest to Waldalgesheim, is that found in the Hungarian Plain (e). The scroll patterns and vine leaves are still readily visible, but now more strongly stylized into geometric motifs, sometimes used as an infill on the major motifs. Even more stylized is the example from La Tène itself (f). Both these examples should belong to the third century BC.

*Scales: a—1:2; e, f—1:1*

**39c**

**39f**

**39e**

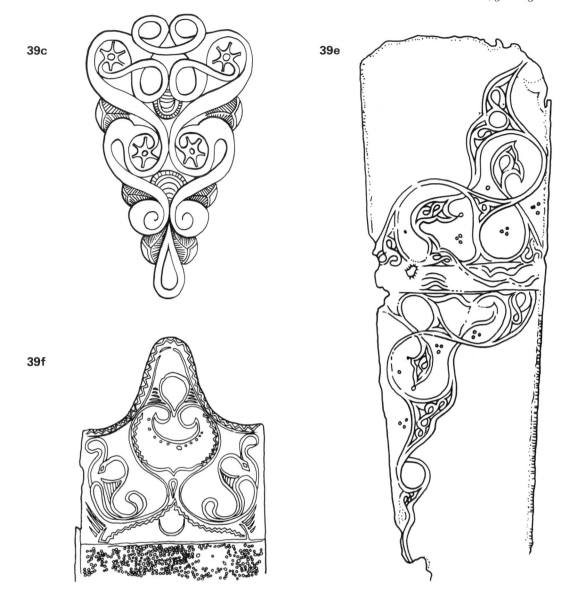

and Hungary. But these products do not seem to emanate from one source. Even the Waldalges-heim find is not homogeneous. Subtle differences in the style of the torc and bracelets suggest they are the work of two different individuals, the wagon fittings of yet a third. The picture of a 'Waldalgesheim Master', inspired by the bucket and gradually developing his style from one object in the grave group to the next, is no longer

tenable, and a case could be made out for the development of the style in northern Italy where the sources of influence were more available.

On the Hungarian Plain iron spears are found incised with a simplified version of Waldalges-heim style, but it was subsequently mainly on iron scabbards that the local artists produced their finest products. Elaborate intertwined patterns run diagonally across the tops of the scabbards, again in imbalanced symmetry—the hallmark of 'Hungarian sword style'. Other regional styles appear on the scabbards—in Switzerland, northern France and Britain, all ultimately descendants of Waldalgesheim. Tendrils are turned into birds' heads or simplified paired dragons derived from the lyre pattern.

The decoration of the scabbards had to be incised on a flat surface. That on curved objects, such as torcs and bracelets, showed an increasing emphasis on three-dimensional effects, especially mouldings and scroll patterns. On both the Early Style and Waldalgesheim style the effect is not strongly marked, but by the third century what Jacobsthal has termed the 'Plastic Style' had developed. Like the various sword styles it has both regional variations and considerable influence on subsequent styles. The third century is noted generally for its heavy ornaments, from brooches to women's anklets. But nothing shows any new sign of Mediterranean influence.

The end of La Tène B and beginning of La Tène C thus marks the widest extension of the La Tène culture. The sword types, the brooches, the various art styles are found in recognisably similar forms from central Turkey to Ireland, and from northern Italy to southern Poland. However, after an initial period in La Tène B when, for instance, brooch types in Switzerland are almost identical in basic characteristics to those in Czechoslovakia and Romania, greater regionalisation becomes apparent, as the period of extensive internal trade and physical expansion ended. By the end of La Tène B only a few prestige items such as sword types had more than local distribution, and even the trade in coral finally disappeared.

In the core area, this localisation was connected with less social differentiation, and after Waldal-gesheim there are no rich burials for another two or three centuries. Only on the fringes is this rule broken. In northern France and Yorkshire, burials with two-wheeled vehicles still occurred occasionally, though there is rarely anything other than the vehicle to pick these burials out from the rest—no imports, no extra weapons or pottery—and they are perhaps only the equivalent of the sword burials in the core area. The south and the east are different, partly because geographically they are closer to the classical cultures of the Mediterranean, partly because they are in areas which were physically conquered, under warchieftains like Brennus who led the attack on Greece. The burial of a warrior at Ciumeşti in Romania is unambiguously a Celtic warrior but Mezek in Bulgaria, with its chariot fittings in 'Plastic Style', is a burial in a chamber—a local rather than La Tène rite. The rich burials of northern Italy such as Montefortino are even more ambiguous, with local Etruscan luxury goods, alongside La Tène swords and helmets. This ambiguity extends to the poorer burials as well. Though we know the names of the Gallic tribes who settled in the north of Italy, Gallia Cisalpina, and though we know in which areas the indigenous tribes such as the Veneti survived, the division between Celtic and non-Celtic is not clearly marked archaeologically. La Tène style objects turn up in native burials as much as native objects appear in Gallic burials, and is a clear warning to those who like to interpret archaeological evidence in purely ethnic terms. Invasions and migrations did take place, archaeological finds can have ethnic significance, but unless we have independent historical corroboration, we may not be able to unravel the complex interrelationship between ethnicity and material culture.

CHAPTER SIX

# *The Economic Revival*

The history of the Mediterranean in the last three centuries BC is dominated by the rise of the Roman Empire. With the final defeat and destruction of Carthage, the way lay open for the piecemeal annexation of the remaining littoral parts of the west Mediterranean, until the circle was completed in 125–120 BC by the incorporation of southern France, linking Spain with northern Italy. But this process was not without its setbacks, one of which was administered from north of the Alps—the invasion of the Cimbri and Teutones into northern Italy at the end of the second century BC—which led directly to the reorganisation of the Roman army on more professional lines by Marius. But this invasion was unconnected with the earlier Gallic invasions. It emanated from the north European Plain, and rather marked a new phase of migration that was mainly to affect central Europe a century later.

The Italian political dominance was accompanied by industrial dominance as well, by Campania, and to a lesser extent Etruria. During the second century, wine amphorae produced in this area, the Dressel Ia form, gradually replaced those from the east Mediterranean from Cos and Rhodes. It was presumably Campanian and Tuscan wine that was transported in them, exported through ports such as Pompeii and Cosa. These amphorae, which first appear at Carthage in contexts predating 150 BC, by the beginning of the first century virtually held a monopoly in the trade with southern France.

Central Italy also was the main source of the fine wares traded in the west Mediterranean. The black slipped table wares, generally termed 'Campanian', may have been produced elsewhere as well, but Campania was certainly the main source. They were mass-produced in standardised forms, turned on the wheel, but employing moulds or templates. Ornamentation however is limited generally to simple stamped decoration such as palmettes, which means they are more difficult to date than their Corinthian and Attic predecessors. Production was certainly underway in the fourth century BC, and continued until about 20 BC, when the market was taken over by the red-gloss wares of Arrezzo in Etruria. These latter show a new level of enterprise with factories organised along capitalist lines, but it is unlikely that the Campanian production was at more than an artisan level.

In the first century this virtual monopoly was extended to bronze vessels as well, and a range of products appeared which achieved the same prestige and even more extensive distribution than the fifth-century Etruscan products. Most were associated with wine drinking: handled flagons, ladles and mixing pans and bowls, which commonly appear with amphorae in graves. Their chronology is difficult to sort out: production was certainly underway by the mid-first century, but may go back to the end of the previous century; and it continued until the decade 20–10 BC, when new types appeared.

In other respects, however, the development of economic institutions in Italy may have been somewhat backward, especially in the case of coinage. The Greek colonies were among the earliest producers of coins, and some issues still rank among the finest ever struck. But the western colonies generally did not follow Athens in the production of low-value coins in bronze; and for

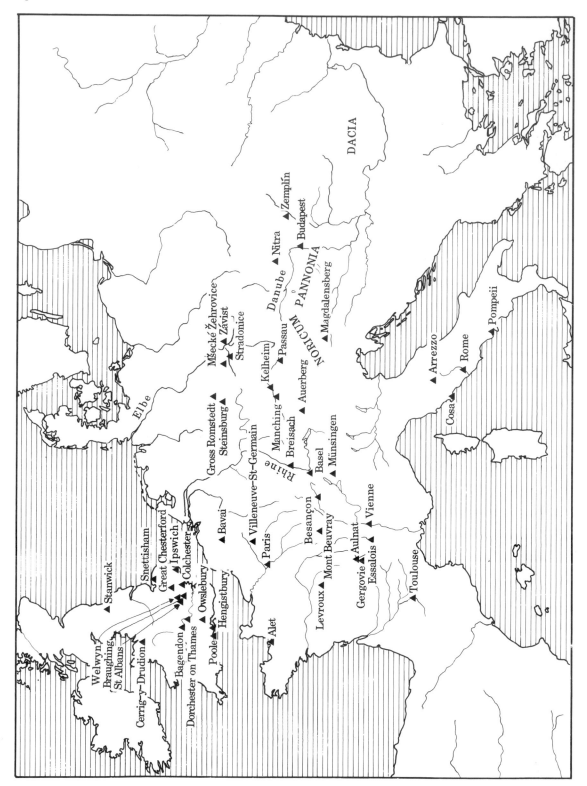

40  Sites mentioned in chapters 6 and 7

**41 Italian traded goods, 2nd–1st century BC**

The most common imports from the Mediterranean into western Europe in the late La Tène are wine amphorae from the west coast of Italy. Fabric analysis shows that they came from a variety of sources, mainly shipped through the ports of Cosa and Pompeii. Two principle forms can be distinguished: a smaller one with a triangular rim, Dressel Ia (a); and the taller Dressel Ib with elongated rim (b). The difference is chronological. Ia is found in deposits at Carthage at about 150 BC, and continues until about 50 BC when it is replaced by Ib, which is the typical form of the second half of the first century BC. Some are stamped with the producer's or exporter's mark, the most common being s or SES with an anchor (c), an abbreviation of Sestius, the name of one of the leading families of Cosa.

Accompanying the wine were sets of bronze drinking vessels, the most common being the jug (d) of which

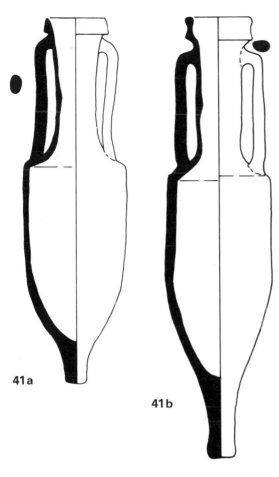

41a

41b

41c

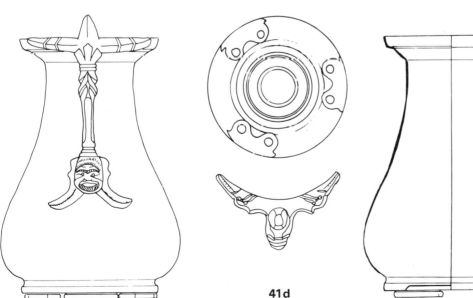
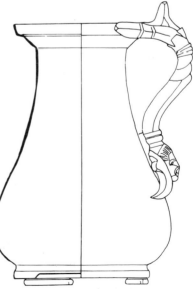

41d

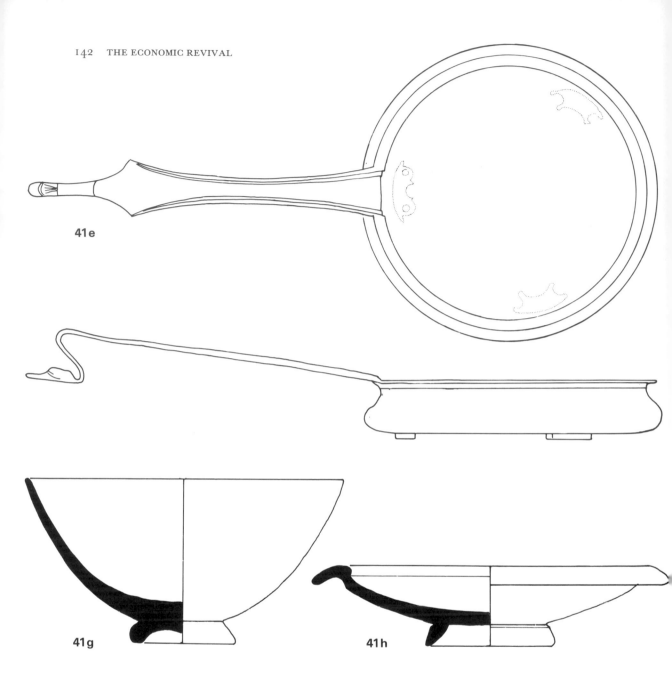

**41e**

**41g**   **41h**

there is an early 'Kelheim type' belonging to the first half of the first century BC, and a later 'Kaerumgaard type'. Equally common is a handled pan named after the burial at Aylesford (e). The amphorae are mainly known from site finds, and have a westerly distribution because of the ease of transport by sea and river; the bronze vessels were more easily transported over the Alps, and occur not uncommonly on oppida in central Europe, and in burials in France, England and on the North European Plain (f).

In addition to these imports there are fine black-slipped vessels, also probably from Campania. These did not reach such a wide area, but are common in central and southern France, and occasionally they reached the Rhine. The bowls (g) and plates (h) were quickly imitated in central France, and provided the antecedents for the red-slipped samian wares of Arrezzo and southern France which largely replaced them after 20 BC.

*Scales: a, b—1 : 10; c—1 : 1; g, h—1 : 2; d, e—1 : 3*

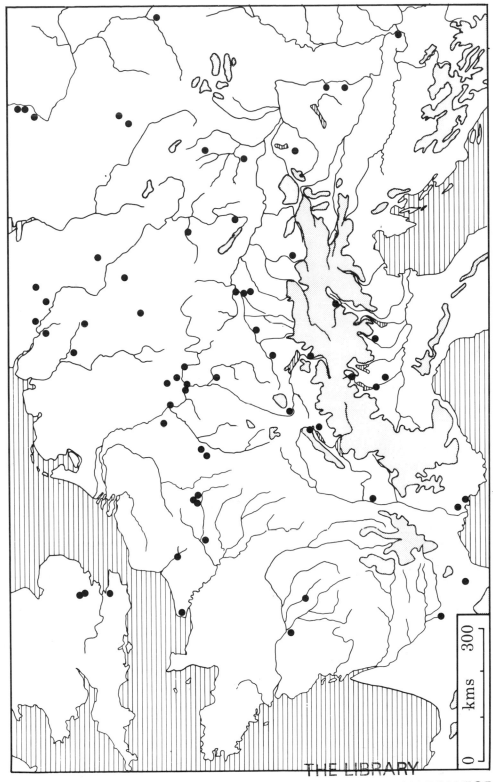

41f

**42** Gallic coinage and its Greek prototypes

Coinage became widely used in Temperate Europe from Romania to France in the fourth and third centuries BC. All the early coins were based upon Greek types, starting with Philip I of Macedonia (359–336 BC). In central Europe it was his silver tetradrachm which was chosen, in western Europe the gold stater with head of Apollo and two-horse chariot or biga (a).

The earliest imitations follow the originals closely, and are virtually indistinguishable, but gradually the coins were simplified, with only a single horse, and often other attributes added, in the case of the coin from Aulnat(b) a triskele on the reverse. The chariot is now only represented by a wheel. This dates early in the second century BC. In other cases the head and the biga became heavily stylized, as on the Gallo-Belgic E coin from Owslebury of the first century BC (c).

The Greek colonies in the west also provided prototypes. The coins of Rhode in northeast Spain have a rose on the back (d). The pattern between the petals became transfigured into a cross on the coins of south-western France (monnaies à la croix), and symbols such as axes and crescent moons were placed in the angles (e). This coinage dating to the second and first centuries BC was the main type used by the tribe of Tectosages and their neighbours, and was imitated as far away as Austria and southern Germany.

Another popular prototype was the coinage of Marseilles, especially the type with a butting bull on the reverse (f). This was mainly used for cast bronze (g) and potin (high tin bronze) coinage which starts in the late second century BC, but mainly dates to the first century BC. In Britain the type is further simplified (h). The coins were cast in moulds by impressing papyrus into clay, and the designs were scratched in the clay using a stylus.

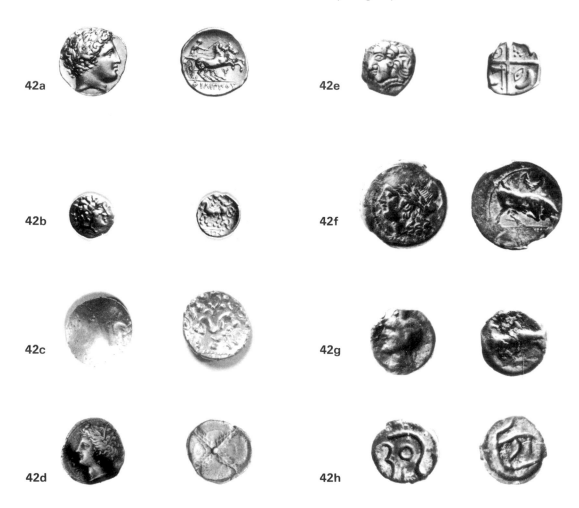

42a

42b

42c

42d

42e

42f

42g

42h

as long as only silver or gold was struck, the growth of market exchange must have been inhibited. Rome did not start low-value bronze production until the principate of Augustus in about 30 BC (it had earlier produced large bronzes), and even then it was Nîmes and Lyons in southern France that were the main mints. Gaul had been producing bronze coinage for at least a generation before this, and may well have been more advanced than Rome in its coin usage, but for some time to come much of the economy must still have been embedded in the social structure.

Economically and politically central Italy may have been dominant; culturally the Greek world still played the leading role. In the realms of literature, philosophy and science Rome still had little to compare, and many wealthy Romans completed their education if not in Athens or Alexandria, then in one of the western Greek colonies such as Marseilles. This influence seems to have extended north of the Alps. Caesar remarks that documents captured from the Helvetii were written in Greek characters, and until the conquest of Gaul all Celtic coins were inscribed in Greek, but changed to Latin script around 50 BC. All the prototypes for pre-conquest coins were likewise Greek; Roman coins are virtually unknown pre-conquest north of the Alps. The earliest copied were all eastern Greek, mainly Macedonian, but occasionally Greek colonies supplied the inspiration, such as Rhode whose rose was simplified into the 'Tectosages cross' found on coins in south-west France. But by the first century BC coins from Marseilles were circulating freely in Gaul, and provided the prototypes for many of the lower value issues.

With the exception of the influence of the Macedonian coin types, which belongs early in the period we shall be discussing, the Hellenistic world of the east Mediterranean had no visible influence on central and western Europe north of the Alps. Trade even with the Hungarian Plain was dominated by Italy, and the world of Alexander and his successors can be ignored for our purposes. With this brief and eclectic summary of a momentous period of Mediterranean history, we now turn to Temperate Europe.

## La Tène C, second century BC

The picture previously drawn of La Tène B–C is largely true of the archaeological record. Trade had ceased with the Mediterranean, the settlement pattern was of small villages and farmsteads, and the burials indicate a simple, ranked, social organisation. But the changes which occurred at the end of La Tène C and especially in La Tène D, in the period 150–50 BC, imply that fundamental political, social and economic changes were taking place, for suddenly we are faced with tribal states who were capable of founding and maintaining large defended urban centres, the 'oppida'. Hints of this change are found only in a small number of sites.

In Czechoslovakia industrial villages re-emerge which are engaged in more than one or two 'central place' activities. The best known is Mšecké Žehrovice in Bohemia, find spot of the famous stone head of a Celt with curly moustache and wavy hair. It was found just outside a double *Viereckschanze*, the square enclosures which in Germany at least had a cult function. Surface finds from around the enclosures show that the settlement was engaged in metalworking, especially iron smelting, and also there is waste from producing bracelets of sapropelite, a type of schist. These bracelets were traded as far away as Switzerland.

Sapropelite bracelets were common in the earliest phase of the next site we must consider—Manching, on the south bank of the Danube in Bavaria. At the end of La Tène B the settlement seems to be merely a small farm or village, though only its 'flat inhumation cemetery' is known. However, the site had unique potential for trade passing east-west along the Danube. Not only could it control river traffic, and the crossing of the Paar, one of the Danube's tributaries, but the land route along the gravel terrace is restricted by marshy ground to the south to a narrow strip, 400 metres across, which the later town was to straddle. Distributions of datable objects, such as the sapropelite bracelets and brooch types, show that this open settlement gradually expanded during La Tène C, and by the end of the period it justifies the adjective 'urban'. Unfortunately we

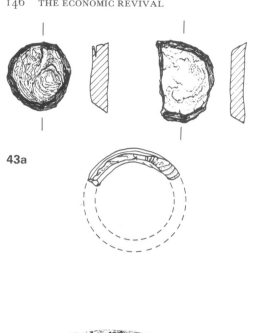

**43a**

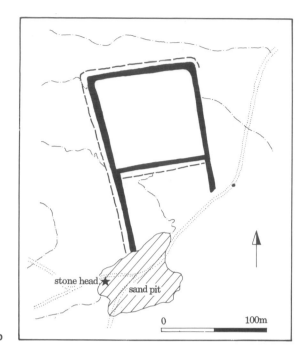

**43b**

### 43 Mšecké Žehrovice

The majority of sites of the early second century in central and western Europe were small farming villages or hamlets. A few sites such as Aulnat in France and Mšecké Žehrovice in Bohemia seem to be somewhat more important, but even these can only be described as 'industrial villages'. Mšecké Žehrovice has not been extensively excavated, but surface finds show that iron was being worked on a considerable scale, and also this was one of the sites producing bracelets of 'sapropelite', a kind of shale. The bracelets were made by hand from flat slabs of sapropelite, and the waste discs from the centre and unfinished bracelets are found in some quantities on the site (a). Bracelets of Bohemian sapropelite reached as far as Switzerland, and are not uncommon in the early phases of Manching (fig 44), but manufacture had ended by the time the Czech oppida were founded at the end of the second century BC.

The only visible features on the site (b) are two joined *Viereckschanzen* (square enclosures). Such enclosures have a wide distribution in late La Tène Europe, from Czechoslovakia to Britain. Two in southern Germany have been extensively excavated, Holzhausen and Tomerdingen. They were both cult sites, enclosing deep shafts which sometimes contained standing posts. Holzhausen had a wooden temple in one corner and a large number of hearths. Their function varies from

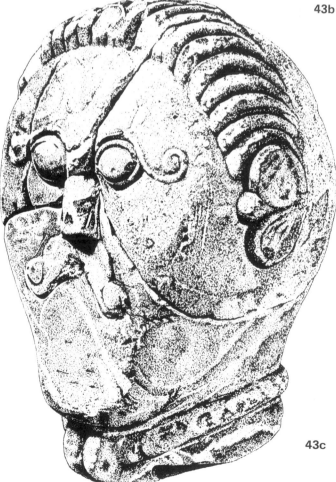

**43c**

one area to another. In Bavaria they are common, almost like parish churches, except they are found in areas of woodland away from areas of settlement. That at Gosbecks Farm, Colchester is more of a 'cathedral', the main cult site of the tribe of Trinovantes. The Czech sites fall somewhere in between—not all areas had them, and they are found inside settlements.

The famous stone head from Mšecké Žehrovice ('Sir Mortimer Wheeler') (c) is also often assumed to be from a cult figure, though outside Provence, stone figures are rare before the Roman conquest, and the funeral stele from Hirschlanden shows that not all figures are from religious sites. The head was discovered broken into fragments and thrown into a pit which contained no other finds. It comes from a sand pit just outside one of the *Viereckschanzen*.

*Scale: a—1 : 2*
*Actual size: b—height 25cm*

---

**44** Manching, Bavaria

The earliest La Tène phase at Manching is represented by two typical flat inhumation cemeteries, Steinbichel and Hundsrucken, which start in La Tène B, and continue into La Tène C. The earliest settlement areas of La Tène B have not yet been located, but the La Tène C1 occupation has been found in the northern part of the occupied area (defined by the distribution of La Tène C1 brooches and sapropelite bracelets). By C2 it was expanding (a) to include most of the excavated area. The occupied zone shows a marked east–west orientation following the route along the Danube towards the ford/bridge over the river Paar.

By La Tène D occupation extended up to the limits of the ramparts. These were themselves only constructed in La Tène D, and up to this time the site had either been open, or at most defended by a palisade. The earliest defences were of *murus gallicus* construction, and huge quantities of timber and iron spikes were used. The rampart was twice repaired before the site was destroyed, apparently violently, around the middle of the first century BC. Both repairs were of Kelheim construction (see fig 45a). To build the defences a stream had to be diverted and an area of boggy ground enclosed (b).

Within the excavated area a pattern of mainly east–west streets is clearly visible (c). Along the main road is a mass of small rectangular houses, perhaps workshops, and elsewhere there are long buildings (warehouses?), and palisade enclosures around large buildings, which may be the residences of the elite. These are especially found in the peripheral areas just inside the ramparts. The roads do not seem to have been surfaced, and a general lack of amenities (water supply, drainage, rubbish disposal) is a feature of the oppida.

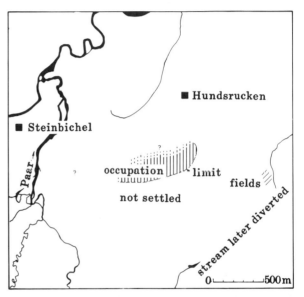

**44a**

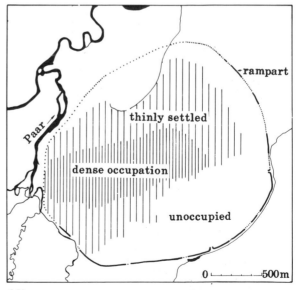

**44b**

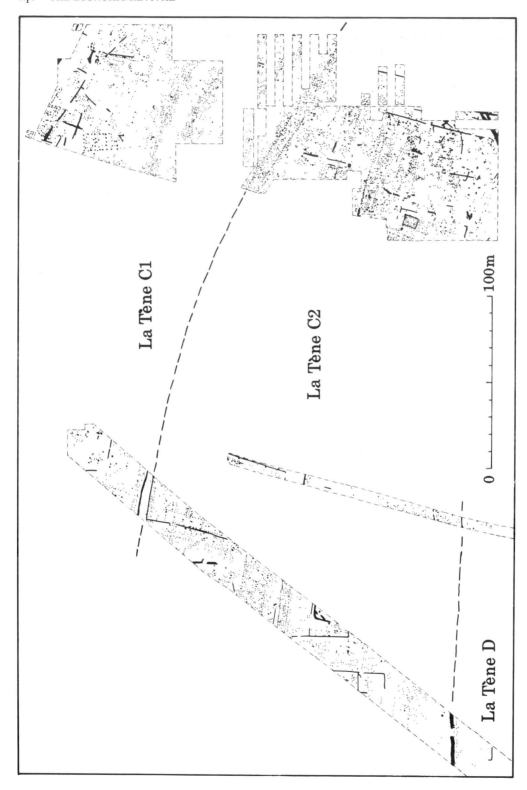

La Tène C1

La Tène C2

La Tène D

100m

0

44c

know little about the early industrial activity, as it is at present impossible to separate it from the later period of La Tène D; but it is likely to have covered a wide range. Manching however is a unique case, and it may be that it started life as a 'port-of-trade' between two tribal areas. The only site which might be comparable with Manching at this stage is Levroux on the western side of the central Massif in France. In area it is about 12ha, but the piecemeal rescue excavations have shown it had an industrial character, which included the manufacture of gold and silver coins; but its exact status requires further research.

The fourth site is Aulnat in central France, in the territory of the Arverni, the most powerful tribe in Gaul in the second century BC. This is another 'industrial village', only 300m in diameter, but it is one of a cluster of at least three villages about a kilometre apart, a situation reminiscent of the early phases of urban sites in the Mediterranean. It started in La Tène B when it already had a largely industrial character. During its occupation—it was abandoned in the mid-first century soon after the Roman conquest—it had been involved at one time or another in the working of gold, silver, bronze, coral, glass, bone, textiles and production of gold and silver coins, and perhaps pottery. Aulnat is also the only site in France to produce imported Mediterranean pottery dating to the end of La Tène C (a lone bronze jug from Slovakia is the only other object in Temperate Europe), though this is probably due to lack of adequate settlement excavation. The imports are 'Campanian' black-gloss wares, and white-ware sherds of unknown origin, but Dressel I amphorae had not yet appeared. In the same deposit was an early gold coin of local type, perhaps datable to the early second century, reminding us that gold coins had already been introduced, probably in the third century. A few original Macedonian gold coins are known in central Europe, but, like the earliest imitations, they are all stray finds without an archaeological context. All are high-value gold, though silver was quickly adopted as the standard in the east. They are widely scattered with no obvious concentrations, and such coins were rarely used for trade; so the mechanism for the adoption of coinage north of the Alps is still obscure. 'Down the line' trade is a possibility, or mercenaries returning from the Mediterranean have also been suggested. But the technology travelled too, as the earliest imitations are of high quality, scarcely distinguishable from the originals. This early coinage probably had little effect on the economy. Along with iron 'currency bars', it took its place as another form of standardised product, for use in only a limited sphere of prestige exchange.

The burial evidence is even less informative. In central Europe burials virtually disappear in the middle of La Tène C, and in the west by the end of La Tène C. At Münsingen the latest burials have few gravegoods, and little care is taken with the graves, and this seems to be the general pattern. Only in the Hünsruck-Eifel, where burials start to reappear after a 200–300 year gap can we see any differentiation appearing—one or two wagon graves with large numbers of local pots, but no trace of imported goods (though these are relatively common in the following century).

The documentary evidence, notably the Greek ethnographer Posidonius, also provides a few hints. He mentions Luernios, who became king of the Arverni around the middle of the second century BC, by scattering gold and silver to his followers from his chariot, and providing a great three-day feast. At this period the Arverni exerted some sort of influence over an area 'from the Rhine to the Atlantic'. When the Romans invaded southern France they felt sufficiently threatened to send an expeditionary force under their king, Bituitos son of Luernios. All this evidence put together shows that trade contacts with the Mediterranean were being resumed, that in some areas social differentiation was becoming marked, and that locally early states were even being formed.

## The oppida

At the end of La Tène C in Czechoslovakia and central Germany, the process of state formation in Temperate Europe achieved a tangible form, in the deliberate foundation of large urban centres, which seem to appear from almost nowhere. A generation or two later similar sites were established in southern Germany and France, where Caesar was to encounter them in his invasion of Gaul. Following his terminology, archaeologists call these sites *oppida*, the Latin word for towns. He spent the winter at one such site, Bibracte, capital of the Aedui, and he mentions meetings of the senate, and the election of the chief magistrate, the *Vergobret*. Bibracte has been identified with Mont Beuvray near Autun, a defended hill-top of 135ha. There can be little doubt that what Caesar is describing is an archaic state with a major urban centre.

Mont Beuvray was clearly chosen for its defensive qualities rather than any other reason such as relationship to trade routes, raw resources or agricultural land. This is true of many oppida— even those on trade routes tend to be on inaccessible hills. Only rarely is defensibility combined with accessibility, for instance islands in rivers (Paris, Breisach) or in river loops (Besançon), which tend to be the sites that still remain in use. The oppida are thus sites which have been deliberately implanted, established as an act of deliberate policy, and not as a process of natural accretion as in Greece and Tuscany.

In some cases we can identify undefended low-lying settlements which were abandoned in favour of the defended sites, and which were about the same size as their successors. Levroux we have already mentioned—the town was transferred to a hill-top only two kilometres away. The same happened at Basel and Breisach on the Rhine, but in both cases the earlier lowland sites had themselves only been in existence for a generation or two before their abandonment, and hardly started much before the beginning of La Tène D. These are relatively small sites, and the norm, especially for the larger oppida such as Mont Beuvray, was for a number of different settlements to combine in constructing the oppidum. So far, however, this has only been clearly identified in the Auvergne, where Aulnat was abandoned at the time of the foundation of the oppidum of Gergovie. Aulnat was a settlement of about 7ha, Gergovie 150ha.

Manching again provides the exception. The old settlement was not abandoned, either because it was now so large that the labour of reconstruc-

tion was too great, or more likely that there was no good defensible site near at hand. It thus represents the one defended oppidum in a not particularly defensive situation. The date of the defences (La Tène D) and their method of construction (*murus gallicus*) is however entirely in line with the western group of oppida such as Mont Beuvray.

At Manching all the buildings are of timber, and this is apparently true of pre-conquest sites in Gaul as well, though oppida that continued in occupation in the Roman period were given stone buildings within a generation or two. Unlike the earlier hillforts, which usually contained only a limited range of house types, the oppida show enormous variation in size and shape, suggesting economic and social complexity. Occasionally there is a rectilinear planned layout of streets, as at Villeneuve-St-Germain near Soissons in northern France. More usual is an irregular layout, with small houses constructed along terraces cut into the hillside. The overall pattern in principle resembles that of the classical cities, with small workshops densely packed along the major thoroughfares, and higher class residences in the more secluded fringes. One feature that is not obviously apparent is public buildings, though we know these must have existed as Caesar mentions 'senates' and 'market-places'.

The 'workshops' are small rectangular buildings, usually no more than 4 × 6m in size, presumably used for both work and habitation. Large buildings also are found—some up to 30m long at Manching may be warehouses or barns—but it is difficult to work out functions of buildings as stratified deposits are usually absent, and several phases of activity may be jumbled together in the top soil. The upper-class dwellings are large wooden buildings, with a wooden palisade or fence forming a courtyard around them. Unlike their classical counterparts, these courtyard households engaged in industrial activities such as bronze and iron working, or coin manufacture, as though some industrial production was under direct upper-class control. Distributions of tools and industrial debris at Manching suggests specific industries may have had their own areas within the town. One street for instance has a high concentration of needles and other items associated with textiles, while the usually ubiquitous traces of metalworking are absent. It is possible that some form of craftsmen's guild system may have been operating.

With the foundation of the oppida most production became centralised, and there was a great upsurge quantitatively, though few technological innovations can be detected. Iron objects, especially mundane items such as nails and cleats, became common, whereas currency bars disappeared. Trade was now in finished objects rather than raw iron. A site like Manching may have been importing its raw materials from some distance: iron ore probably came from the oppidum of Kelheim 50km down river, and graphite clay for making cooking pots from Passau 200km down river. Over 75 per cent of the

---

**45** Rampart types of the late La Tène

The normal method of constructing defensive ramparts in Temperate Europe involved the use of both timber and an earth and rock infill, and occasionally drystone walling to revet the front and back. A vertical front wall was normal, while the ditch was little more than a quarry to provide material for the rampart. The main weapon for fighting was the spear, and for hand-to-hand fighting the sword, and for these defence relied on height.

From the late Bronze Age the front and back of the rampart was linked by cross-pieces in various ways. If enough timber was used, this could create an effect of a string of isolated chambers which could then be filled with earth and rock—the 'box' rampart found at the Heuneburg during Hallstatt D. More normally there were vertical posts back and front, and the 'timber lacing' just linked these posts, and the front was revetted by timbers (the Hollingbury type), or by vertical stone walling (the Preist-Altkönig type). This was especially typical of the fifth century, both on the Continent and also in Britain.

An alternative construction popular in the fifth century involved no vertical posts, only horizontal, both parallel to the line of the rampart and at right angles. The ends of the posts often protrude through the front and back of the drystone walling. It occurs on the continent but is especially common in Scotland. In Britain it dies out quickly, but it survived until the first century on the continent, when a more sophisticated form appeared in which the timber joints were nailed with large iron spikes up to 30–40cm long, and the rear wall revetted with an earthen bank (a). This is what Caesar termed the *murus gallicus*, and he remarks on its effectiveness against both fire and the battering ram. The Preist construction was also developed until it consisted of merely a front wall revetting an earthen bank (b the Kelheim construction). This is the standard construction on oppida in central Europe, while the *murus gallicus* has a more westerly distribution.

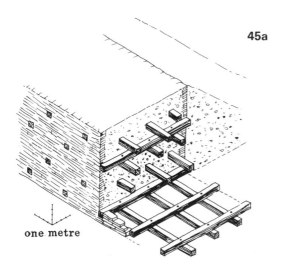

**45a**

one metre

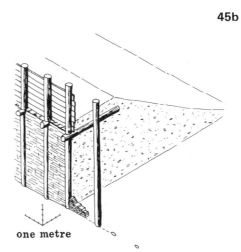

**45b**

one metre

**46a**

**46** Buildings inside oppida

All the buildings in pre-Roman contexts in Temperate
Europe are of timber. Those on the oppida are very
varied in both size and shape, and indicate complex
economic and social functions. Unfortunately it is
often hard to reconstruct them as most are on hill-tops
or ploughland where stratified deposits and floor levels
have disappeared.

There was already a long tradition of settlement
planning on hill-forts. Villeneuve-St Germain near
Soissons in northern France (a) had a rectilinear
system of streets bordered by large houses with fences
around them. These palisade enclosures can be
interpreted as high status dwellings, the equivalent of
the courtyard house in Greek and Roman contexts.

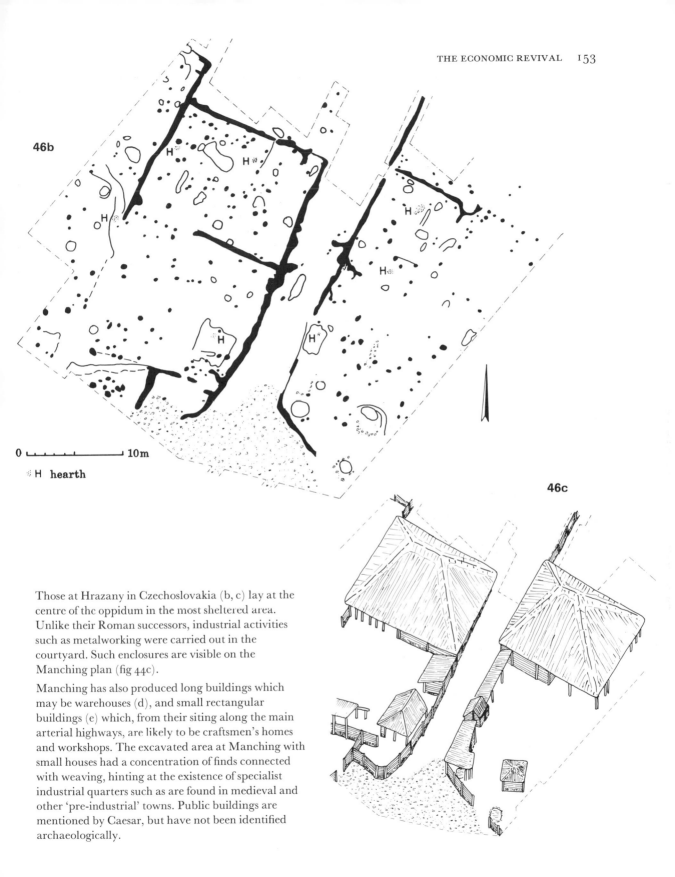

**46b**

0 ⌞—⌟—⌟—⌟—⌟ 10m

∷ H hearth

**46c**

Those at Hrazany in Czechoslovakia (b, c) lay at the centre of the oppidum in the most sheltered area. Unlike their Roman successors, industrial activities such as metalworking were carried out in the courtyard. Such enclosures are visible on the Manching plan (fig 44c).

Manching has also produced long buildings which may be warehouses (d), and small rectangular buildings (e) which, from their siting along the main arterial highways, are likely to be craftsmen's homes and workshops. The excavated area at Manching with small houses had a concentration of finds connected with weaving, hinting at the existence of specialist industrial quarters such as are found in medieval and other 'pre-industrial' towns. Public buildings are mentioned by Caesar, but have not been identified archaeologically.

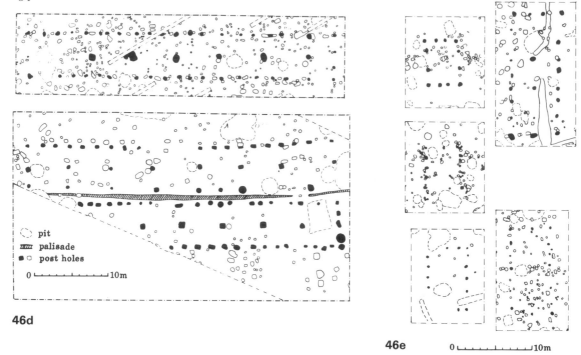

pit
palisade
post holes
0 ⊢———————⊣ 10m

**46d**

**46e**      0 ⊢———————⊣ 10m

pottery was now made on the fast wheel, including 20 per cent fine red-and-white painted wares bearing elaborate geometric and curvilinear patterns. This pottery and some of the coins are the only objects which can claim any artistic quality; personal ornaments such as brooches and belt-hooks were now being mass-produced according to stereotyped patterns.

To what extent the whole population was nucleated within the oppida is still unclear. Some courtyard buildings at Manching look like farms. The relative lack of diagnostic coins and painted pottery in the surrounding areas could either mean that there was no surrounding population, or that the finer objects were not reaching them—or, certainly in some areas, that the basic field-work has not yet been done. Small silver coins probably minted at Stradonice in Czechoslovakia generally are not found more than 30km from the site, whereas its painted wares seem to have reached virtually the whole of Bohemia. Though there were several major oppida in Bohemia all densely occupied, Stradonice seems to have held a special position in terms of the range of its industries and its external contacts. It is the only

site to have produced coins in quantity, and it is clear that a fully monetised economy was certainly not operating at this period.

Inter-regional trade is as hard to detect as local trade. Individual objects such as coins could travel considerable distances—there are several western Gaulish coins from Czechoslovakia, and the Stradonice silver coins are based on those used by the Aedui at Mont Beuvray—but coinage was not used for inter-regional trade. Individual pots too were widely traded: there are graphite ware cooking pots at Aquileia on the Adriatic Coast, and at Aulnat several hundred kilometres from Manching, the nearest centre of manufacture. There are three main sources of graphite clays: at Passau on the German-Austrian border; in southern Bohemia near the oppidum of Třísov; and more scattered sources in Moravia. The clay was exported to several production sites—Hallstatt, Budapest, Třísov, Manching, and probably others—and the finished products not uncommonly reached Romania, southern Poland, central Germany and Switzerland. The fine red and white painted wares were probably also widely transported, but no detailed fabric studies are yet

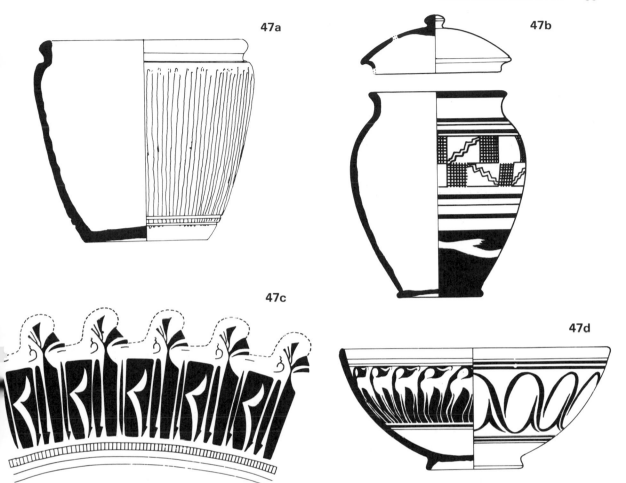

**47a**

**47b**

**47c**

**47d**

**47** Late La Tène pottery

During La Tène C, the second century BC, pottery in Temperate Europe started to be mass produced. To a certain extent each urbanised oppidum such as Manching produced its own pottery, even importing the clay if necessary. But some more specialised centres appeared, such as Sissach in Switzerland, which were the antecedents of the mass production centres of the early Roman period like Lezoux.

About 25 per cent of the pottery was still produced by hand, but the everyday cooking and eating vessels tended to be wheel made. The *Graphittonkeramik* cooking pot (a), made of a clay containing graphite, was manufactured at a number of oppida such as Manching and Třísov, and was widely traded, reaching Poland, Romania, Italy and France.

The finest products were the painted wares made in fine off-white fabrics. The production centres are widely distributed, from southern France to southern Poland, and certain centres specialised in its production, such as Zemplín in Slovakia, Budapest, Stradonice in Bohemia, Manching and Sissach. The normal product had painted red and white bands, like the example from Manching (b), sometimes painted over with simple geometric patterns in mauve paint. More rarely curvilinear patterns from La Tène Art appear. Roanne in central France produced especially elaborate designs, which might include stylised animals such as horses (c) or deer (d). The samian production centres of La Graufesenque and Lezoux started by producing these painted wares in the late first century BC.

*Scale: 1 : 4*

available. In the west, graphite slipped pottery from southern Normandy was reaching Hengistbury Head in southern England, in some quantities.

How this trade system functioned is far from clear, but certain individuals seem to have travelled considerable distances. It is easier to identify women in foreign contexts as their brooches and other trinkets can be distinctive. From Manching come two groups of three foreign objects found in close proximity to each other: three brooches of a central Alpine/north Italian type (possibly the Ticino valley), and brooches and a belt fitting of north-west German type. In a cremation cemetery at Vilanów near Warsaw were found two Nauheim brooches, typical female ornaments for Czechoslovakia/southern Germany, but rare in Poland. We have documentary evidence for long-distance marriage alliances, for instance between Arminius the German leader, and a daughter of the king of Noricum.

With the Roman capture of southern France in 125–121 BC, the floodgates were opened for Mediterranean trade through France, and the Alpine routes too flourished. Once again the graves of the Ticino Valley were rich in bronze vessels imported from Campania, but more important now were the more easterly passes in Austria. The kingdom of Noricum is mentioned on a number of occasions in Latin sources for the quality of its iron, Pliny stating that it was only rivalled by that of the Parthians and the Chinese. High-quality iron swords made of iron strips welded together were being produced in the Alps, especially Switzerland, from the second if not the third century BC, but the Noricum exports to Italy included tools such as anvils, rings, hooks, and iron vessels. This information comes from trading accounts scratched on the walls of cellars at the Magdalensberg, probably the ancient Noreia, capital of Noricum. Here there was an enclave of Italian traders, who mention their trading partners in various towns in Italy, and, in one case, Mauretania in north Africa.

Italian traders seem to have controlled the French river routes as well. Both Posidonius and Caesar mention their activities, but nowhere do they mention Gallic traders. Posidonius writes

that in central France it was possible to acquire a slave for an amphora of wine—'a servant for a drink'— though other goods and raw materials were coming back, like the hunting dogs from Britain that Strabo mentions. Three sites seem to have played a key role in this trade. Vienne on the Rhône was a border town on the edge of the Roman Provincia, controlling the river routes up the Saône and Rhône, and also the land route on to the upper Loire. Here, controlling the headwaters of the Loire was the small oppidum of the Palais d'Essalois, a site which is still littered with hundreds of fragments of Dressel I amphorae. Toulouse performed a similar function to Vienne on the upper Garonne, on the route to the Atlantic at Bordeaux. Through these sites goods reached the north in ever increasing quantities. The Campanian fine wares are not uncommon in central France, and reached the central Rhine. The wine amphorae are found on the Mosel, in northern France and southern England, the bronze vessels reached central England, Denmark, northern Germany and Poland. More rarely silver vessels and glass from Italy travelled similar distances. The amphorae are much more common in the west as it was easier to transport them up the rivers than over the Alps. The bronze and silver vessels, and occasionally the amphorae, are mainly found in burials, but they also occur in hoards, and in fragments on settlements. They were clearly reaching the north in considerable quantities.

The mechanisms for trade seem to have varied from region to region. At the Magdalensberg the Italian traders operated a monopoly, doubtless under royal control. The Aedui in central France were content to extract tolls from the passing trade, and the right to collect them was auctioned each year, the proceeds going to the state. Monopoly control of the trade was less feasible here, as all areas, excepting Vienne and Toulouse which were under Roman control, could be by-passed. None the less the Aeduan Dumnorix attempted to obtain a monopoly by packing the auction with his armed followers. In southern England, Hengistbury Head near Christchurch may have acted as a 'port of trade', controlling the tin trade, and acquiring wine via the Loire or Garonne. The impact of this trade even on minor farming sites can be gauged from the increasing size of grain storage pits at Owslebury, which was acquiring wine, silver coins and bronze belt fittings through Hengistbury Head.

This trade may have been the direct cause of the state formation, and the move to defended oppida in western Europe. Caesar says that hardly a year passed without one Gallic state making war on another. Victory in war could extend territorial limits, but it also provided tribute, booty and slaves. It could both extend control over trade routes and provide the goods with which to trade. In the west it is clearly the trade which comes first, and the oppida second. The Arverni, perhaps because of their military power, were one of the last tribes to construct an oppidum—Gergovie was not founded until the Roman conquest or even later. Urbanism was not necessarily a sign of civilisation and power, it was more a sign of weakness. It does not however explain the early move to defended sites in central Europe. Filip has suggested Germanic pressure from the north, which was certainly a reality by the end of the first century BC. There was also the expanding power of Burebista, king of the Dacians in Romania.

However, if we are to trust our historical sources, the formation of the state had already happened before the upsurge of trade in the first century, with the hegemony of the Arverni. They are mentioned in even earlier contexts at the time of Hannibal's invasion of Italy. The initial phase of the formation of the tribal states may rather have been connected with renewed problems of over-population, coming after the period of migration, and the renewal of Mediterranean trade may be a secondary, almost irrelevant factor. The tribal states of the Celts were certainly very different in size and demography from the city states of the Mediterranean, but at present neither literary nor archaeological sources can tell us much of their development.

# CHAPTER SEVEN

# The Roman Empire and Beyond

Caesar's conquest of Gaul, effectively completed by 51 BC, saw the establishment of the Roman frontier along the Rhine. In the succeeding decades the western Alps were gradually assimilated, and in central Europe the first moves were made into the Hungarian Plain. In 15 BC the king of Noricum died, bequeathing his kingdom to the Roman people, and opening up the rest of Pannonia and southern Germany for conquest. By 14 BC the Rhine–Danube frontier had been established, and, despite subsequent attempts by Drusus and then Germanicus to extend to the Elbe, this was to remain the boundary, excepting the addition of Britain under Claudius in the west, and of Dacia under Trajan in the east. Before we evaluate the immediate effect that incorporation into the Roman Empire had on the areas we have been considering, we must first discuss those areas which were not, or only later, conquered—Britain and Germany.

## Britain

The southern parts of Britain had lain on the fringe of trade systems of the late Hallstatt and early La Tène periods. At least some of the fashions in weaponry had reached the Thames area in both periods, and in personal ornaments especially brooches during La Tène A, which were disseminated throughout virtually all the British Isles. At the same time the more geometric version of the Early Style of La Tène Art was also adopted, and, more rarely, some of the orientalising motifs such as the palmettes on the hanging vessel from Cerrig-y-Drudion in North Wales. Had we located burials of this period in southern England, Greek and Etruscan vessels might well have been found also, as the skeomorphic Greek handle attachments incised on the pottery from Chinnor suggest such items were reaching the south-east.

Britain was one of the first areas to demonstrate the increasing regionalisation of the middle phases of the La Tène period. The Münsingen and Dux brooch styles, ubiquitous on the continent, are virtually unknown in Britain, though the British styles of brooches do show some cognisance of continental trends. Some influence of Waldalgesheim style is also found in the Insular styles, but our chronologies of British La Tène Art are so vague, that it is impossible to say how and when this influence was introduced. Pottery styles too no longer follow the continental, indeed in some areas such as Wessex and Yorkshire the tradition for producing fine pottery disappeared. This could relate to changes in the social structure, to the organisation of production and trade, and ultimately be due to the collapse of the La Tène A trade system centred on the Hunsrück-Eifel.

The fourth and third centuries were thus periods of relative isolation for Britain, though some general trends are visible which continued into the late Iron Age. One of these was the gradual abandonment of the hillfort. Hillforts were rare in eastern England at all periods, on the chalk wolds of Yorkshire all had been abandoned by the end of the Bronze Age. South-east England, like other areas of the continent, saw a spate of hillfort construction in Hallstatt D/La Tène A, but with certain exceptions most had been finally abandoned by the fourth century.

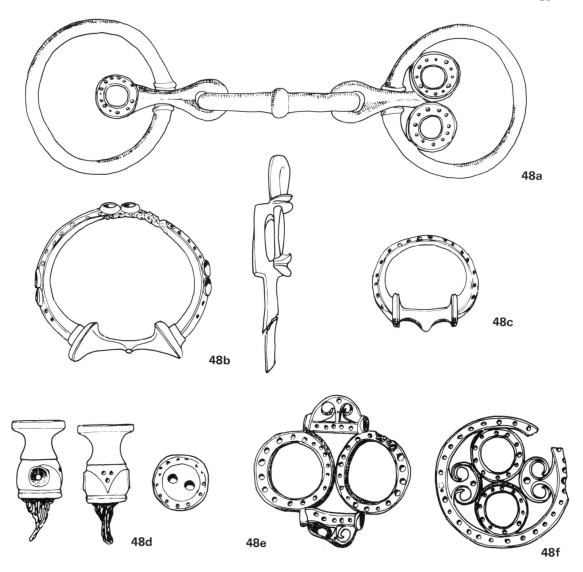

48a

48b

48c

48d

48e

48f

## 48 British La Tène Art

Though luxury items of classical origin were reaching Britain in the first centuries BC–AD, and industry was becoming centralised, local production of prestige goods by no means faltered, as it did over the rest of central and western Europe. In fact it was the period when it reached its zenith, and even the Roman conquest did not immediately destroy it. Partly this was due to the need for items unavailable from the classical world, such as chariot fittings, torcs, shields and mirrors, whereas bronze and silver vessels were available and show less artistic development.

The bronze industry was highly specialised—the smith at Gussage All Saints was only producing fittings for vehicles and harness, not personal ornaments such as brooches and bracelets, nor weapons, nor bronze vessels. None the less he had to produce a range of fittings, as the hoard found just outside the Yorkshire oppidum of Stanwick demonstrates. Each set of harness fittings required two bits (a), a large terret (b) and two small terrets (c) which were fitted to the yoke and through which the reins passed, and two linch pins to hold the wheel on to the axle (d is only the upper part of the pin). In addition a number of loops

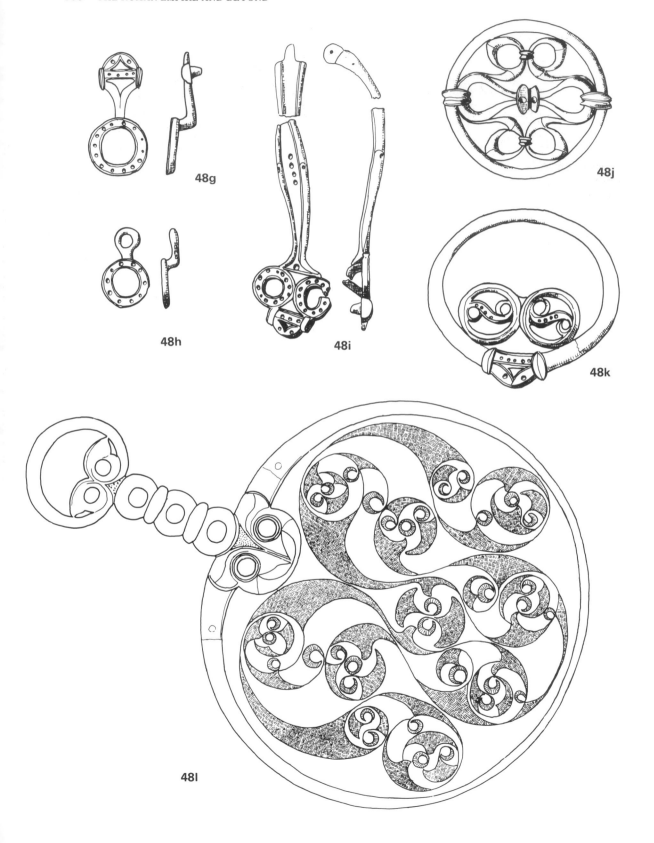

48g

48h

48i

48j

48k

48l

**48m**

(e, f) and strap ends (g, h) were needed for the harncss, and an optional range of further embellishments both for the harness and the chariot itself (i).

Each set was made with matching decoration, and the Gussage smith certainly had a range of different styles to offer. The Stanwick finds belong to four sets, and two harness mounts are illustrated to show other styles, one with moulded 'trumpet shapes' (j), and the other with decorated 'lips' protruding (k). The Stanwick sets need not be from one workshop as they were deposited as scrap.

Each class of object had its own style and tradition of decoration, though cross influences can be seen, for instance between torcs, mirrors, and helmets. Decoration on the mirrors demanded an engraved technique on the back of the mirror (they were apparently hung upside-down on the wall with the polished bronze surface concealed until needed). The earliest mirrors had a restrained geometric ornament, but by the first century AD the finest, such as that from Holcombe in Devon (l), had a highly developed and florid abstract form, with reserved areas infilled with basket cross-hatching.

Basket cross-hatching also appears on the gold torc from Snettisham (m) filling in the curvilinear shapes on the terminals. The rest of the pattern was carried out in strong relief, a characteristic also found on the gold torcs from Ipswich (n). The Snettisham finds are from a hoard dated by coins to about the middle of the first century BC, and the finds consist mainly of scrap, whereas the Ipswich torcs include examples which were unfinished.

*Scales: a—l—1 : 2*

48n

During the second century Sussex and eastern Hampshire gave up the hillfort way of life. Precisely what this signifies is still unclear, but it could be a change to a more centralised political system which could effectively limit localised warfare—a change perhaps from a simple to a complex chiefdom if not state system of social organisation.

Not until the second century, or even as late as the early first century BC, was sustained contact with the continent renewed. In the south-east this was first detectable in the introduction of gold coins of types also found in northern France, and this contact was maintained for at least two or three generations, until the Roman conquest of Gaul. Secondly there was the adoption of the potter's wheel, though, like the coinage, the social and economic context in which this was done is obscure. The cremation burial rite prevalent in northern France and western Germany also appears in Kent and Essex, though with regional idiosyncracies—for instance, swords and spears virtually never appear in these burials in Britain. In part we know there was immigration into Britain, but the continental names that are found—the Atrebates and Belgae—are on the

fringe of the areas most influenced from the Belgic areas on the continent. Ideas also flowed the other way, as British styles of hillfort construction— complex entrances, ramparts of dumped soil with sloping 'glacis' front—were adopted on the Atlantic coast of France.

The second point of continental influence can be more sharply defined: the port of Hengistbury Head, which has already been mentioned as a direct recipient of Mediterranean goods—wine amphorae, and even Campanian black-gloss ware. This was also probably a second entry point for the potter's wheel, as some of the earliest wheel-turned pottery in Wessex imitates the Normandy-Breton fine wares. The wheel-turned styles of Cornwall, Dorset and Hampshire are very different from those of eastern England, and certainly have a separate origin. The Breton links are confirmed by the silver coinage assigned to the north Breton tribe of Coriosolites which are also found at Hengistbury, probably passing through the port site of Alet at St Malo, the sister port of Hengistbury. The hinterland of Hengistbury can be fairly well defined. The graphite slipped wares hardly passed beyond the port, but the amphorae reached central Hampshire, the Isle of Wight, southern Dorset, and western Cornwall; the imported coins penetrated even further inland to the Thames and Severn. These contacts are confirmed by the imported pottery from Hengistbury which includes decorated Glastonbury style pottery from Cornwall and Somerset.

According to Caesar the cross-channel trade was controlled by the Veneti of southern Brittany, but virtually no coins or other imports are known from that area. Caesar's activities in the Atlantic, culminating in the destruction of the Venetic fleet, may have adversely affected the cross-channel trade. The later Dressel Ib amphorae, which appear about the middle of the first century BC, are virtually unknown at Hengistbury—but the trade did not completely collapse. Early Augustan amphorae from southern France (Pascual I) are known from Hengistbury, Poole Harbour and Owslebury, and central Gaulish fine wares are also known at Cleavel Point near Poole, which may have replaced Hengistbury as the major port. By the first century AD the trade had ended, and eastern England was the main recipient of imported goods.

The shift in emphasis to the east reflected the changes induced by the Roman conquest of Gaul. The major market, especially for food stuffs, was now the army of occupation in Gaul, though we are unsure where its bases were. The earlier phase of contact between about 50 and 15 BC is difficult to define, as there is no major centre through which goods passed, but there is evidence for increasing social differentiation from Kent to East Anglia. Firstly there is a number of rich burials which, in addition to large numbers of local pots, contain imported Mediterranean goods—bronze Campanian vessels, Italian silver cups, Dressel Ib wine amphorae, north Italian silver brooches. Of more local origin are large iron fire-dogs, wooden buckets with decorative bronze fittings, Kimmeridge shale vessels, and occasionally defensive weapons (shields, mail corselet) but never offensive weapons. These rich burials continue on until after the Roman conquest.

---

**49** Hengistbury Head

Hengistbury Head is a peninsula which cuts off Christchurch Harbour from the open sea (a). It controls the river routes of the Avon and Stour into the chalk heartlands of Dorset and Wiltshire. It had been occupied in the late Hallstatt period and at various times during the La Tène period, and at some time the headland had been cut off by a massive defensive earthwork. It was at the end of the second century BC and during the first half of the first century that it rose to importance, possibly virtually controlling all the trade from the continent to the southern part of England.

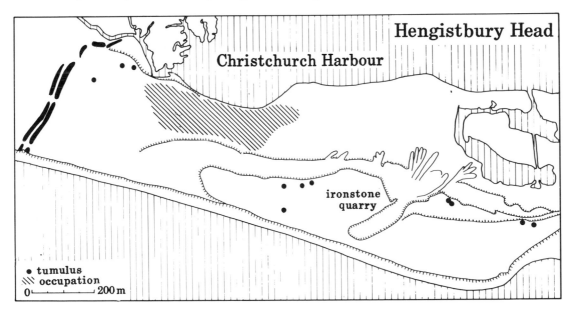

Hengistbury Head

Christchurch Harbour

ironstone quarry

• tumulus
occupation
0 ————— 200 m

49a

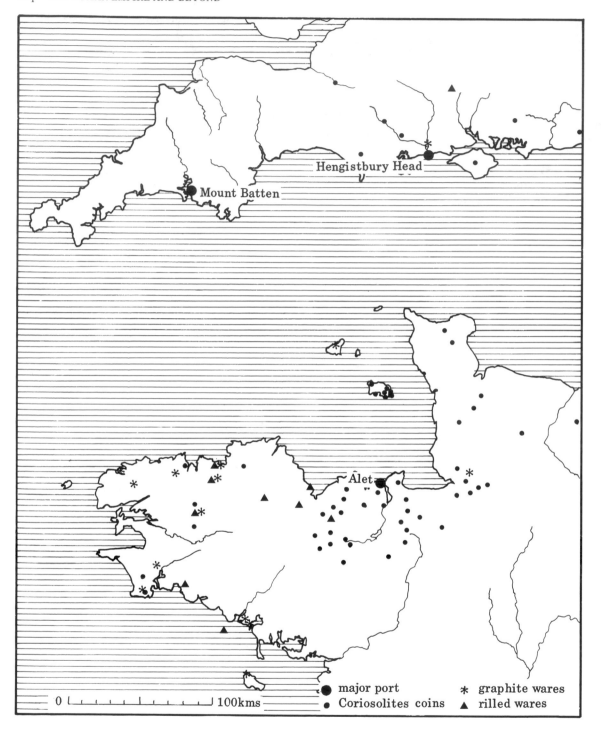

Hengistbury Head

Mount Batten

Âlet

0 ———————————— 100kms

● major port
● Coriosolites coins
✳ graphite wares
▲ rilled wares

49b

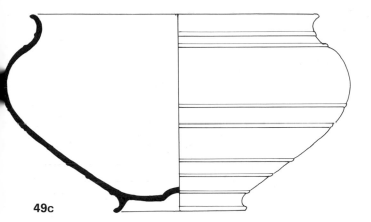

**49c**

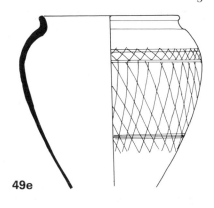

**49e**

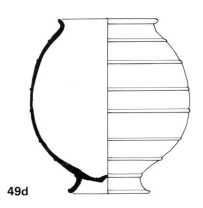

**49d**

It is the most prolific site for Dressel Ia amphorae in Britain, which perhaps reached here via the Carcassonne Gap route in southern France. It is the coarse pottery which shows its hinterland most clearly (b). From the nearest part of France (Brittany and Normandy) there is fine wheel-turned pottery with cordons (c, d) which may have come via the port of Alet at St Malo, and the pottery with graphite slip (e) comes from a similar area. Coins of the Breton tribe of Coriosolites also occur at Hengistbury, but none is known of the Veneti of southern Brittany, whom Caesar claimed had a monopoly of the cross-channel trade. Pottery is also known of clays found only on the Lizard in Cornwall, and sherds occur of Somerset and Dorset types as well. Wine amphorae, which presumably came through Hengistbury, occur in Cornwall, Dorset, the Isle of Wight and Hampshire.

*Scales: c, d, e—1 : 4*

In East Anglia where such burials are not known, the concentration of wealth is indicated by gold torcs, especially those from Snettisham and Ipswich. In both cases the context of the finds is unknown, though Snettisham consisted of two or three separate hoards, and included other items such as coins. The Ipswich torcs were unfinished, and the Snettisham finds may also have included scrap waiting to be melted down. How much earlier this social differentiation started is not clear—Snettisham should date to about the middle of the first century BC, and Caesar implies the existence of an elite chieftain class in the south-east. In about 20–15 BC this process reached its climax, with the establishment of a number of tribal kingdoms under individuals such as Tasciovanus and his son Cunobelin, who not only produced coins inscribed with their own names, but referred to themselves as 'kings'. Independent historical sources confirm Cunobelin's claim calling him 'king of the Britons'. By the time of the Roman conquest kingship had been established over most of the east of England, among the Atrebates, Catuvellauni, Iceni, Brigantes and Dobunni.

The second phase of contact starting around 15–10 BC was brought about by both internal and external changes. The Roman army, now more obviously the main source of influence, was concentrated on the Rhine frontier. Much river trade doubtless passed through the Rhine mouth across the North Sea, but the newly established road network through Bavai in northern France to

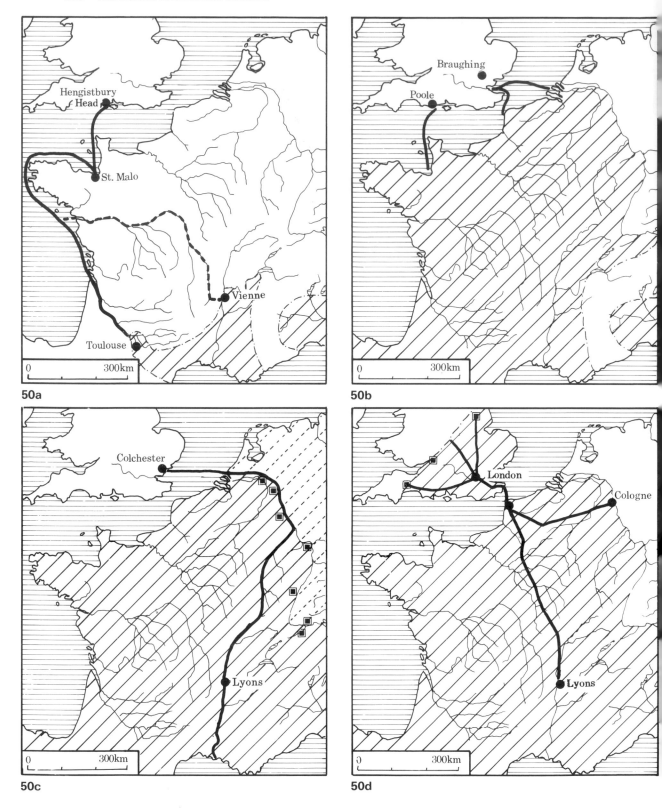

**50a**

**50b**

**50c**

**50d**

**50**  The changing relationship between Britain and the Roman empire

The conquest of southern France in 125 BC gave Rome control of the two major trade routes through France. The eastern runs up the Rhône valley to Switzerland, southern Germany, the Paris Basin, and the Loire, and near the frontier, the town of Vienne developed rapidly, specifically controlling the route to the upper Loire. The western route is over the Carcassonne Gap to the upper Garonne at Toulouse. This latter was the easier route to Britain, and it was probably via here that wine travelled to St Malo and Hengistbury Head, though the Loire route may also have functioned.

After Caesar's conquest of Gaul in 58–51 BC, trade contacts across the Channel were more diffuse, and a number of short crossings may have been functioning. We do not know the disposition of the legions in the generation after Caesar, but they seem to have been widely scattered. Caesar's treaties after his invasion of Britain may have favoured links in eastern Britain as the distribution of Dressel Ib amphorae suggests, but the Atlantic route was still functioning, as Spanish Pascual I amphorae turn up in Hampshire and Dorset. Poole Harbour may have replaced Hengistbury Head as the major entrepôt. In eastern England there was no obvious port site operating, and goods reached a wide area around the Thames estuary, though Braughing in Hertfordshire, perhaps the capital of the developing Catuvellaunian state has an unusual concentration of imports.

Augustus' decision to conquer Germany radically altered the situation in Gaul, with a concentration of troops on the Rhine frontier. The need to supply this new market caused the emphasis in trade to fall on the eastern Rhône–Saône–Mosel route, and all early imports from the Mediterranean may have reached Britain via this route. Within a decade or two, power had shifted from Braughing to Colchester, one of the closest British ports to the Rhine market, and Rhenish pottery (Gallo-Belgic wares) appears there in quantity. Eventually Colchester may have exercised a monopoly in the lucrative cross-Channel trade.

With the conquest of Britain the situation changes again, though it took a decade or two for Colchester to lose its supremacy. Partly the market had shifted— Britain had its own four legions to supply and three of these had come from the Rhine. But the new need was for an administrative centre as close as possible to the shortest Channel crossing, and so to the overland route to Rome, but sufficiently inland to maintain contact with the forward legions. Colchester was too far to the east, but London was ideally situated for both purposes, as well as providing a port with major river access to the centre of the new province.

Thus, if we accept there was likely to be a time-lag to adjust to changed circumstances, the relative importance of Hengistbury Head, Colchester and London in their relationship with Rome can be explained in simple geographical terms.

---

the middle Rhine provided an alternative connection. Imported goods from the Mediterranean now came up the Rhône–Rhine routes. The second change was the development of major centres of population in eastern England, some open settlements like Braughing, others, like Colchester, the British version of oppida.

Colchester (Camulodunum) has many of the characteristics of a town. It was one of the residences of the royal dynasty of Cunobelin, and the royal graves are probably those in the large tumulus at Lexden which have produced amphorae, Italian bronzes, remains of a mail corselet and a silver coin of Augustus in a setting. The royal palace may have been at Gosbecks where there was also a shrine (a *Viereckschanze*) which after the Roman conquest acquired an amphitheatre as well. The industrial and trading area lay at Lexden commanding the highest tidal part of the river Colne. Unlike a Roman town the population was not nucleated, and the whole was enclosed by massive linear earthworks enclosing at least 20 square kilometres. The two major Catuvellaunian centres inland may have started a bit earlier. Coins of Cunobelin's father Tasciovanus are much commoner at Braughing, and at St Albans (Verulamium), and, though he struck coins at Colchester (inscribed CAM), those inscribed VER (for Verulamium) are much more common. Braughing consists of a small defended enclosure surrounded by a large scattered open settlement, and may well have been the earlier royal residence. St Albans is again a scattered settlement, like Colchester, with linear dykes enclosing the whole complex which includes several cemeteries.

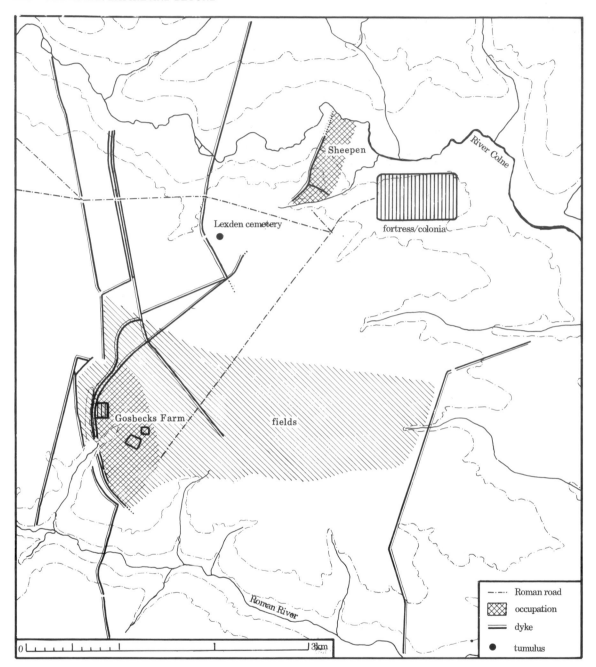

51a

**51** Colchester, Essex

The earliest evidence we have for the existence of
Camulodunum (the fort of Camulos, god of war) is on
inscribed coins of chieftains such as Tasciovanus,
which should date to about 15 BC. The earliest
occupation from the settlement dates to about AD 10,
by which time it was the capital of Tasciovanus' son
Cunobelin. By the time of the Roman conquest in
AD 42, massive linear earthworks had been built
around the site, enclosing some 2000ha (a). Much of
the area enclosed included farmland and also the
cemeteries, such as the massive tumuli at Lexden
perhaps the burial place of the royal family itself.

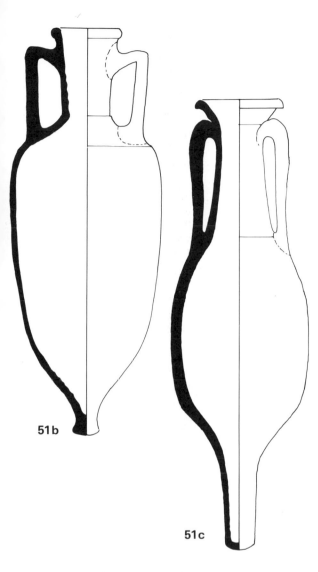

**51b**

**51c**

There were two centres of occupation. One lay around the religious sanctuary at Gosbecks Farm where a square enclosure has been found underlying the Roman temple. Adjacent is a sub-rectangular enclosure which looks like a native farming estate, and could be the royal residence, and around it the aerial photographs show an extensive system of fields. The second centre of activity is the Sheepen site where excavations have revealed evidence for trading and industrial activity, including the minting of coins.

Colchester was in close contact with the Rhineland (see fig 50), and Gallo-Belgic pottery from that area is common. There are also numerous fragments of amphorae which were used to import wine, olive oil and fish paste. The Dressel 2–4 amphora (b) comes from Italy or southern France, and was probably for wine, the Dressel 7–11 (c) are Spanish and were for fish products. It is interesting to note that from a pit at Skeleton Green, Braughing, which contained fragments of Spanish amphora, there were also bones of the Spanish mackerel *Scomber colias*. Samian pottery was also imported both from Italy (Arrezzo) and southern France (d).

Such was the importance of this site that Claudius himself travelled to Britain to take part in its capture. A fortress and possibly a second small fort were established, and initially the road system for the new province was centred on Colchester, where a Roman colony and Imperial cult centre were also founded. Within a couple of decades it was superseded by London as the major city of the province.

*Scales: b, c—1:8; d—1:2*

**51d**

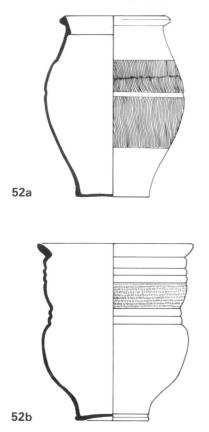

52a

52b

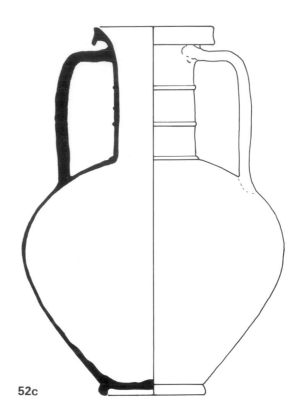

52c

**52** The Gallo-Belgic pottery industry

The Gallo-Belgic pottery industry appears around 15 BC, with centres of production on the lower and middle Rhine, the Mosel and northern France. The arrival of the Roman army on the Rhine frontier at this time is certainly closely connected. The precise origins of the industry are still unknown, but it arrived fully developed. It certainly did not originate from the local late La Tène pottery industry, and an origin somewhere in central France is most likely.

The potters produced a range of beakers and jars in fine slipped or plain wares, often decorated with fine rouletting, like the butt-beaker (a) and the girth-beaker (b). The latter certainly finds its origin in middle-late La Tène ceramics in central France. Other innovations were flagons and double-handled flasks (c), the latter in a distinctive white fabric. The most common products were plates and platters (d), either in a light grey ware with a black polished surface (*terra nigra*) or a fine red-slipped ware (*terra rubra*), often stamped with the maker's name (e).

Platters were unknown in late La Tène contexts, except as imitations of Mediterranean types, and these Gallo-Belgic platters are mainly imitations of Campanian and Arretine samian forms.

The earliest occurrence of the Gallo-Belgic types is on the forts of the Rhineland such as Haltern or Oberaden, founded during the campaigns of Drusus and Tiberius, but they also occur in native contexts, such as the rich cremation burials from Goeblingen-Nospelt in Luxembourg. They were extensively traded along the Rhine, reaching Britain around the turn of the millennium. By about AD 10–20 workshops had been set up in England, mainly in the Colchester area, perhaps under royal patronage, though it is still difficult to distinguish imports from native production. Certainly of local production are the distinctive butt-beakers, Camulodunum 113 (a), which were extensively traded over southern and eastern England. The Gallo-Belgic industry continued until about AD 60–70.

*Scales: a, b, c, d—1 : 4; e—1 : 1*

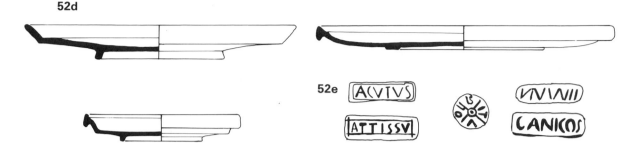

52d

52e

The Rhineland influence is most clearly visible in the pottery, the unusual 'Gallo-Belgic' industry which produced plates imitating Campanian and Arretine wares (black slipped 'terra nigra' and red slipped 'terra rubra'), fine rouletted beakers (butt beakers, girth beakers), and various flagons and flasks all in the Graeco-Roman tradition. The plates often bear the stamps of the potters, and show links with the Mosel, and especially Bavai, a major production centre. Colchester started producing its own versions made by potters doubtless brought in under royal patronage, and their wares reached as far as the Humber and central Hampshire. Amphorae too were imported in large quantities, containing not only wine, but olive oil, and fish paste from southern Spain. Arretine red-gloss wares, which had by now replaced the black Campanian vessels, are also not uncommon at Colchester, but they were increasingly replaced by the developing samian industry of southern France. Colchester was the main, perhaps the only port for this trade in the later periods, and it may well have been 'administered trade' under direct royal control. Not surprisingly British exports on the Rhine are rare, but not unknown, and include enamelled harness equipment from Paillart (Oise), and a bronze mirror from a burial at Nijmegen.

The early rich burials are clustered around St Albans and Braughing, as might be expected from the 'tribute' distribution found in complex chiefdoms. The later ones are more widely scattered from Kent to Cambridgeshire, and are in fact almost on the periphery of the Catuvellaunian kingdom, a pattern which is also found in the early Danish state of the tenth century AD. Gold coins on the other hand show a fairly even distribution, though the bronze is more nucleated in the major centres. If market exchange utilising low value coinage was operating, it only involved the major centres, and had hardly penetrated the countryside. On the fringe of the coin distributions of Cunobelin a number of minor centres appeared—such as Dorchester-on-Thames and Great Chesterford, which could have operated as 'gateway communities' for trade beyond the Catuvellaunian state. Fine pottery certainly travelled beyond the coin distribution.

Around this central state there developed a number of secondary states under kings producing their own inscribed coinage. That of the Dobunni, based in Gloucestershire, was certainly in close contact with the Catuvellauni along the Thames valley, and its oppidum of Bagendon, north of Cirencester, was importing Gallo-Belgic pottery in quantity, and more rarely Arretine and south Gaulish samian. To the south the Atrebates, under their kings Commius, Tincommius and Verica, at times were able to rival the developing Catuvellaunian kingdom, though both the latter are mentioned in the historical sources as petitioning for help from the imperial court at Rome. At the time of the conquest, it was in their kingdom in west Sussex that the Romans found their staunchest allies. The Iceni to the north in East Anglia seem also to have been anti-Catuvellaunian, and later pro-Roman, and before the conquest were relatively isolated from the main trade system. The kingdom of the Brigantes may be a later development, when it formed a client kingdom on the northern fringe of the initial Roman province. Its main centre was at Stanwick, the finest

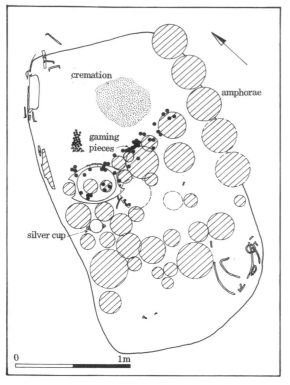

**53a**

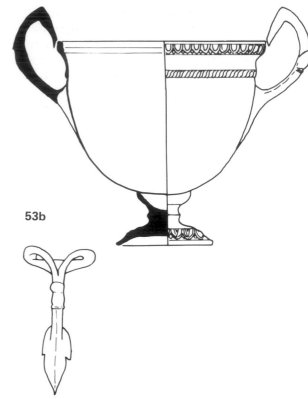

**53b**

**53** Welwyn Garden City

Burials are virtually unknown in the Iron Age in south-eastern England until the first century BC, when cremations similar to those in neighbouring areas of the continent appear. Normally there are between one and four pots in the grave, and the occasional brooch or other personal item. However, there is a group of richer burials which have many more pottery vessels, as well as local luxury items (shale vessels, mirrors, bronze bound buckets and firedogs), as well as imported luxuries (wine amphorae and bronze and silver vessels).

The burial at Welwyn Garden City is the most recently excavated of this rich class (a). It was part of a small cemetery of about a dozen burials, but none of the others had rich gravegoods, though not far away, at Welwyn, two rich graves were found last century. The Welwyn Garden City burial was in a rectangular pit with no trace of any surface mound. It was the cremation of a man of about 35 who had been wearing

a bear skin—the bear's burnt phalanges were found mixed with the human bones.

The imported items included five wine amphorae and a bronze Campanian pan (see fig 41e), and a silver cup of Italian origin similar to one from Welwyn (b). A set of coloured glass gaming pieces may also be an Italian import. There was an iron object which may be the boss of a shield, and several of these rich burials have produced defensive weapons (shields and a corselet) but never offensive weapons.

The earliest of these burials are found in the area of Hertfordshire where the kingdom of the Catuvellauni was developing, but by the late first century BC and early first century AD they are found in a wide arc around the oppidum of Colchester, extending from north Kent to Northamptonshire and Cambridge-shire. They must represent the elite class of the kingdom of Cunobelin.

*Scale: b—1 : 2*

surviving British oppidum enclosing about 330ha, which controlled the major land routes to the north and north-west, while maintaining sea links via the estuary of the Tees. Not only was it importing Gallo-Belgic wares and samian, but also Roman tiles to be used for buildings as yet undiscovered.

Unlike the continental wares in the late La Tène, the importation of foreign luxury goods did not cause the home industry in luxury items to collapse, rather the first century BC and first century AD see the culmination of Insular La Tène Art. Production of fine metalwork, though centred in the eastern kingdoms, is also found in western areas, such as the bronze smiths who produced the beautiful engraved mirrors from Birdlip and Holcombe. Wooden vessels, buckets and handled cups were ornamented with decorated bronze, and one bronze vessel of a type made in western Britain found its way to Poland. Various styles of harness and chariot fittings with simple but effective ornament are found throughout most of the British Isles. Display weapons, especially shields such as that from the Thames at Battersea, demonstrate craftsmanship of the highest order and production of these masterpieces was to continue even after the Roman conquest.

By the time of the Roman conquest, centralised tribal states under kings had become the norm in the east of England. Continental trade may well have been the basis of the power of the elite class, and imported goods and inscribed coinage are largely confined to these areas. Further west and north the hillfort tradition continued, judging from the quality of the native metalwork, under a chiefdom level of society. Though larger tribal entities were recognised, at the time of the Roman conquest these western tribes failed to act as cohesive entities, and among the Durotriges of Dorset, for instance, each hillfort defended itself and fell. Britain by the early first century AD thus presented a patchwork of different social structures, from the centralised state to the low-level chiefdom.

## Germany

The highland area of the German Mittelgebirge,

extending through Hesse, Thuringia, northern Bavaria and into Bohemia, had been one of the areas in which La Tène culture had developed in the fifth century. A number of hillforts, some of very large size, a hundred or more hectares in area, had been established, some extending back into Hallstatt D. Though not as rich as the Hunsrück-Eifel in La Tène A, occasional gold objects or imported bronze vessels turn up in the richer burials. The defended sites, such as the Steinsburg bei Römhild in Thuringia and Závist in Bohemia, were abandoned during La Tène B, and archaeologically they are virtually a blank for two centuries. This was however the earliest area, extending now further eastwards into Moravia, for the foundation of defended oppida at the end of La Tène C, about the middle of the second century BC. Earlier forts like the Steinsburg and Závist were reconstructed, but new sites were also established such as Stradonice. By the early first century BC many of those sites were thriving centres of trade and industry.

Further north, on the North European Plain, a very different settlement pattern and culture had come into existence. Fortified sites were virtually unknown, and those that did exist were small in size. Settlements above the size of villages were unknown, and compared to central Europe industrial organisation was at a low level. The potter's wheel, for instance, was not introduced, though known in adjacent areas. Coinage was not adopted, and imported goods from the Mediterranean only rarely found their way this far north. Burials, where known, contain a minimum of gravegoods—usually no more than a rough urn to contain cremated remains. The economy was basically agricultural, the social level essentially tribal or low-level chiefdoms. By the first century BC these groups, from southern Poland to Jutland, had developed burial rites and a distinctive material culture which distinguishes them from their central European neighbours, and which is usually termed 'Germanic'.

At about the same time this society began to expand. The first evidence is literary—the appearance of the Cimbri and Teutones in central Europe and northern Italy at the end of the second century. Archaeologically it is first detectable in the mid-first century with the brief appearance of northern style burials and pottery in Hesse, and more permanently in northern Bohemia. The chronological details of the next half century are obscure. Some of the oppida in the German Mittelgebirge were abandoned not long after 50 BC, some survived well into the second half of the first century. One site which may have been an early victim was Manching, and its east gate shows evidence of hasty reinforcement. It has been suggested that it was destroyed in the Roman advance in 15–14 BC, but the brooch series ends too early, and elsewhere the Romans tended to support native urban settlements, even in hostile areas. Manching was probably a deserted waste when the Romans arrived. All we possess for the latest La Tène in Bavaria are a few graves with objects which are more Germanic than central European.

The fate of Bohemia is better documented as there is historical evidence to supplement the archaeology. All five oppida were abandoned at about the same time, in the last quarter of the first century BC. In two cases, Závist and Hrazany, the gates had been blocked by clay revetments which were subsequently destroyed by fire. The culture of the oppida was replaced by one of 'Germanic' type with open villages and cremation cemeteries, centred on the agricultural löss soils of northern Bohemia. In 14 BC a Roman army on the upper Main in northern Bavaria had encountered the tribe of Marcomanni. A decade later they were established in Bohemia under their leader Maroboduus. The only discrepancy between the archaeological and historical sources relates to the origin of the Marcomanni—the material culture most closely resembles that of the middle Elbe rather than the Mittelgebirge. Maroboduus was eventually expelled, and spent the rest of his days in notorious debauchery in Aquileia on a pension from the Roman state.

Further east the situation was more complicated. In southern Poland, western Slovakia and northern Hungary, the material culture was essentially the same as central Europe—the same painted wares, graphite vessels, brooch types. Urbanisation, when it appeared, was different. A small defended hillfort acted as the nucleus around which large open industrial settlements developed, as at Budapest. These sites, such as Zemplín and Nitra, controlled the valley routes into the High Tatry of northern Slovakia, a major source of copper, where there had been a rich and flourishing culture in the late Bronze Age. After this nothing is known until the appearance in the first century BC of small hillforts, around which cluster small open settlements. These clusters include ritual sites, with cremated remains and burnt-offerings, such as fragments of central European brooches, and of the now ubiquitous Campanian bronze vessel. Southern Poland was eventually incorporated into the Germanic area, and individual groups spread as far east as Romania. The Zemplín–Budapest sites, however, remained in occupation for some decades after the Roman conquest of Pannonia, and Germanic metalwork penetrated only slowly into the valleys of the Tatry.

The area, however, was finally dominated by a Roman client kingdom under Vannius. The process of differentiation in the Germanic cultures was already underway in the second half of the first century BC, and the early types of Campanian vessels occur sporadically in graves in Poland and northern Germany. Italian traders are mentioned east of the Rhine, though certain tribes such as the Suebi deliberately excluded them, or only traded booty on a tribal basis. At first we seem to be dealing with individual lineages which were acquiring power rather than specific individuals. The cemetery of Gross Romstedt in Thuringia demonstrates this well. On the lower Elbe males and females were buried in separate cemeteries. Gross Romstedt is an all-male cemetery belonging to the end of the first century BC/early first century AD. The gravegoods seem to represent two different status hierarchies. One is military, and some of the objects are clearly symbolic (miniature spears, empty scabbards, fragment of shields), but the top of the hierarchy is represented by a complete set—sword, spear, shield and spur. A second system is represented by more domestic goods, including Campanian bronze vessels. Often individuals have high or low status in both systems, but they do not correspond exactly, and graves rich in domestic goods can be poor in military terms. In

Bohemia and Slovakia this took on a different form with certain cemeteries showing considerably greater wealth in imports than others. In Denmark on the other hand, rich imports turn up in a ritual context or in hoards—the silver cauldron from Gundestrup (from Romania), the bronze cauldron from Brå or the wagons from Dejbjerg, both of central European origin, and it is in such contexts that the Campanian bronzes make their appearance.

The move to the Danube frontier proved a major stimulus to this trade, and eventually, in the mid-first century AD, had led to the establishment of small scale chiefdoms in certain areas, not only along the frontier, but in northern Germany and Denmark. Bronze vessels, and especially Roman republican silver coins were the main items traded, but the elite class, characterised by the rich graves of Lübsow type, also contain silver vessels and glassware, as well as gold and silver objects of more local origin. But beyond this the process of centralisation did not go. Even by the end of the late Roman period, hillforts which might act as centres of production were virtually unknown, and urbanism in any form did not appear until the ninth or tenth century AD.

## The impact of conquest

The effect of the imposition of Roman power varied both with time and place. The experiences of previous conquests, the increasing professionalisation of the army, and to a lesser extent the administration, meant that the invaders entered with a preconceived model of what was required. This was certainly so in Britain, where by this time the layout of the fort was becoming fairly stereotyped, though with subtle differences which might allow one to distinguish, for instance, a fort of Agricola from one of Severus. But when we turn to Gaul only a few of Caesar's camps are recognisable, and in small scale excavations in urban contexts, buildings such as barrack blocks even on more permanent bases may not be so readily identifiable as on later British sites. The problems become greater with earlier conquests, as layout of forts, their distribution, even their existence become less predictable. Thus the conquest of Britain can be reconstructed in considerable detail from the archaeology; that of southern France not at all.

The Romans also imposed their ideas of civilisation upon the conquered. Not only did urbanism have to be introduced into areas where none had existed before, but even in areas of advanced culture the settlement pattern eventually had to conform to Roman administrative needs. Old towns were abandoned, new ones founded. This had no connection with previous enmity or assistance—in no case, to my knowledge, was a hostile population removed from a defended town. Witness how Alesia, scene of the final defeat of the Gallic rebellion in 52 BC developed as a major Roman town, whereas Bibracte, capital of Rome's allies the Aedui, was abandoned within a couple of generations, for Autun (Augustodunum), a few miles away.

If we consider Roman priorities in newly conquered territory, the first would be to impose adequate military control. This would involve establishing a hierarchy of sites, with an administrative centre preferably as close to Rome as possible, but in touch with the major military bases. These legionary bases needed to be spread around at key points, but sufficiently close to each other for mutual support if necessary. Lines of communications needed to be secured by subsidiary forts, controlling ports and river crossings. In Britain it was this initial military requirement that virtually dictated the civilian settlement pattern in south-eastern England. Settlements were established outside the forts, but when the military moved on the civilians often stayed.

This process was accelerated by the second need—a fast and efficient means of communication. For this roads were constructed from one nodal point to the next, deflected only by problems of terrain, such as river crossings. In this process native settlements were ignored, and even major centres of population by-passed. Southern Tuscany provides the most instructive example. The towns of Etruria possessed an antiquity and prestige equal to that of Rome herself, and had served as market and administrative centres each with their own radiating network of roads. In the third century BC the developing needs of the

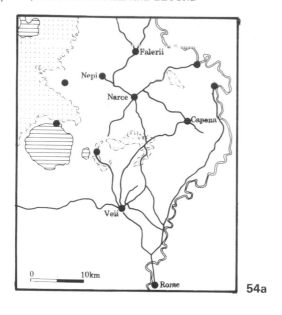

54a

54b

**54 The Roman impact on southern Etruria**

The effect of the administrative needs of the developing Roman Empire are clearly visible immediately north of Rome. In the seventh–sixth centuries (a) a number of defended settlements such as Veii, Falerii, Narce, and Rome itself were developing as service centres for their surrounding countryside. They were also interlinked with one another, but only by winding cross-country routes. During this period many of these service roads were improved by providing paved surfaces and by the construction of cuttings, and doubtless bridges.

As Rome gradually conquered Etruria in the fourth and third centuries, speed of communication between centres, and especially with Rome itself, became paramount. The earlier routes, the Amerina to Nepi and the Clodia, were mainly improved and straightened service roads, but by the end of the third century fast long-distance routes were being established. The Amerina was extended probably in 241 for access to Umbria, and Falerii Novi was founded on it, replacing the old less accessible centre.

In 220, with the conquest of the Faliscan area, the Via Flaminia was established, the main long-distance route to Rimini and the Adriatic, and probably in 154 BC the Via Cassia, which led to northern Italy via Arrezzo. The new roads chose the most direct routes, and Veii for instance was completely by-passed. By AD 100 (b) former centres such as Falerii and Narce had been abandoned as new centres developed on the main routes, while Veii, though still occupied, was declining, and was itself finally abandoned in the fourth century AD.

Roman Empire demanded a network of fast straight roads radiating from Rome. Many of the Etruscan towns were by-passed. Some were actually refounded at nodal points on the road system like Falerii Novi. The ancient town of Veii, on the other hand, continued to act as a market centre, but gradually faded away, and was finally abandoned in the late Roman period. Britain provides similar examples. The native settlements at Canterbury and Leicester developed into Roman towns as they lay at natural strategic points. St Albans merely changed its focus to the area around the ford over the Ver where the Roman fort had been established. Bagendon was abandoned for Cirencester, Maiden Castle for Dorchester, both new sites alongside Roman forts. This basic re-orientation of urban settlement pattern to the needs of Empire in Etruria took about 200 years, in central France about half a century, in south-eastern England it was achieved within a couple of decades.

From a geographer's point of view this imposition of the road system brought changes in the types of central place system operating. The oppida and early towns in Tuscany, in central France and south-east England, all equate more or less to the 'solar central system': large central places which held monopolies for their territories in providing services. In Tuscany this system had already started to change, and the appearance of secondary centres around the main sites provided a competitive system on Christaller's 'marketing principle'. With the imposition of the road pattern in southern England, this produced a competitive system based on the 'transport principle'. The development of the lower-level central places was encouraged by military and administrative needs: an early network of minor forts replaced by posting stages for official travellers, often at crossroads which could develop into minor towns.

The Romans also attempted to impose their concept of social organisation upon the conquered—a landowning 'senatorial' group, a rich merchant and industrial class of 'equites', a free class of artisans and retailers, peasant agricultural communities and a slave class. The landowning elite was the key to successful administration of the towns and it was encouraged to participate in urban life—a contrast with medieval towns which were run by the merchant classes. This elite was already in existence in societies which had already achieved some form of state organisation. At Mont Beuvray their stone-built courtyard houses are identifiable within a decade or two of the conquest, and these probably had timber predecessors. In chiefdom societies, the change from power based in lineage to one based on landownership probably represented no great difficulty, given official encouragement. Areas such as Wales, northern England or northern Gaul, where less potential existed for creating such a class, often remained under direct military control.

It was in the second and third classes, those of merchants and artisans, that the greatest adjustment had to be made. The artisan quarters at Mont Beuvray and Manching suggest generally that they suffered a lowly status, and some might even be under direct elite control. The houses are minute, with minimal storage facilities, and con-

trast strongly with the artisan and traders quarters at the Auerberg, a hill-top Roman trading centre founded in southern Germany at the beginning of the first century AD. It is possible that a merchant class did not even exist in Gallic society, as all the evidence suggests that the profitable foreign trade was in Italian hands even before the conquest. But the trading class was of necessity mobile, and this gap in society was generally filled by outsiders until native society was able to develop.

The extent to which the countryside became fully integrated with the imperial economy also varied considerably. At one end of the scale there is the rapid development of the estates with palatial country houses of the Somme valley, at the other, in a not dissimilar landscape, the peasant farms of the chalk wolds of eastern Yorkshire. This difference has often been simplified into native resistance or acceptance of Romanisation, but it is more likely to be connected with the social structure and rights of land tenure of the indigenous population. Roman archaeologists have tended to lump the natives into broad categories, without investigating the subtle differences in pre-existing patterns which dictated subsequent development.

The outward trappings of Roman life, its material culture, were quickly adopted within the limits of each society to accept and afford them. Over much of Temperate Europe trade had already dulled the taste of the elite classes by supplying them with the generally boring mass-produced metalwork of the classical world. The products of late La Tène industry showed even greater poverty of innovation, and only Britain could offer something that was different, exciting and a challenge to Roman taste. But even the Insular Art of the mirrors and shields faltered within a generation before the onslaught of Roman provincial art. Technically the Italian bronze vessels were superior to anything available locally. In the realms of stone and bronze sculpture, increasingly used in religious and official contexts, there was virtually no Celtic tradition, and almost all the figures that grace books on 'Celtic art' are either not Celtic, or of Roman date.

55a

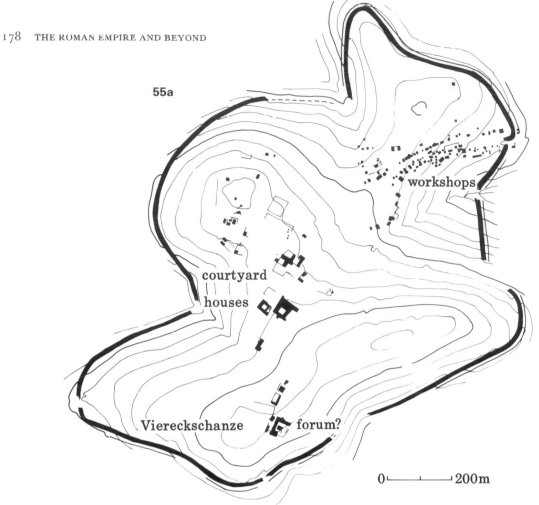

workshops

courtyard

houses

Viereckschanze      forum?

0 ⊢――┴――⊣ 200m

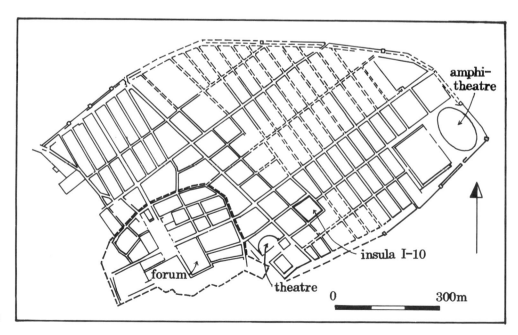

amphi-
theatre

insula I-10

forum

theatre

0 ――――――――― 300m

55b

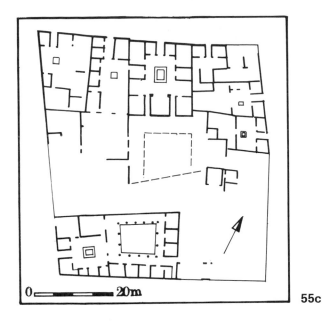

0 ————— 20m

**55c**

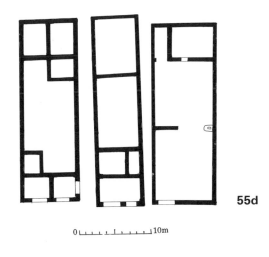

0 �⌊⌊⌊⌊⌊⌊⌊⌊⌊ 10m

**55d**

**55** Iron Age and Roman towns

Pre-Roman oppida on the continent shared much in common with their Mediterranean counterparts, and at the time of the Roman conquest, the Romans had few problems in imposing their system on the native pattern. In some cases there was even a grid-system of streets, as at Villeneuve-St Germain (fig 46), which need only be provided with paved surfaces, as on the Titelberg in Luxembourg. In others there was no such regularity, as at Mont Beuvray, the ancient Bibracte (a). Here the stone built Roman houses are scattered with no regular system throughout the enclosed area. None the less there are similarities. The small workshops cluster along the main thoroughfare, the elite courtyard houses lie in more secluded areas, away from the hustle and bustle.

Generally the public buildings are at the furthest point from the entrance. In Roman towns with gates on all sides, this usually means the centre of the town, but at Mont Beuvray, with only one entrance, the public buildings are at one end of the site. At Pompeii (b) they are also displaced, but this is because of the complex history of a site which had expanded in size. The forum lay in the centre of the older area.

Similarity of outer form may, however, mask major differences in function. Iron Age oppida tend to be larger than their Roman counterparts. In Britain this is because the settlement is not strongly nucleated, for instance at Colchester (fig 51a), but this is not true of the continental sites. Manching was much larger than for instance Roman London. Though the former may have had some open spaces, and the latter may have had suburbs, the density of Manching houses suggests it may have had a larger population than Londinium. This may be due to a less developed urban system, in which only major centres existed, and no secondary urban centres to compete with them as occurred in the Roman period.

In Roman towns courtyard houses (c) were occupied by the land-owning elite, and rich merchants, though at Pompeii in the first century AD the landowners start drifting towards their country estates, a trend that became marked in Britain in the fourth century AD. The equivalent structures on the oppida are palisaded enclosures (fig 46), though these show more industrial activity than the classical courtyard houses. This suggests a different organisation of trade and industry, and it may also be reflected in the size of artisan houses. On oppida they tend to be small (fig 46), in Roman towns they have spacious living and storage facilities (d). The status and wealth of the Roman artisan and trader seem to be very different from their Iron Age counterparts..

In pottery styles we can detect a distinctive change, as the Mediterranean range of vessels contrasted with those of Temperate Europe. Bowls and pedestal jar were replaced by plates, jugs and two-handled flasks which carry implications not only of eating habits but of cuisine as well. The Gallo-Belgic pottery industry, with its emphasis on platters, was not merely a revolution in standards and scale of production, but of domestic life as well. In central France, where imitation of Campanian plates started early, and in south-eastern England with its Gallo-Belgic wares, the Roman invasion merely reinforced a trend that had already started. In northern Gaul the change occurred a generation after the conquest, and the spread was by diffusion rather than invasion. The rise of the samian industry in Italy and Gaul brought this Mediterranean style to Wales and northern England, to the limits of the Empire, in areas where pottery had not been in regular use during the Iron Age.

The impact on industry is less easy to measure. Metal and stone extraction were Roman state monopolies, and in Britain, for instance, within a decade the army was involved in lead and silver extraction in the Mendips, and doubtless there was a similar take-over of the iron industry.

Industrially the army was probably less influential—of necessity it was largely self-supporting for its metallurgical requirements and technologically the Romans had little to offer the native industries. It did, however, rely considerably on native pottery, where possible using established potteries, even where this meant long-distance transportation. As late as the second century Hadrian's Wall relied on central France for its fine samian ware, and southern Britain, especially Dorset, for its cooking pots. The textile and leather industries must have received similar financial stimulus. But only in peripheral areas is production likely to have increased noticeably, with the centralisation and rationalisation of artisan production.

Almost universally, however, the imposition of Empire produced a rise in living standards. Peace was imposed, with access to a wider, international market. Standards of housing improved for all classes, not just the ostentatious elite with their hypocausts, mosaics and painted wall plaster. Social differentiation was encouraged and increased, but the artisan class saw a comparable rise in their status and opportunities, and in the long term, it was perhaps only the rural peasantry who suffered. Defeat has its compensations.

# Notes and bibliography

This bibliography makes no pretence to list even all the major works on any topic. Rather it acts as a pointer to the sources of some of the ideas expressed, to useful syntheses, or to the more accessible English articles.

## 1 Attitudes to the Past

*Introduction*

The origin and impact of the 'Three Age System' and subsequent events in Scandinavian and British archaeology are discussed in:

G. Daniel *A Hundred and Fifty Years of Archaeology* London 1975

The Kossinna school of Germanic archaeology is effectively attacked in:

H. J. Eggars *Einführung in die Vorgeschichte* Munich 1959

The major essays by Marshall Sahlins demonstrating the general lack of labour and productivity in simple societies are to be found in:

M. Sahlins *Stone Age Economics* London 1972

A background to the changing conceptual framework of the 1960s, especially the idea of 'independent invention' and its impact on British prehistory:

A. C. Renfrew *Before Civilization* London 1973

*Diffusion*

The extreme form of hyperdiffusion is:

W. J. Perry *The Growth of Civilization* London 1924

Despite the obviously racist nature of the theory, it still unhappily appears without discussion of even the factual framework in such popular works as:

T. Heyerdahl *The Ra Expeditions* London 1971

Examples of west-east diffusion are discussed below in Chapters 4 and 7.

*Trade*

The original fundamental work on exchange, studying the obligations and motivation of giving, receiving and reciprocating is:

M. Mauss 'Essai sur le don: forme et raison d'échange dans les sociétés archaïques' in *L'Année Sociologique* 1923–4, and published in English as *The Gift* London 1954

An equally influential book of the same period studying the Kula ring of the Trobriand Islanders was:

B. Malinowsky *Argonauts of the Western Pacific* London 1922

The development of the 'substantivist' as against the 'formalist' school of economics was propounded in a series of papers in:

K. Polanyi, C. Arensburg and H. W. Pearson (eds.) *Trade and Market in the Early Empires* Glencoe 1957

and is further discussed by Sahlins in *Stone Age Economics*.

A more marxist approach to production and exchange can be found in the writings of C. Meillassoux, including the concept of 'Prestige Goods Economics' which has influenced a number of writers on Iron Age Europe. The various types of trade (down-the-line, directed, etc.) and their identification in the archaeological record are described by:

A. C. Renfrew 'Trade as action at a distance: questions of integration and communication' in J. Sabloff and C. C. Lamberg-Karlovsky (eds.) *Ancient Civilization and Trade* Albuquerque (1975) 3–59

*Social structure*

The three most influential recent volumes on social organisation are:

E. R. Service *Primitive Social Organisation* New York 1962

E. R. Service *The Origins of State and Civilisation* New York 1975

M. Fried *The Evolution of Political Society* New York 1967

Interest in burial rites was mainly stimulated by such works as:
J. A. Brown (ed.) *Approaches to the Social Dimensions of Mortuary Practices* Society for American Archaeology Memoir No. 25, 1971
This included:
L. Binford 'Mortuary practices: their study and their potential', reprinted in L. Binford *An Archaeological Perspective* New York (1972) 208–243

A recent series of papers on interpretation of burials is:
R. Chapman, I. Kinnes and K. Randsborg (eds.) *The Archaeology of Death* Cambridge 1981

The 'potlatch', a word taken over from the American Indians of the north west coast, signifies the deliberate destruction of wealth for social advancement. Examples of these societies, the Nootka and Kwakiutl, are described in:
C. Daryll Forde *Habitat Economy and Society*, 8th Ed. London 1963

*Spatial organisation*
The two geographical works most influential on archaeology published in the 1960s were:
P. Haggett *Locational Analysis in Human Geography* London 1965
M. Chisholm *Rural Settlement and Land Use* London 1962

The former was a source book for recent developments in quantitative and theoretical geography, including the German school of Christaller and Lösch which developed 'Central Place Theory'. Chisholm revived the theories of the nineteenth-century German agrarian writer von Thünen, which inspired the archaeological field method of 'Site Catchment Analysis'. The influence of geography on anthropological analysis of third world and historical economics produced the important publication:
Carole A. Smith (ed.) *Regional Analysis* London 1976, and her own contribution, 'Exchange systems and the spatial distribution of elites: the organisation of stratification in agrarian

societies' 309–374, has had a major influence on my own approach to the Iron Age. Other interesting spatial models have been developed from archaeological data by:
V. Steponaitis 'Location theory and complex chiefdoms: a Mississippian example', in Bruce Smith ed. *Mississippian Settlement Patterns* New York (1978) 417–453
K. Randsborg *The Viking Age in Denmark: the formation of a state* London 1980

I have developed models for studying the impact of a move to defensive sites in an Iron Age context:
J. Collis 'A theoretical study of hill-forts' in G. Guilbert (ed.) *Hill-fort studies: papers presented to Dr. A. H. A. Hogg* Leicester (1981) 66–76
J. Collis 'Gradual growth and sudden change: urbanisation in temperate Europe', in A. C. Renfrew and S. J. Shennan (eds.) *Ranking, Resource and Exchange: aspects of the archaeology of early European society* Cambridge 1982

For consideration of post-Roman developments which hold some interesting parallels for the Iron Age see:
R. Hodges *Dark Age Economics: the origins of towns and trade AD 600–1000* London 1982

An interesting if controversial application of Christaller's 'Central Place Theory' is:
I. Hodder and M. Hassall 'The non-random spacing of Romano-British walled towns' *Man* New series 6 (1971) 391–407

For the nature and spatial layout of urban sites the seminal study is:
G. Sjoberg *The Pre-industrial City, past and present* New York 1960

Alternative models are to be found in:
J. E. Vance 'Land assignment in the pre-capitalist and post-capitalist city', *Economic Geography* 47 (1971) 101–120
J. Langton 'Residential patterns in pre-industrial cities', *Transactions of the Institute of British Geographers* 65 (1975) 1–27

*Chronology*
The most accessible source for the chronology of early Iron Age Greece is:
A. M. Snodgrass *The Dark Age of Greece* Edinburgh 1971

The chronology for Bronze Age Europe is developed in:

H. Müller-Karpe *Beiträge zur Chronologie der Urnenfelderzeit nördlich und südlich der Alpen* Berlin 1959

and for Hallstatt C and D:

G. Kossack *Südbayern während der Hallstattzeit* Berlin 1959

The major historical and modern sources for La Tène chronology are:

H. Hildebrand 'Sur les commencements de l'âge du fer en Europe' *Congrès Internationale d'Anthropologie et d'Archéologie Préhistorique*, Stockholm, Band 2, (1874) 592

O. Tischler 'Ueber Gliederung der La Tène-Period und über die Dekorirung der Eisenwaffen in dieser Zeit' *Correspondenz-Blatt der deutschen Gesellschaft für Anthropologie, Ethnologie und Urgeschichte* 16–11 (1885) 157–161

P. Reinecke *Mainzer Aufsätze zur Chronologie der Bronze- und Eisenzeit* Bonn 1965, a collection of all his important papers from before the First World War

F. R. Hodson *The La Tène Cemetery at Münsingen-Rain* Bern 1968

J. R. Collis *Defended Sites of the Late La Tène*, British Archaeological Reports, Supplementary Series 2 Oxford 1975

Recent developments and results of dendrochronology are discussed in:

M. Baillie *Tree Ring Dating and Archaeology* London 1983

E. Hollstein *Mitteleuropäische Eichenchronologie* Mainz 1980

## 2 The Old Order

A detailed if undigestible factual account of the European Bronze Age with extensive bibliography is:

J. M. Coles and A. F. Harding *The Bronze Age in Europe* London 1979

The development of late Bronze Age sword types is discussed by:

J. D. Cowen 'Eine Einführung in die Geschichte der bronzen Griffzungenschwerter in Suddeutschland und den angrenzenden Gebieten'

in *Bericht der römisch-germanischen Kommission* 36 (1955) 52–155

*The origin of iron working*

Useful sources on the technology of iron work are:

H. H. Coghlan *Notes on Prehistoric and Early Iron in the Old World*. Pitt Rivers Museum Occasional Papers on Technology 8 Oxford 1956

R. F. Tylecote *Metallurgy in Archaeology* London 1962

R. Pleiner *Iron Working in Ancient Greece* Prague 1969

On the production of sword blades in the Alps in middle-late La Tène see:

R. Wyss 'Belege zur keltischen Schwertschmiedekunst' in *Provincialia Festschrift für Rudolf Laur-Belart* Basel/Stuttgart (1969) 664–681

The finds from Alaca Hüyük and other early finds of iron in Anatolia including Kültepe and the Hittites are most accessibly published in:

Seton Lloyd *Early Highland Peoples of Anatolia* London 1967

C. Burney and D. M. Lang *The People of the Hills* London 1971

O. Gurney *The Hittites* (revised edition) Harmondsworth 1962

Information on the early finds in Europe:

B. Stjernquist *Simris II: bronze age problems in the light of the Simris excavation* Bonn/Lund 1961

J. Vladar 'Osteuropäische und mediterrane Einflüsse im Gebiet der Slowakei während der Bronzezeit' *Slovenská Archeologia* 21 (1973) 253–257

*The end of Mycenaean Greece*

General books on Greece are mentioned in the notes on the Proto-Geometric section below. The possibilities of invasion are discussed in:

V. R. d'A. Desborough *The last Myceneans and their Successors* London 1964

The case for a climatic cause of the collapse of Mycenaean civilisation is made by:

Rhys Carpenter *Discontinuity in Greek History* Cambridge 1965

A published example of a regional survey showing the lack of 'Dark Age' sites is:

W. A. McDonald and G. Rapp *The Minesota Messenia Expedition: reconstructing a bronze age regional environment* Minneapolis 1972

For Mycenaean trading sites on the Italian coast:
R. Whitehouse, 'The earliest towns in peninsular Italy' in A. C. Renfrew (ed.) *The Explanation of Culture Change* London (1973) 617–624

*Iron working in Greece and Proto-Geometric Greece*
The most comprehensive survey of Greece in this period and the Geometric period, with good critical awareness is:
A. M. Snodgrass *The Dark Age of Greece* Edinburgh 1971
V. Desborough *The Greek Dark Ages* London 1972 gives a more traditional view

*Late Bronze Age Europe*
The main source of information is again:
J. M. Coles and A. F. Harding *The Bronze Age in Europe* London 1979

Additional sources used are:
D. Longley and S. Needham 'Egham: a late bronze age settlement and waterfront' *Current Archaeology* 68 (1979) 262–267 deals with Runnymede
F. E. Barth 'Das prähistorische Hallstatt: Bergbau und Gräberfeld', in D. Straub (ed.) *Die Hallstattkultur: Frühform europäischer Einheit* Linz (1980) 67–79

# 3 Reawakening in the East

*The ninth century*
The three main general books on the Geometric period in Greece are:
A. M. Snodgrass *The Dark Age of Greece* Edinburgh 1971
V. Desborough *The Greek Dark Ages* London 1972
N. Coldstream *Geometric Greece* London 1977

For Lefkandi see:
M. P. Popham and L. H. Sackett *Lefkandi I: The Iron Age: the settlement* London 1980

The potential for southern Euboea as an early centre of iron working is discussed in:
S. C. Backhuizen Greek steel *World Archaeology* 9 (1977) 220–234

Books on the Phoenicians are:
D. B. Harden *The Phoenicians* London 1962
S. Moscati *The World of the Phoenicians* London 1968
V. Karageorghis *Kition: Mycenean and Phoenician discoveries in Cyprus* London 1976

*Greece and Cyprus in the eighth century*
The best general book on Urartu is:
B. Piotrovsky *Urartu* London 1969

Most books concentrate on the art and artefacts:
B. Piotrovsky *Urartu, the Kingdom of Van and its Art* London 1967
G. Azarpay *Urartian Art and Artefacts* Berkley 1968
M. N. van Loon *Urartian Art* Istanbul 1966

The burials at Salamis have been published in a series of monographs by the excavator V. Karageorghis, but he has also written a more general overview:
V. Karageorghis *Salamis* London 1969

*Italy in the eighth century*
The most recent general synopsis as well as information on Quattro Fontanili are the papers in:
D. Ridgway and F. R. Ridgway *Italy before the Romans: the iron age, orientalizing and Etruscan periods* London, New York, San Francisco 1979

# 4 The Trade Explosion

*Greece in the seventh century*
The two general sources for Archaic Greece are:
A. M. Snodgrass *Archaic Greece: the age of experiment* London 1980
L. H. Jeffery *Archaic Greece: the city states c. 700–500 BC* London 1976

The most accessible sources on Greek colonisation are:
T. J. Dunbabin *The Western Greeks* Oxford 1948
T. J. Dunbabin *The Greeks and their Eastern Neighbours* London 1957
J. Boardman *The Greeks Overseas* Harmondsworth 1964
J. M. Cook *The Greeks in Ionia and the East* London 1962

A. G. Woodhead *The Greeks in the West* London 1962

*Etruscan civilisation*
General books on the Etruscans are:
D. Strong *The Early Etruscans* New York 1968
R. Bloch *The Etruscans* London 1968
H. Hencken *Tarquinia and Etruscan Origins* London 1968
For early Rome there is a series of monographs by E. Gjerstad, though he places too much ethnic significance on pottery styles. For an introduction there is:
R. Bloch *The Origins of Rome* London 1960

More specialised reports or illustrations of orientalising grave finds and sites:
H. Hencken *Tarquinia, Villanovans and Early Etruscans* Cambridge, Mass 1968
L. Parelia *La Tomba Regolini Galassi del Museo Gregoriani Etrusco La Civilta nell' Italia centrale nel se. VII v.c.* Rome 1947
P. Romanelli *Palestrina* Naples 1977
G. Camporeale *Tombe del Duce* Firenze 1967
J. B. Ward Perkins 'Veii: the historical topography of the ancient city', *Papers of the British School at Rome* 16 (1961) 1–23

*Situla Art*
*The two major sources on Situla Art are:*
W. Lucke and O. H. Frey *Die Situla in Providence, Rhode Island* Berlin 1962
O. H. Frey *Die Entstehung der Situlenkunst* Berlin 1969

Other sources, giving a more general background are:
L. H. Barfield *Northern Italy before Rome* London 1971
J. V. S. Megaw *Art of the European Iron Age* London 1970.
Catalogue for the Internationaler Ausstellung Situlenkunst, Vienna 1962 *Situlenkunst zwischen Po und Donau*

*Central and western Europe in the seventh century*
There is no general source dealing with Hallstatt C, only a number of regional studies and site reports, some of which are quoted here:

G. Kossack *Südbayern während der Hallstattzeit* Berlin 1959
G. Kossack *Gräberfelder der Hallstattzeit am Main und frankische Saale* Kallmunz 1970
G. Kromer *Das Gräberfeld von Hallstatt* Firenze 1959
F. E. Barth 'Das prähistorische Hallstatt: Bergbau und Gräberfeld' in D. Straub (ed.) *Die Hallstattkultur: Frühform europäischer Einheit* Linz (1980) 67–79
R. Pittioni *Urgeschichte des österreichisches Raumes* Vienna 1954, for Alpine sites such as Klein Klein
E. & J. Neustupny *Czechoslovakia* London 1961
J. Alexander *Yugoslavia* London 1972
Drawings of the hoard from Llyn Fawr can be found in:
W. F. Grimes *The Prehistory of Wales* Cardiff 1951
Reviews of British beaten bronze metalwork and its continental affinities are dealt with by:
C. F. C. Hawkes and M. A. Smith 'On some buckets and cauldrons of the Bronze and Early Iron Ages' *Antiquaries Journal* 37 (1957) 131–198
J. M. Coles 'European bronze age shields' *Proceedings of the Prehistoric Society* 28 (1962) 156–190

*Hallstatt D*
T. Talbot Rice *The Scythians* London 1957 deals generally with the Scythians including the Hungarian finds.
S. I. Rudenko *The Frozen Tombs of Siberia* London 1970 shows the wealth of organic materials not normally preserved in the rich Iron Age tombs.

General books and articles discussing the nature of the relationship between southwest Germany and the Mediterranean are:
W. Kimmig 'Early Celts on the Upper Danube' in R. L. Bruce-Mitford (ed.) *Recent Archaeological Excavations in Europe* (1975) 32–64
W. Kimmig *Die Heuneburg an der oberen Donau,* Tübingen 1978
F. Fischer 'ΚΕΙΜΗΛΙΑ: Bemerkungen zur kulturgeschichtlichen' Interpretation des sogenann-

ten südimports in der späten Hallstatt-und frühen Latènekultur des westlichen Mitteleuropa' *Germania* 51 (1973) 436–459.

S. Frankenstein and M. J. Rowlands 'The internal structure and regional context of early iron age society in south west Germany' *Institute of Archaeology, London, Bulletin* 15 (1978) 73–112

P. S. Wells *Culture Contact and Culture Change* Cambridge 1981

Articles and books on specific sites are:

G. Riek *Der Hohmichele: ein Fürstengrabhugel der späten Hallstattzeit bei der Heuneburg* Berlin 1962

H. Zürn An anthropological Hallstatt stele (Hirschlanden) *Antiquity* 38 (1964) 224–6

H. Zürn *Hallstattforschungen in Nordwürttemberg Stuttgart 1970* (Hirschlanden, Grafenbühl, Mühlacker)

K. Spindler *Magdalenenberg: der hallstattzeitliche Fürstengrabhügel bei Villingen* vols 1–6 Villingen-Schwenningen 1971–1980

J. Biel 'The late Hallstatt chieftain's grave at Hochdorf', *Antiquity* 55 (1981) 16–18

R. Joffroy *L'Oppidum de Vix et la Civilisation Hallstattienne Finale dans l'Est de la France* Dijon 1960

R. Joffroy *Le Trèsor de Vix* Paris 1962

A. van Doorselaer 'Resultaten van zes opgravingscampaynes op de Kemmelberg' *Archaeologia Belgica* 161 (1974)

One of the most provocative and stimulating essays on Hallstatt D, but one with which I do not totally agree is:

L. Pauli Untersuchungen zur späthallstattkultur in Nordwürttemberg *Hamburger Beiträge* 2–1 (1972) 1–166

## 5 The Tide Turns, 500–250 BC

*The classical world of Greece*
A recent general view of the development of Athenian coinage is:

K. Rutter 'Early Greek coinage and the influence of the Athenian state' in B. Cunliffe (ed.) *Coinage and Society in Britain and Gaul: some current problems* London (1981) 1–9

The development of market exchange is discussed in:

K. Polanyi 'Aristotle discovers the economy' in K. Polanyi, C. Arensburg and H. W. Pearson (eds.) *Trade and Market in the Early Empires* Glencoe (1957) 64–94

*The classical world of Italy and northern Italy and southern France*
The main sources have been quoted in Chapter 4. The major synthesis on the countryside is:

T. W. Potter *The Changing Landscape of South Etruria* London 1972

The evidence for Etruscan towns is summarised in:

F. Coarelli (ed.) *Etruscan Cities* London 1975

For southern France there is no general book of synthesis, but there is a large number of articles on individual sites. Some of the key articles and books are:

P. A. Fevrier 'The origin and growth of the cities of southern Gaul' *Journal of Roman Studies* 63 (1973)

M. Louis, O. Taffanel and J. Taffanel *Le Premier Age du Fer Languedocien* Bordighera 1960 (for Cayla de Mailhac)

F. Benoit 'Fouilles d'Entremont 1946–1967' *Gallia* 26 (1968) 1–31

J. Jannoray *Ensérune* Paris 1955

H. Rolland *Fouilles de Glanum* Paris 1946, 1958

H. Rolland *Fouilles de Sainte Blaise* Paris 1951, 1956

*Orientalising in central Europe—La Tène A*
Regional studies of the Hunsrück-Eifel culture are:

A. Haffner *Die westliche Hunsrück-Eifel-Kultur* Berlin 1976

H. E. Joachim *Die Hunsrück-Eifel-Kultur am Mittelrhein* Köln 1968

For the only rich grave excavated recently:

J. Keller *Das keltische Fürstengrab von Reinheim* Mainz 1965

For the relationship to metal resources:

J. Driehaus 'Fürstengräber und Eisenerze, Mittelrhein, Mosel und Saar' *Germania* 43 (1965) 42–49

The two major hillfort excavations are:
G. Riek 'Ein Fletthaus der Wende ältere-jüngere Hunsrück-Eifel-Kultur bei Befort, Luxemburg' *Germania* 26 (1942) 26–34
R. Schindler 'Die Altburg bei Befort in Luxemburg' *Hémecht* 21 (1969) 37–50
R. Schindler *Die Altburg von Bundenbach* Mainz 1977

The Dürrnberg excavations are published in:
E. Penninger *Der Dürrnberg bei Hallein I* Munich 1972
F. Moosleitner, L. Pauli and E. Penninger *Der Dürrnberg bei Hallein II* Munich 1974

The major books and articles on La Tène Art are:
P. Jacobsthal *Early Celtic Art* Oxford 1944
J. V. S. Megaw *Art of the European Iron Age: a study of the elusive image* Bath 1970
M. Lenerz de Wilde *Zirkelornametik in der Kunst der Latènezeit* Munich 1977
O. H. Frey and F. Schwappach 'Studies in early Celtic design' *World Archaeology* 4 (1973) 339–356

*La Tène B–C—the age of migration*
The major study for central Europe is:
J. Filip *Keltové ve středni Evropě* Prague 1956
Some of the content is summarised in his useful popularising account:
J. Filip *Celtic Civilisation and its Heritage* Prague 1978 (2nd ed.)
A synthesis of La Tène burial rites is provided by:
H. Lorenz 'Totenbrauchtum und Tracht: Untersuchungen zur regionalen Gliederung in der frühen Latènezeit' *Bericht der Römisch—Germanischen Kommission* 59 (1978) 3–378
F. R. Hodson *The La Tène Cemetery at Münsingen—Rain* Bern 1968

For Waldalgesheim and the disputed origin of Waldalgesheim style:
J. Driehaus 'Zum Grabfund von Waldalgesheim' *Hamburger Beiträge zur Archäologie* 1–2 (1971) 101–113
C. Peyre 'Y a-t-il un contexte italique au style de Waldalgesheim?' in P.-M. Duval and V. Kruta (eds.) *L'Art Celtique de la Periode d'Expansion, IVᵉ et IIIᵉ siècles avant notre ère* Geneva/Paris 1982

O. H. Frey 'Du premier style au style de Waldalgesheim: remarques sur l'evolution de l'art celtique ancient', in P. M. Duval and C. F. C. Hawkes (eds.) *Celtic Art in Ancient Europe* (1976) 141–163

For the sword styles and the site of La Tène itself:
J. M. de Navarro *The Finds from the Site of La Tène—I. Scabbards and the swords found in them* London 1972

## 6 The Economic Revival

For the Campanian pottery and bronze industries:
J.-P. Morel *Céramique Campanienne: Les formes* Rome 1981
J. Werner 'Zur Bronzekanne von Kelheim. Rückblick und Ausblick' *Bayerische Vorgeschichtsblätter* 43 (1978) 1–18
D. P. S. Peacock 'Roman amphorae in pre-Roman Britain', in J. Jesson and D. Hill (eds.) *The Iron Age and its Hill-Forts* Southampton (1971) 161–188
D. P. S. Peacock 'Recent discoveries of Roman amphora kilns in Italy' *Antiquaries Journal* 57 (1977) 262–269

The period La Tène C and La Tène D is summarised in:
J. R. Collis *Oppida: Earliest towns north of the Alps* Sheffield 1984

## 7 The Roman Empire and Beyond

For Roman frontier policy in Germany, and archaeological evidence for the Rhine frontier:
C. M. Wells *The German Policy of Augustus* Oxford 1972
H. Schönberger 'The Roman Frontier in Germany: an archaeological survey' *Journal of Roman Studies* 59 (1969) 144–197

For general summary of the British Iron Age:
B. W. Cunliffe *Iron Age Communities in Britain* London, Henley and Boston 1978 (2nd ed.)
T. C. Champion 'The iron age: southern Britain and Ireland' in J. V. S. Megaw and D. D. A. Simpson (eds.) *Introduction to British Prehistory* Leicester (1979) 344–445

For major sites:

B. W. Cunliffe *Danebury: Anatomy of an Iron Age Hillfort* London 1983

B. W. Cunliffe *Hengistbury Head* London 1978

J. R. Collis *Oppida: Earliest towns north of the Alps* Sheffield 1984

C. F. C. Hawkes and M. R. Hull *Camulodunum* Oxford 1947

C. Partridge *Skeleton Green* Britannia Monograph Series No. 2, London 1981 (for Braughing)

The burial rites are discussed by:

J. R. Collis 'Pre-Roman burial rites in north-western Europe' in R. Reece (ed.) *Burial in the Roman World* London (1977) 1–13

R. Whimster *Burial Practices in Iron Age Britain* Oxford 1981

C. Haselgrove 'Wealth, prestige and power; the dynamics of late iron age political centralisation in south-east England', in A. C. Renfrew and S. Shennan (eds.) *Ranking, Resource and Exchange: aspects of the archaeology of early European Society* Cambridge (1982) 79–88

The Germanic Iron Age is usefully summarised in:

M. Todd *The Northern Barbarians 100 BC–AD 300* London 1975

The Iron Age in central Europe and the development of the kingdom of Vannius is discussed in several articles in:

B. Chropovsky (ed.) *Symposium: Ausklang der Latène-Zivilisation und Anfänge der germanischen Besiedlung im mittleren Donaugebeit* Bratislava 1977

The adjustment of the settlement pattern to Roman imperial needs in Etruria is discussed in:

T. W. Potter *The Changing Landscape of South Etruria* London 1972

An article suggesting the Roman expansion was limited by the low level of native social organisation:

W. Groenman—van Waateringe 'Urbanization and the northwest frontier of the Roman Empire', in W. S. Hanson and L. J. F. Keppie (eds.) *Roman Frontier Studies 1979* (1980) 1037–1044

# Index

Adria 104, 108
Aedui 150, 154, 175
Aegina 107
Aeschylus 103
Agighiol 11
Agora 41, 103
Agricola 175
Aix-en-Provence 110
Alaça Hüyük 27, 30–2
Alb-Salem ware 81, 99
Alesia 175
Alet 140, 162, 165
Alexander 108, 145
Alexandria 65, 145
Al Mina 39, 40, 45, 51, 64
Altintepe 48
Amasis 65
amber, 26, 79, 94, 118, 126
amphorae 95, 107, 139, 141, 142, 149, 162, 163, 165, 169, 171, 172
Amphitrite potter 124
Andros 41
Aphrodite 58
Appenwihr 79, 82
Aquileia 154, 174
archaic states 19
Areopagus 42
Argishti I 48
Argos 51
Aristotle 106
Arminius 156
Arrezzo 25, 139, 140, 142, 169–71, 176
arrows 45, 90, 93, 102
Arverni 149, 157
Asperg 64, 82, 94, 99–101, 113
Athens 15, 16, 18, 23, 33–6, 39–42, 45, 51, 52, 56–8, 62–4, 103–6, 139
Atrebates 162, 165, 171
Auerberg 140, 177
Aulnat 127, 140, 144, 146, 149, 150, 154
Autun 150, 175
Aylesford 142

Bad Canstatt 84
Bagendon 140, 171, 176
band 19
Bargeroosterveld 27
barter 18
Barth, F.-E. 75, 184, 185
Basel 140, 150
Basse Yutz 104, 118, 120, 123
Battersea 173
Bavai 140, 165, 171
beaked flagons 66, 84, 95, 97, 112–14, 118, 123–4
bearskin 172
Befort 114, 187
Belgae 162
Bell im Hunsrück, 64, 102
Besançon 140, 150
Bibracte 150, 175, 179
Biel, J. 93, 186
big man 18, 19
Birdlip 173
Biskupin 38, 64, 81

Bituitos 149
Bituriges 120
black-figure ware 23, 84, 95, 97, 112–13
black gloss ware 139, 142, 149, 156, 162, 170–1
Bocchoris 66
Bogazköy 27, 31, 32
Bologna 40, 60, 64, 69, 70, 73, 104, 109, 112
Bordeaux 156
Bourges 120
Brå 175
Braubach 121, 123
Braughing 140, 166, 167, 171, 188
Brennus 138
Brezje 69, 70, 73
Brigantes 165, 171
Britzgyberg 64, 82, 84, 113
Budapest 140, 154–5, 174
Bundenbach 104, 114, 187
Burebista 157
Byblos 39, 40

Ca' Morta 118
Caere 66
Caergwyle 37
Caesar, G.J. 150–1, 153, 156–8, 163, 165, 167, 175
Čaka 26–7
Camillus 59
Campanian pottery 139, 142, 149, 156, 162, 170–1
Camp du Château 113
Camulodunum 167–8
Canterbury 176
Carcasonne Gap 113, 120, 165, 167
Carthage 39, 40, 139, 141
Catuvellauni 165, 167, 172
Cayla-de-Mailhac 78, 104, 113
central places 18, 20–2, 99, 145, 182
Cernunnos 12, 14
Cerrig-y-Drudion 140, 158
Chalkis 43–4, 51, 62, 64
chariot fittings 159, 161, 173
chariots 65, 67, 73, 114, 118, 138
chiefdom 18–19, 21
Chinnor 104, 118, 158
Christaller 177
Cimbri 139, 173
Cirencester 171, 176
Çiumeşti 138
Claudius 158, 169
Cloaca Maxima 108
coinage 18, 25, 106–7, 144–5, 149–50, 154, 157, 161–3, 168–9, 171, 175
Colchester 16, 21, 140, 147, 161–8, 170–2, 179
Cologne 166
Commius 171
compass 35–6, 54, 123
coral 99, 118, 124, 127, 138, 149
Corinth 41, 45, 51, 56–8, 62, 64
Coriosolites 162, 165
Cosa 139, 140–1
Croesus 58, 63, 106
Cumae 23, 40, 51, 64–5
cunicula 108
Cunobelin 165, 167–8, 171–2
currency bars 127, 149, 151

Dejbjerg 175
Delian League 19, 108
Delos 20
Delphi 20, 103–4, 126
dendritic system 21–2
dendrochronology 23
Dietikon 130
diffusion 9
Dionysus of Syracuse 108
Dipylon 54, 56
Dobunni 165, 171
Dodona 20, 103–4
Dorchester-on-Thames 140, 171, 176
down-the-line trade 16–17, 176
Dressel amphorae 139, 141, 149, 156, 163, 167, 169
Driehaus 116, 136
drinking horns 93, 99, 113, 118
Drusus 158, 171
Dumnorix 156
Dürkheim 118
Dürrnberg bei Hallein 64, 81, 104, 118, 120–1, 127, 187
Dux 158

Eberdingen–Hochdorf 82, 93, 99, 113–14, 186
egalitarian society 19
Eigenbilsen 104, 118, 123
Elba 40, 51
Enkomi 27, 29, 33–4, 50, 52
Ensérune 104, 113, 186
Entremont 104, 110, 112, 186
Erbenheim 26, 29, 37, 74
Erebuni (Erevan) 40, 48, 50
Eretria 43–4, 62, 64
Erstfeld 104, 118–9
Essalois 140, 156
Este 69–71, 79, 83–4, 104, 112
ethnicity 10
Euripides 103
Ewart Park, 37

faience 26, 33, 43, 45, 59–60, 65–6
Falerii 176
Federsee 37
Filip, J. 157
firedogs 51, 53, 163, 172
Fried, M. 18, 182

Gallo-Belgic pottery 167, 169–71, 173, 180
Gánovce 27, 32
Gergovie 140, 150, 157
Germanicus 158
glass 79, 99, 101, 127, 132, 149, 156, 172, 175
Glastonbury 163
Goeblingen–Nospelt 170
Gordion 40, 46, 48, 50
Grafenbühl 84, 186
Graphittonkeramik 155
Graufesenque, La 155
Great Chesterford 140, 171
Gross Romstedt 19, 140, 174
gryphons 15, 48, 50–1, 53, 57, 95, 107
guilds 23
Gundestrup 11, 175
Gündlingen 29, 74, 76–9
Gussage All Saints 20, 154, 161

Halle 26–7
Hallstatt (site) 23, 27, 38, 64, 69, 70, 74–6, 78, 81, 104, 118, 154, 184–5
Haltern 170
Hama 23, 40, 46
Hannibal 157

harness fittings 37, 74, 78–9, 90, 93, 123, 159, 161, 171, 173
Hart-an-der-Alz 26–7
Hattusilis 32
Hattussas 31–2
Helvetii 145
Hemigkofen 28–9, 37, 74
Hengistbury Head 21, 140, 156–7, 162–4, 166–7, 188
Herodotus 65
Hesiod 9
Heuneburg 15–16, 18, 21–2, 64, 81–2, 84, 88–91, 94–5, 99, 101, 113, 120–1, 124, 126, 151, 185
Hildebrand, H. 23, 183
hillfort 18, 21, 37–8, 78–9, 81–3, 88, 99, 101–2, 112–4, 158, 162, 173–4
Himera 113
Hirschlanden 93, 99–100, 147, 186
Hodson, F.R. 134, 183
Hohmichele 84, 89–90, 92, 99, 102
Holcombe 161, 173
Hollingbury 151
Holzhausen 146
Horath 121
horse bits 41–2, 59, 159 see also harness fittings
Hradenín 64, 78
Hrazany 153, 174
Hurbanovo 104, 131
hyperdiffusionism 14

Iapygian painted wares 58
Iceni 165, 171
Idaean Cave 40, 43, 57
inscriptions 73, 113 see also writing
Ipswich 140, 161, 165
iron working 15, 24, 28, 34, 36, 43, 60, 74, 78, 156
Ischia 46
Istros 64–5
ivory 33, 45, 51, 53, 106

Jacobsthal, P. 120, 129, 136, 138, 187
Jason 57
Jenišovice 37
jet 26
Jogasses, Les 102, 121
Johannisberg 64, 102

Kaerumgaard 142
Kanesh 27, 32
Karmir Blur 40, 47, 50
Kastenwald 79, 118
Kelheim 140, 142, 147, 151, 187
Kemmelberg 64, 102, 186
Kerameikos 54
Kimmeridge 163
Kition 39–40, 184
Klein Aspergle 84, 104, 113, 120, 124
Klein Klein 64, 73, 79, 185
korai and koroi 63
Kossinna 9, 181
Kramer, W. 132
Kuffarn 69–70, 120
Kültepe 32

La Graufesenque 155
La Tène (site) 23, 104, 136, 187
Lausitz 38, 81
Lefkandi 40–1, 44–5, 54, 58, 62
Leicester 176
Les Jogasses 102, 121
Les Pennes 104, 112
Leubingen 26–7
Levroux 140, 149–50
Lezoux 155

Libenice 131
lignite 199
Linsenflaschen 120–1, 123
Livy 120
Llyn Fawr 64, 74, 185
London 22, 166–7, 169, 179
Lorenz, H. 132, 187
lotus buds, flowers 48, 50–1, 53, 66, 123–4
Lübsow 175
Luernios 149
Lydia 46, 106–7
Lyons 145, 166

Magdalenenberg 64, 82, 84–5, 89, 186
Magdalensberg 16, 23, 140, 156
Magdalenská Gora 69–70, 79
Maiden Castle 176
Manching 22–3, 140, 145, 147, 149–51, 153–5, 174
Marcomanni 174
Marius 139
market exchange 18, 106, 171
Maroboduus 174
Marseilles 21, 64–5, 82, 94, 104, 110, 112–13, 144–5
Marzabotto 104, 108–9, 112, 132
Matzhausen 104, 120
Mauenheim 99, 104, 113
Mauss, M. 181
Megara 64
Megiddo 40, 46
mercenaries 63, 65, 149
Messenia 33
Mezek 104, 138
Mindelheim 29, 64, 74–5, 77, 79, 81
mining 38, 75, 78–9, 81, 106–7, 118
Mithras 12
Montefortino 138
Mont Beuvray 150, 154, 177, 179 see also Bibracte
Montfercault 131
Mont Lassois 15–16, 18, 64, 82, 95, 101, 113, 121, 124, 126
Mötschwyl 135
Mount Batten 164
Mšecké Žehrovice 140, 145, 146
Mühlacker 99, 186
Müllendorf 37
multiple brush 35–6, 54
Münsingen 23, 25, 104, 118, 127, 134, 140, 149, 158, 187
murus gallicus 116, 147, 150–1
Mycenae 27, 33, 41

Nages 113
Narce 176
Naucratis 21, 64–5
Nauheim 156
Naxos 64
Nebringen 104, 132
Nepi 176
Neuwied basin 104, 126
Nijmegen 171
Nîmes 145
Nimrud 51, 53
Nitra 140, 174
Nora 40, 60
Noreia 156
Noricum 156
Noves 113

Oberaden 170
Oedipus 57
Olbia 64–5
Old Smyrna 39
Olympia 20, 40, 57, 103–4

oppida 21, 135, 142, 146–7, 148, 150, 152–3, 155, 157, 167, 173–4, 177, 179
orientalising 15, 56, 62, 65, 69, 123
Otzenhausen 116–17
Owslebury 140, 144, 157, 163

Paillart 171
Palais d'Essalois 140, 156
Palestrina (Praeneste) 64, 66–7, 73, 185
Panticapaeum 64–5
Paris 140, 150
Pascual amphorae 163, 167
Passau 140, 151, 154
Pécs-Jakobhegy 64, 78–9, 81
Pegasus 50, 57
Pennes, Les 104, 112
Peoples of the Sea 33
Perachora 40, 57
Perati 27, 33–4
Pergamum 104, 126
Perry, W. J. 14, 181
Philip I of Macedonia 108, 144
Philistines 23, 33
Phocaea 64
piling 30, 36, 43
Písek 104, 120
Pithekoussai 40, 45–6, 51, 57–60, 64–5
Platěnice 64, 78
Pliny 156
Polanyi, K. 17–18, 181, 186
polis-state 62, 108
Pompeii 139, 140–1, 179
Poole 140, 163, 166–7
population movement 10
Populonia 64, 66
port of trade 16, 22, 56, 65, 149
Posidonius 149, 156
potlatch 20, 182
potters' wheel 15, 34–5, 53, 66, 95, 154, 162, 173
pre-industrial city 22
Preist 151
Providence, Rhode Island 70, 73
Psammetichos I 63, 65
Pylos 27, 33

Ramsauer, J.G. 75
ranked society 19
reciprocity 17
red-figure ware 23, 108, 112–14, 118, 124
redistribution 17
regional analysis 20
Reinecke, P. 23, 134, 183
Reinheim 104, 114, 123–4, 186
Rhode 144–5
Rhodes 39
Rimini 176
rite of passage 20
Roanne 155
Rome (city) 16, 22, 66, 104, 126, 140, 176, 185
Römerhügel 84
Roquepertuse 113
Runnymede 27, 37, 184

Sahlins, M. 9, 17, 181
St Albans 140, 167, 171, 176
St Blaise 112, 186
St Colombe 84, 95
St Jerome 126
St Malo 162, 165–7
St Sulpice 104
Salamis 40, 50, 52, 184
Salins 104, 113

salt 38, 75, 78–9, 81, 118, 121
Saluvii 110
samian 25, 142, 155, 169, 171, 173, 180
Samos 39, 40, 57, 65
sapropelite 145–7
Sarduri II 50
Sartrup 37
scarab 45, 159
schist 99, 145, *see also* sapropelite
Schwarzenbach 104, 116–17, 123–4
Scoglio del Tonno 34
Service, E.R. 18–19, 181
Sestius 141
Severus 175
shale 26, 172 *see also* schist
Sidon 16, 39–40
silk 84, 90, 99, 114
Simris 27
Sissach 155
Situla Art 69–71, 73, 79, 93, 112–13, 118, 120, 185
Sjoberg, G. 182
Smyrna 40
Snettisham 140, 161, 165
Snodgrass, A.M. 57, 182, 184
Soissons 150
solar central place 21–2, 177
Solon 63
Sophocles 103
Sopron–Burgstall 64, 79, 81
Sparta 33, 58, 62, 64, 97, 106
sphinx 15, 50–1, 53, 57, 66, 73
Spina 69, 104, 108–9, 112
stamnos 114, 118, 124
Stanwick 140, 159, 161, 171
Steinsburg bei Römhild 140, 173
Stična 69, 83
Stonehenge 26–7
Strabo 156
Stradonice 140, 154, 155
stratified society 19
Suebi 174
Syracuse 40, 46, 64, 66, 107

Talhau 84, 95
Taranto 27, 34
Tarentum 97
Tarquinia 40, 61, 64, 66, 185
Tasciovanus 165, 167–8
Teishebaini (Karmir Blur) 47, 50
Tène, La (site) 23, 104, 136, 187
terra nigra, rubra 170
Teutones 139, 173
Thebes 15, 57
Theley 114

Thomsen, C.J. 9
Ticino 112, 114, 118, 156
Tincommius 171
Tiryns 27, 33, 36, 40, 41
Titelberg 179
Tomerdingen 146
Toprakale 40, 50
Toulouse 140, 156, 166–7
Trajan 158
Trebenište 64, 82
Treveri 116, 126
tribe 19
Trier 116
Trinovantes 147
tripod cauldrons 43, 48, 50, 53, 57, 66–7, 84, 93–5, 114
Třísov 154–5
Troy 27, 32
Trundholm 37
Tyre, 16, 39–40

Ur 32
Urartu 43, 46–7, 49, 51, 57

Vače 64, 69–70, 73, 79
Vannius 174, 188
Veii 40, 59, 60, 64–5, 67, 109, 176, 185
Veneti (Brittany) 163, 165
Veneti (Italy) 138
Vergina 27, 36
Verica 171
Verulamium 167 *see also* St Albans
Vettersfelde 64, 81
Vetulonia 64, 66
Vienne 104, 112, 140, 156, 166–7
Viereckschanzen 145–6, 167
Vilanów 156
Villeneuve–St-Germain 140, 150, 152, 179
Vix 82, 84, 94–5, 99, 102, 114, 186
Volterra 40, 61
Vulcii 40, 61

wagon fittings 37, 123
wagons 37, 78, 90, 95, 102, 127, 129, 149, 167, 175
Waldalgesheim 104, 114, 126, 128, 137–8, 158
Wasserburg in Buchau 27, 37
Wells, P.S. 118, 186
Welwyn 140, 172
Welwyn Garden City 172
writing 28, 57, 62, 97

Zagora 40–1
Závist 64, 82, 140, 173–4
Zemplín 140, 155, 174